CONTENTS

To Suzie

Through the
LOOKING GLASS

Elizabeth Wilson is Senior Lecturer in Social Sciences at the Polytechnic of North London. She has written for a number of journals, newspapers and magazines, and is the author of several books, including *Women and the Welfare State* (1977), *Only Halfway to Paradise* (1980), *Mirror Writing* (1982), *Adorned in Dreams: Fashion and Modernity* (1985) and *Halluci-nations* (1988).

Lou Taylor is Principal Lecturer in Dress History in the Art and Design History Department at Brighton Polytechnic. She organised the Fashion Gallery and Mariano Fortuny exhibition at Brighton Museum. She is consultant for the major british Council travelling exhibition 'British Fashion in the Eighties' and for design awareness courses run by Courtaulds and Littlewoods. She is the author of *Mourning Dress: A Costume and Social History* (1983).

Frontispiece *Remove the six layers of clothing worn by the woman of 1883 (left) and she would be left wearing a pair of combinations very similar to Hennes' design (right) for spring 1989. What separates the two is more than a hundred years of fashion and social change – which is the subject of this book.*

Through the LOOKING GLASS

A History of Dress
from 1860 to the Present Day

Elizabeth Wilson and Lou Taylor

BBC BOOKS

This book accompanies the BBC TV series *Through the Looking Glass*, first broadcast on BBC 2 from November 1989. The series was produced by Suzanne Davies and Robert Albury and prepared in consultation with the Continuing Education Advisory Council.

Cover illustrations

Front: *Centre left* Sewing machinists from the *Tailor and Cutter*, 1907 (Hulton Picture Company); *bottom left* Dress pattern catalogue, 1942 (Private collection)
Back: *Centre top* Salford second-hand clothes market in the 1890s (Salford Cultural Services); *centre* Victorian corset, 1893 (Hulton Picture Company)
All remaining photographs are stills from the BBC television series.
The dress in the photograph centre front is by Workers for Freedom.
The clothes are modelled by Lysette Anthony.

Published by BBC Books,
a division of BBC Enterprises Limited,
Woodlands, 80 Wood Lane, London W12 0TT

First published 1989
© Elizabeth Wilson and Lou Taylor 1989

Reprinted 1989 (twice)

ISBN 0 563 21441 4 paperback
ISBN 0 563 21443 0 hardback

Set in 11 on 14pt ITC Garamond Light Condensed by Ace Filmsetting Ltd, Frome
Printed and bound in Great Britain by Richard Clay Ltd, Bungay,
Colour separations by Technik Ltd, Berkhamsted
Jacket and cover printed by Richard Clay Ltd, Norwich

$\mathscr{A}$CKNOWLEDGEMENTS

We are especially indebted to Suzanne Davies, Producer BBC Continuing Education, whose vision of this book carried us through the complex work of marrying two divergent (though complementary) approaches to the study of dress: one centring on a dress and social history base, the other taking the more interpretive sociological approach of 'cultural criticism'.

Our book is published to accompany the BBC Continuing Education television series *Through the Looking Glass* produced by Suzanne Davies and Robert Albury. Suzie's support and ideas have been of vital importance throughout the writing and illustrating of this book.

We should also like to thank Martha Caute of BBC Books for her patience and good humour in bringing the book together, Karen Willie for the picture research and Claire Robertson for the design.

We thank also Amy de la Haye for her advice on Chapters Three and Four, Mrs Sheila Shreeve, Honorary Curator of Costume at Willenhall Lock Museum for detailed information and illustrations for Chapters Three and Four, Ann Wise, Curator of Costume, Worthing Museum, for especially photographing the wall-map dress on page 115, Avril Hart of the Textiles Department of the Victoria and Albert Museum for detailed advice on the Utility Clothing Scheme, and Dr Paddy Maguire, Department of Humanities, Brighton Polytechnic, for advice on analysing prices. We have found *Costume*, the journal of the Costume Society, edited by Anne Saunders, to be an invaluable source for detailed dress history study, and we are grateful to the staff of St Peter's House Library, Brighton Polytechnic, which contains not only a first-rate collection of dress, textile and social history books and period magazines, but also houses the Alison Settle archives of dress history papers.

Finally, we should like to thank the following graduates of Brighton Polytechnic for their kindness in letting us quote from their undergraduate studies, researched as integral parts of Lou Taylor's dress history courses on the Polytechnic's Design History BA Honours Degree: Cindy Greenslade, Susannah Handley, Amy de la Haye, Peter Hill, Kathy Hogan, Jill Mardle, Troy Morgan, Katy Steele and Nicola White.

Comparative money values

The price of a given garment in the past means little when taken in isolation. The amount it cost when new needs to be seen in the context of prices and incomes at the time. A haute couture evening dress from the London salon of Redfern in 1906, for example, cost 18 guineas (£18.90p). This seems miraculously cheap until we take into account that the pound sterling was worth £36.49p at today's values. This means that the equivalent price of the Redfern gown today would be approximately £693. Moreover, while an Edwardian society lady could readily spend that amount on a dress, many families were struggling to survive on 'round about a pound a week', equivalent of £36.49p today, less even than social security for a family in 1989.

We have therefore in the text added the approximate 1989 equivalent in square brackets after the original sum. These present-day 'purchasing power of the pound' equivalents also, however, need to be considered in the light of other expenditure that had to be made at the time.

A well-paid secretary in the late 1920s, for example (see Chapter 3), earned at most £3.50p per week. This was more than a coalminer at the same period, and would appear to give her plenty of scope to save for a rayon dance dress at 18s 11d (or 90p), which is the equivalent at today's prices of about £16.50p. Yet she might be living in a hostel, paying rent, food, heating, bus fares, hire-purchase commitments on a winter coat and other expenditure and actually be able to save almost nothing. Equally, a young shop assistant who earned 10s 6d per week [under £5] and who lived at home would in all likelihood pay most of her wages into the family purse and be left with very little pocket money. For her, even the cheapest silk stockings at 4s 6d (equal to £4 today) would take a whole week's wages and were thus an impossible luxury. Today, on the other hand, income tax, credit repayments and often mortgage costs make much greater inroads on income.

In the 1950s teenagers were relatively much better off than their parents had been in the 1930s. There is evidence that in this period of high employment adolescent earners were not expected to pay such a large proportion of their wages into the general family housekeeping fund, but even when a good proportion of a young woman's wage went towards her keep, she could still afford nylons at 5s to 10s [equal to £2.25 to £4.50p], and even a good quality cotton summer dress at £5 [£45], although expensive, was a purchase she could have saved for.

We are grateful to Dr Paddy Maguire, of the Department of Humanities at Brighton Polytechnic, for his advice on this method of assessing prices and to the Bank of England for their January 1989 Retail Price Index figures relating to the period covered in this book (see the appendix on page 233).

For those who are unfamiliar with pre-decimal coinage, some equivalents are as follows:

Pre-decimal	Decimal
£1 (20s or 240d)	£1 (100p)
15s	75p
10s	50p
5s	25p
4s	20p
3s	15p
2s 6d (half a crown)	12½p
2s	10p
1s	5p
6d	2½p
3d	1½p

One guinea was equal to £1 1s 0d, or £1.05p.
One new penny (p) is equal to approximately 2 old pennies (d).
There were 12d to 1 shilling(s).

1

VICTORIAN REVELATIONS
1860-90

Introduction

To the enthusiast, fashion is the most seductive of addictions. We have only to turn the pages of *Vogue* to be immersed in a sensuous world of colours and tactile luxury:

Fitted salmon silk double-breasted jacket . . . burgundy elastic halterneck . . . salmon pink satin-finish Lycra skirt with taupe stretch lace hem . . . burgundy mousseline scarf trimmed with gold coins . . . dusty rose pleated satin Belgrave shoes. . . .

Long silk crepe tunic . . . with ankle-length crystal-pleated cream silk crepe skirt . . . cameo earrings. . . . Finely textured bright yellow wool bouclé. . . . Black suede high heels. . . .[1]

It was not so different in the 1860s:

A dress of lilac silk covered with clouds of tulle in the same shade in which clusters of lilies of the valley were to be drowned. A veil of white tulle was to be thrown like a mist over the mauve clouds and the flowers, and, finally, a sash with flowing ends should suggest the reins on Venus's chariot.[2]

Fashion, a potent source of pleasure, also, however, meets with widespread disapproval. To enjoy dress is to risk accusations of vanity and triviality, and the fashionable are condemned as heartless for their indifference to the sufferings both of the exploited workers who make their clothes and of the birds and animals whose lives are sacrificed to their vanity.

Yet dress is not trivial. It is a necessary form of communication, particularly in urban society, and we use it all the time to convey unspoken signals to those around us. Sometimes judged immoral, it is also a system of coded moral precepts: the way we dress conforms to a whole range of moral and social customs and attitudes, and often, even today, we flout sartorial conventions at our peril.

Opposite This close-fitting, upholstered 'princess-line' dress, worn by an unknown woman (c. 1881), is cut in the new all-in-one style. Both dress and corset would have been boned to mould her body to the hourglass shape.

11

Fashion is about pleasure and danger, conformity and the breaking of taboos. It expresses our 'deeply felt need to be superficial';[3] – our love of style for its own sake. This consumerism, this love of surface beauty and novelty is, in itself, neither admirable nor wicked. It is ambiguous, offering pleasure and enrichment on the one hand, waste and envy on the other.

This book, and the television series it accompanies, explore what ordinary women and men, as well as the rich and fashionable, wore in the past and are wearing today, their strategies for following the fashion, or simply for getting by. We have tried to convey the feel of clothes, as well as describing how they were and are produced, and how different social groups and classes have dressed at different periods. We have tried at the same time to steer a path between uncritical admiration of the beauty of haute couture (exclusive high fashion design) and wholesale condemnation of fashion for its extravagance and exploitation.

We therefore reject a tradition in dress history which overemphasises the fashions of the rich, and haute couture in particular. This tradition is, in general, uncritical of fashion. By contrast, the tradition of theoretical explanation in fashion literature has tended towards the opposite extreme. Many of the best-known books on the theory of fashion proceed from the assumption that all fashion is irrational, and is therefore either ugly and immoral or just silly – something that needs to be explained away.[4] To some people, all fashion is ridiculous, and especially the perpetual change that lies at its heart. The dress reform movements of the nineteenth century expressed such a view; they constituted an 'attack on the concept of fashion itself'.[5] Writers and reformers longed for an unchanging form of dress, not recognising that ideas about what is beautiful change over time, and from one social grouping to another.

Fashion theorists have tended to rely on a single explanation – whether it be sex, status, or economics – for the fashion phenomenon they find so strange. Dress historians, too, often adopt a simple 'reflection' theory of history, whereby a given social fact – the emancipation of women, say – produces an immediate and clear symbol in the shape of 'short skirts'. Human behaviour is much more complex than this, and cultural symbols more subtle. While we do not deny that social change, eroticism, the display of wealth, or just general showing off play an important part in fashion, it is the combination of these with other components that makes fashion what it is.

It is our belief that no one explanation is sufficient to grasp the multifaceted phenomenon that is fashion. Neither events nor artefacts can ever be reduced to a single objective meaning in this way.

Fashion is in a sense curiously elusive, escaping attempts to pin it down to a single explanation. This may be because it is a kind of meeting point for intersecting aspects of our culture. Fashion is perhaps most usefully seen as a field where economics and industry meet aesthetics and art; where individual psychology meets the social organisation of a group, a class, an age. In other words what each of us actually wears is determined simultaneously by a variety of factors: income, personal preference and mental set come up against dominant aesthetic trends, and the group norms of class. All these are framed by the economics of the industry.[6]

We use dress to present ourselves as clothed, social, gendered (that is, masculine or feminine) individuals. Our image in the looking glass seems to reflect something deeply important about us: our identity. We are made to feel we 'choose' our appearance, and up to a point we do; but it is also determined for us, not only by the looks with which we were born, but also by the clothes we can obtain or must wear. This book is concerned largely with the processes which come before that moment of choice in front of the mirror. In it we hope to 'deconstruct' the fashion image, and expose the many pieces which go to make the puzzle of that final image, the secret of where it comes from and what it means.

Wealth and poverty in Victorian Britain

Victorian Britain was the first urbanised society in the world, and the rise of great cities filled with individuals who were strangers to one another had important consequences in terms of dress. There had been large and important cities in Britain for centuries, but it was not until the Industrial Revolution, which began in the second half of the eighteenth century, that Britain as a whole became an urban society. Towns in the north of England were doubling their size every ten years in the early nineteenth century. London was already a city of one million inhabitants in 1801; one-twelfth of the total population of the country lived in London, and one-fifth (20 per cent) in a town of one sort or another. By 1851, 38 per cent of the population lived in cities, and London's population was over two and a quarter million. By 1901, 75 per cent of the population was urban.[7] By 1860 Victorian Britain was approaching its peak of prosperity and confidence as the leading and most highly industrialised nation in the world.

The Industrial Revolution – the change from production in the home or in small adjacent workshops to factory production – together with

13

the rise of urban society, constituted a social upheaval of immense proportions. It was an upheaval so truly momentous that it is hard for us today fully to comprehend what the experience of living through it must have been: 'All that is solid melts into air. . . . All fixed, fast-frozen relations . . . are swept away.'[8] The turbulent new world of the industrial city and the commercial metropolis fragmented the old way of life.

Precisely because the world of the Victorians was changing so fast, clear distinctions in male and female roles, and the preservation of distance between the classes, seemed of paramount importance. The clothes men wore became the most immediate and one of the most important signals of status, occupation and aspirations. What women wore symbolised their sexual status. Victorian journalism is filled with descriptions of the more successful courtesans and prostitutes whose silk dresses, combined with too-easy manners, told the observer all. Middle-class women had to be careful to dress in styles that proclaimed both their class status and their unquestioned virtue.

The changing and, many felt, deteriorating position of women in the nineteenth century was probably one reason why differences between male and female dress became more marked. In the eighteenth century male dress, court and formal wear at least, had been flamboyant; men, like women, wore coloured silks and velvet, lace and embroidery. Both sexes used cosmetics. By the mid-nineteenth century male garb had become sober and reserved, and dark colours only were worn. The clothes of upper- and middle-class women remained as fragile, elaborate and colourful as ever.

Huge differences in wealth and poverty persisted. Yet the dynamism of Victorian society was due to its relative fluidity. The middle ranks of society were expanding throughout the eighteenth century and in the late eighteenth century and early nineteenth century a new group of entrepreneurs were making fortunes in the textile industry in Manchester and Lancashire as a whole. Steel in Sheffield, engineering in Birmingham and a host of new industries marked the rise of a wealthy industrial class. In general these families were not accepted in aristocratic society, nonetheless the boundaries between classes were less clear cut than they would have been in earlier times, and by the last quarter of the nineteenth century the merging of the aristocracy and the wealthy industrialist class had begun. Not only did the industrialists aim for an aristocratic way of life, acquiring titles and land in some cases, but some members of the aristocracy became involved in business and finance.

The uncertainties of class were most marked in the shifting centre. The progressive section of the professional upper middle class formed an energetic, dynamic and often highly creative reforming group. They felt

A middle-class Victorian family, such as this one photographed in Bournemouth in 1883, displayed their social aspirations through fashionable clothes purchased from tailors, department stores or private dressmakers.

themselves to be altogether a cut above families who were 'in trade' and whose vulgarity and philistinism they despised. The lower middle class was amorphous territory. The novels of Charles Dickens, covering, approximately, the period from the 1830s to 1860, are full of characters of ambiguous social status: the genteel poor, the *nouveaux riches*, the *déclassés* and also members of the 'underclass' (those who were outside normal employment, living right at the margins).

Differences in income between the working and the professional classes were greater in the nineteenth century than they have since

15

become. At the same time the lower middle class and the respectable working class were close together in terms of income. In the mid-nineteenth century, £300 [£9519] was frequently cited as being the minimum sum required if you were to lead a middle-class style of life. Most white-collar workers – clerks, curates, teachers – earned less than this and very little more than a skilled artisan. The artisan did not need to 'keep up appearances' to the same extent, so may well have felt better off.[9]

The middle class was much smaller than it is now, as a proportion of the population; not more than about 13 per cent. There were correspondingly more factory operatives, agricultural workers and struggling general labourers. There was immense diversity within this large sector of the population as well. There were regional differences and differences which cannot be reduced to income alone. For example, a Wiltshire farm labourer was one of the poorest and worst paid workers in the land and ate only the simplest food, but his life expectancy and that of his children was rather better than that of a Durham miner. Yet the mining family ate considerably more meat and its members had at least a change of clothes, unheard of for the rural farmworkers of the south-west of England. Such variations could be reproduced at every level of society.[10] Approximately ten per cent of the working population came within the top group of skilled artisans[11] and their families, and within each trade there would be different grades of skill and remuneration. Among car-

Foremen during the construction of the 1862 British International Exhibition in London wearing a variety of ready-made clothing, some ill-fitting and possibly second-hand. The top hat was a mark of respectability for artisans as well as gentlemen by this date.

penters, for example, there were the young men working for the 'low speculating builders':

As a rule . . . they are men of dissipated habits . . . and they have seldom a second suit to their backs. They are generally to be seen on a Sunday lounging about the suburbs of London with their working clothes on, and their rules sticking from their side pockets – the only difference in their attire being, perhaps, that they have a clean shirt and a clean pair of shoes.[12]

On the other hand:

The more respectable portion of the carpenters and joiners 'will not allow' their wives to do any other work than attend to their domestic and family duties, though some few of the wives of the better class of workmen take in washing or keep small 'general shops'. The children of the carpenters are mostly well brought up, the fathers educating them to the best of their ability. . . . Before the men leave their work in the large shops, it is usual for them to change their working clothes for others which they keep in a little cupboard under their bench. Their appearance in the street is as respectable as that of any tradesman.[13]

In this fast-shifting society, the vision of 'the rich man in his castle, the poor man at his gate' was a nineteenth-century fantasy of what pre-industrial life had been like; nevertheless it was of vital importance to the Victorian bourgeoisie for the lower orders to know their place. The poor were meant to look poor. By the mid-century, however, middle-class Victorians frequently expressed anxiety and resentment because the working class were beginning, or so it appeared, to aspire to consumer luxuries.

John Thomson's photograph of 1876 shows a London street dealer in fancy goods. His customers wear plain unfashionable dresses covered with utilitarian pinafores.

The bourgeoisie regarded these new trappings of a middle-class way of life as their preserve, to be jealously guarded. As one writer expressed it in 1860:

Even those old and wholesome and self-imposed sumptuary limits have been extravagantly exceeded which, in the last century, at once denoted and defined the station and duties of each class. In the progress of society, by the extension of education, by the prevalence of luxury, and by the suggestion of new wants, by the crush of every rivalry and by the pressure of every disappointment, all the old landmarks have been swept away.[14]

A Conservative MP wrote in 1881:

[There is] a huge and constantly increasing class who have wide wants and narrow means. Luxury has soaked downwards and a raised standard of living among people with small incomes has created an enormous demand for cheap elegancies . . . cheap clothes and cheap furniture, produced as they must be by cheap methods.[15]

This belief that the lower middle classes and the working classes were wallowing in luxury was another bourgeois myth, but sharply felt precisely because of the uncertainties of the Victorian economy. The mid-Victorian bourgeoisie was immensely self-confident and many were proud of their new consumer society, in which wants you never knew you had could suddenly be satisfied. Theirs was a period of constantly increasing prosperity; but even within the bourgeoisie fortunes were frequently made and lost owing to the vagaries of the stock market and the fluctuating fortunes of trade.

For the working-class family, even the artisan class, on the other hand, any improvement in living standards was always precarious, dependent upon the chief wage earner remaining healthy and in work. An accident, or a temporary recession in his trade, immediately threatened the fragile stability of the artisan, and unskilled workers never rose above a bare subsistence.

Some members of the middle class did react against the consumer society. For example, John Ruskin, the influential art critic and social reformer, in *Unto This Last*, written in 1862, made a plea for restrictions on luxury and a more just division of wealth. There were many reformers, both women and men, who did try to help the poor and change society.

Among the largest groups in society at this time were domestic servants, both male and female. Their status in life was extremely variable, ranging from the aristocrat's housekeeper in Charles Dickens's *Bleak House*, whose son is himself a powerful self-made industrialist, to the workhouse skivvy employed in return for board and keep by an artisan family. It was particularly for women, however, that domestic service offered the opportunity of work in the towns at a time when they had

Hannah Cullwick, a maid-of-all-work, photographed in 1879 by Arthur Mumby, who secretly married her. She has pinned up her cheap cotton print dress while working, showing boots and petticoat beneath.

been, or were in the process of being excluded from many other occupations. In 1851 there were twice as many domestic servants as female textile workers and four times as many as there were textile factory workers. The other two most important occupations for women were dressmaking and agriculture, and between 1851 and 1881 the number of women working in agriculture declined sharply.[16] (In the last quarter of the nineteenth century the number of domestic servants began to decline.) The large numbers of servants employed in Victorian households used to be interpreted as evidence of 'conspicuous consumption', but more recently it has been suggested that the terms 'servant' or 'housekeeper' in census returns often referred to female kin of the head of household: that many were part of the family economy, performing women's productive (but unpaid) work in the home.[17]

During the nineteenth century uniforms of all kinds developed, including servants' uniforms: these uniforms provided another way of telling who was who in the great cities. The much more sober and restrained dress adopted by men is often itself seen as a kind of bourgeois uniform for the new business class, a more 'democratic' style of dress for a society moving away from aristocratic privilege and hierarchy. It has even been described as a male 'renunciation' of fashion.[18] Dark, uniform clothes, it is argued, symbolised the bourgeois work ethic, *laissez-faire* economics and the virtues of thrift.

Yet the styles of male dress did continue to change, although more slowly than women's, so it is not really true to say that men moved right outside fashion. Rather, the dress of women and men in the nineteenth century emphasised gender difference (that is, the differences between masculinity and femininity).

Men did not always dress drably in any case. There was a fashion in the 1860s for the shapeless, sack-like jacket (and an equally shapeless hat) worn with check trousers, and in this decade tweed suits began to be worn. Young men about town were quite dashing. Augustus Sala, a novelist and journalist, described the well-dressed clerks as they walked to work along the Strand in terms which convey the continuation of dandified ostentation:

These are the dashing young parties who purchase the pea green, the orange and the rose pink gloves; the crimson braces, the kaleidoscopic shirt-studs, the shirts embroidered with dahlias, deaths' heads, race horses, sunflowers and ballet girls. . . . These are the glasses of city fashion, and the mould of city form, for whom the legions of fourteen, of fifteen, of sixteen and of seventeen shilling trousers . . . are made. . . .

For them the shiniest of hats, the knobbiest of sticks, gleam through shop windows; for them the geniuses of 'all round collars' invent every week fresh yokes of starched linen, pleasant instruments of torture. . . . There are some who wear peg-top trousers, chin-tufts, eye glasses and varnished boots. . . .

You may know the cashiers in the private banking houses by their white hats and buff waistcoats; you may know the stockbrokers by . . . the pervading *sporting* appearance of their costume.[19]

Women's dress was none the less much more elaborate than men's. The 'submissive' look of the 1840s – the sloping shoulders, childlike ringlets and poke bonnets – had given way by the 1860s to a bolder aesthetic. Women now were wearing Zouave jackets (a short braided bolero), low chignons and flat, oval, pillbox or pork pie hats. The invention of chemical aniline dyes had brightened the appearance of the Victorian lady all too successfully, and women often wore a garish medley of colours: for

Cartes de visites *were small photographs, taken from the late 1850s. Usually people looked rather stiff in these photographs, but this unknown woman, in an early semi-tailored walking dress of the mid-1860s, is wearing her husband's bowler.*

example a jacket of magenta (also known as Solferino) might appear over a dress with a pink or mauve and pink bodice and a crinoline of light green with olive green chevrons round the hem, all worn with a yellow hat decorated in red.[20] Colours as loud and ostentatious as this would have been considered unladylike before the Crimean War.

The crinoline, so often seen as literally the cage of the Victorian lady, replaced up to twelve layers of heavy full petticoats. The lightness of the hoops and the lack of constriction round the waist were seen as a positive liberation, at least to begin with. By the mid 1860s, however, crinolines had themselves become absurdly wide, and, however much they freed the legs, they caused severe mobility problems when they reached a width of 6 feet (1.8 metres). Princess Pauline Metternich wrote in the 1860s that:

to walk with so immense a paraphernalia around one was not very easy . . . to be able to sit so as not to cause the rebellious springs to fly open required a miracle of precision. To ascend a carriage when the evening toilettes were made of tulle and lace required a great deal of time, much quietness on the part of the horses and much patience on the part of husbands and fathers.[21]

From 1865 to the 1880s women's dress was becoming generally even more elaborate. Surviving examples of fashionable clothing from this period show increasingly heavy boning stitched down bodice seams, sleeves set narrowly into tight-fitting shoulders (with neat perfumed sachets under each armpit to catch unladylike perspiration). In the 1850s and 1860s detachable 'undersleeves' in fine white, embroidered muslin were tied on to the inside elbow of day dresses and covered the lower arm and wrist with that dainty rim of white so essential to a genteel lady. By the 1870s, fabrics and appliqué decoration weighed garments down. The weight of wool and thick silk dresses with their built-in linings would seem intolerable today. Men, too, of course, wore heavier clothing than is customary now. Perhaps, for both sexes, this did not seem so oppressive in draughty, ill-heated houses; while men riding or walking to work, at least, travelled in the open air much more than they do now.

Beneath her dress the mid-Victorian woman wore a chemise, stockings, heavy boned corsets coming down over the diaphragm, waist, hips and stomach, two or three petticoats, hoops, bustle or tournure, and open legged drawers beneath. The function of these crotchless drawers, which seem positively indecent to us, was to cover the knees and upper calves.

The crinoline was frequently mocked and made the subject of jokes and badinage. In *Punch*, any women who wore the garment tended to be the butt of humour. When working-class women tried to follow the fashion, *Punch* weighed in with a level of ridicule that implied real resentment towards those who aped their betters. Cartoons of the 1860s often show working-class women (servants, usually) placing themselves in ridiculous and indecent situations by insisting on wearing the crinoline which, for example, billows up in the wind to reveal underwear as they are scrubbing the steps.

By 1865 the crinoline began to fall out of fashion, but by 1870 had been replaced by the even more cumbersome bustle. This was solidly built from horse-hair, steel bones and calico.

The new 'Dolly Varden' silhouette was so called because it was vaguely reminiscent of the 1780s styles worn by Dolly Varden, a character in Dickens' novel *Barnaby Rudge*, published in 1841. It made fashionable the 'Grecian bend' figure with light drapery looped up into a 'polonaise' skirt over the hips and bottom. In the late 1870s the bustle was abandoned, although it reappeared in the 1880s in a more exaggerated form, sometimes protruding as much as two feet (0.6 metre) behind the wearer. In between, tight-fitting cuirasse (hour-glass shaped) bodices were worn with slim skirts with fishtail trains. These princess line, tie-back dresses were secured from thigh to lower calf by a series of tapes set in the side seams and tied behind the legs. This made walking difficult, especially in the more extreme evening clothes.

Seasonal styles were increasingly emphasised by Paris, the capital of fashion. Paris had led western European style since the time of Louis XIV in the late seventeenth century, and there had been internationally known dressmakers before the Revolution of 1789. In the mid-nineteenth century a new development reinforced the dominance of Paris: the couturier (top designer) as we understand the term today appeared. This occurred in the extravagant atmosphere of the Second Empire (1852–70), when Napoleon III and his wife the Empress Eugénie presided over a society bulging with new wealth. A group of dress houses and drapers' shops opened luxurious salons, among them Aurelly, Barenne, Palmyre et Vignon and the elegant drapers Gagelin and Opigez. It was the Englishman Charles Worth, though, who more than anyone else developed what was to become the modern haute couture industry.

Worth wooed his clients assiduously, sending examples of his work to the Queen of Spain, to Bavarian and other German princesses and to Sweden. To begin with his clientele was not particularly distinguished, but once Worth established himself as couturier to Princess Pauline Metternich and to her friend the Empress, his name and fortune were assured. Gradually the famous courtesans of the period began to wear, and thus advertise his creations. Cora Pearl, for example, wore designs so advanced that no society lady would have dared to appear in them. The social rivalry between these women of the *demi-monde* and the ladies of the court fuelled the extravagant display of dress.

The influence of the Paris couturier grew so strong that styles became increasingly international. Society women in the major cities of Europe

Opposite *Ready-made underwear for women was sold from the late 1840s. The bustled fashions of the 1870s required support and shaping from hour-glass corsets, tournures and petticoats, all of which were available from department stores and by mail order.*

and the United States wore Paris designs. Every capital city had its own couturiers, but all followed the French styles.

Those who wore such styles justified the luxury and extravagance as bringing work to thousands. When a recession brought unemployment to the silk town of Lyons in the late 1850s, the Empress Eugénie wore dresses made of a heavy brocaded silk which she considered old-fashioned, but which was made in Lyons. The strategy was so successful that Eugénie's 'political dresses' as she called them, created a new fashion for the material, so that the workers in the silk town were once again able to work. The technology of fashion changed only slowly and much of the couture work was done by an army of highly skilled but underpaid cutters, seamstresses, tailors and embroideresses. In the 1890s the House of Doucet was employing 2500 hand embroidery workers.[22]

Fortunes were spent on clothes. Some dresses cost the equivalent of about £3500 to £8400 at today's values. One dress, sent by the fashionable dressmaker Madame Retz to Russia, was made of Chantilly lace and Indian cashmere at a cost of £10 400, again at today's values.[23] 'On certain toilettes,' one commentator observed, 'as much as six or seven hundred yards of ruched tulle or goffered ribbon are placed . . . the luxury of some of the ladies' dresses is perfectly astounding.'[24]

We too are apt to react to this extraordinary luxury with amazement mingled with disbelief. The middle-class Victorian woman did not dress as elaborately as the Empress Eugénie, but, married or unmarried, she is

In spite of the restraints and encumbrances of heavy dresses with bustles, women in the 1880s were beginning to lead more active lives – playing sports, mountaineering, exploring or just having fun.

today likely to be seen as an object of pity. The word 'enslavement' is often used to describe her lot, and her elaborate finery is often assumed to be a badge of her trapped and powerless condition. Yet despite their clothing, middle- and upper-class women were becoming increasingly active, walking, playing croquet and practising archery, and travelling not only in Europe but all over the world. Such women were exceptions, but were less unusual than we might think.

Women of the aristocracy continued to enjoy more freedom in their personal lives in practice than the women of the bourgeoisie, but Victoria's court under the influence of Prince Albert adopted wholesale the bourgeois virtues of the Victorian family. (This was despite the fact that Queen Victoria never allowed industrialists at court, maintaining their exclusion rigidly throughout her life.)

The 'new' ideal of the Victorian bourgeois family and of middle-class gentility, refinement and respectability had been built up in the period from 1780 to the 1840s.[25] Women were the guardians of the home, where they were to create a haven of peace and a refuge for the head of the family from the coarsening world of capitalism outside. John Ruskin summed up the ideal in a famous passage in *Sesame and Lilies*, published in 1865:

The woman's . . . intellect is not for invention or recreation, but sweet ordering, arrangement and decision. . . . By her office and place, she is protected from all danger and temptation. The man . . . must encounter all peril and trial . . . . But he guards the woman from all this. . . . This is the true nature of home – it is the place of Peace; the shelter not only from all injury, but from all terror, doubt and division.[26]

Femininity was a middle-class status symbol, and the fragile looks, housebound lives and pious and moralistic restrictions on female behaviour was a badge of class belongingness as much as a way of policing women. In particular – in part owing to the middle-class religious revival of the early nineteenth century – the new sexual morality opened an unbridgeable divide between the virtue of the 'lady' and the 'coarseness' associated with the moral laxity of the working woman.

Yet even in the sexual realm there was more diversity than is usually acknowledged. Although the 'fallen woman' was a central figure of Victorian moral mythology, in real life a lapse from virtue and even adultery and divorce did not always mean absolute social extinction for the middle-class woman.[27] There is also evidence that Victorian middle-class women were by no means all the sexless sepulchres of virtue that the stereotype has led us to assume.[28] In general, nonetheless, Victorian middle-class women were hedged in, treated as minors and prevented from having access to an independent income and status.

25

One woman of this period was Marion Sambourne, who was married to Linley Sambourne, a successful *Punch* cartoonist in the second half of the century. The Sambournes' social position was full of the middle-class ambiguity we have mentioned. Marion's father was a successful businessman, but their own social world touched on more elevated as well as bohemian circles.

Her clothes seem to have been a source of anxiety rather than pleasure. In the 1880s she was patronising a dressmaker, Madame Bosquet, and many of her diary entries refer to 'Madame B', her haughty ways and her exorbitant prices: 'To Madame B. waited an age' . . . 'Madame cross and getting dearer' . . . 'Madame B asked ridiculous prices, ordered nothing.'[29] Marion Sambourne's diaries contradict the idea of the idle middle-class Victorian wife. In the early years of her marriage at least, she made clothes for herself and her daughter by hand, as well as altering and mending dresses. She also made sofa covers, lampshades and other household items.

Class and gender fused together in the edifice of social ritual which served to maintain class boundaries and which it was the role of the middle-class woman especially to maintain. A woman could make or break the social standing and future of her entire family by her failure to understand or interpret correctly the accepted rules of social etiquette.

Victorian etiquette was elaborate, and dress an important part of it.[30] Social calls, entertaining, relations with the opposite sex, the organisation of meals and of the household, and particularly the vital events of life: birth, marriage and death − all these had their appropriate ceremonies and forms of dress. For example, dress was of vital importance in marking off the different periods of the day with their various activities. It would be unheard of for a wealthy married woman to wear the same clothes all day. She would have morning clothes, dresses for wearing in the house, afternoon tea dresses, dinner dresses and ballgowns, walking outfits and so on. The male wardrobe also contained numerous different outfits for different activities.

The most extreme example of the way in which clothes were used to signify the particularities of social life in minute detail was mourning dress. The escalation of the cult of mourning the dead reached epidemic proportions, especially after the death of Prince Albert in 1861. Queen Victoria spent the rest of her life in mourning. In the upper and middle classes, propriety required absolute adherence to the rules of mourning. Periods of mourning were rigidly laid down: from two and a half years by a widow for her husband, two years for parents down to three months in half mourning by a niece for her aunt. Each period had its own clothes: full crape and bombazine for deepest mourning (when even *shiny* black material was forbidden), down to specific shades of heliotrope (a dull mauve) and grey for half mourning. Every detail was prescribed, down to the black silk ribbon to be slotted through the hems of drawers and petticoats. *Sylvia's Home Journal* listed a widow's complete mourning wardrobe, which should consist of: three dresses, two mantles, two bonnets, twelve collars and cuffs, four pairs of black silk stockings, twenty-four handkerchiefs with black borders and two widow's caps.

To observe mourning properly was very expensive. In 1887 Peter Robinson's cheapest 'economical' weeds (mourning dress) cost £2 19s 6d [£100] and were made of a cheap mourning fabric called Borada crape. Textile manufacturers and department stores latched on to the commercial possibilities of this stable market and exploited it for all they were worth.[31]

For the poor, to bury their dead respectably and for the widow to afford mourning was a question of family and community decency. A pauper's grave was the ultimate shame and disgrace, and not to dress in mourning was the next worst thing. Few could afford new clothes. The black dye-bath was the solution. Young women in service were usually given durable and economical mourning dress – following a death in their employer's family, of course, not their own. Again, as the working classes copied middle-class behaviour, the more fortunate were quick to condemn:

If the poor were wise, their funerals would be as simple as possible . . . decent mourning, but without any of the undertaker's trappings on their persons would be sufficient. The poor forget that during life the condition of the dead was entirely different, and that there ought to be a consistency in everything belonging to the various ranks of society.[32]

The long campaign begins

No sooner was the ideology of exaggerated femininity apparently firmly in place, than it began to come under attack from within. Middle-class women – although only a small and untypical section – began to protest at the dependent and infantilised status of women, and by 1848 had begun to organise as a political feminist movement to improve their situation both inside and outside marriage. The education of women, entry into the professions, married women's property and her status within marriage all became the focus of feminist attention and campaigning.[33] By 1860, there had already been a change in the divorce laws (in 1857), Girton College and several academic girls' schools had been founded, and, in the pages of *Punch* at least, the 'girl of the period' was setting dangerous standards of unfeminine behaviour. In 1859 a Society for Promoting the Employment of Women was founded to deal with the plight of ladies of 'gentle birth' – many of them spinsters, the 'surplus women' of the nineteenth century – who had fallen into poverty. Many were governesses, working for a pittance; many others were needlewomen, as poor as the working-class women who worked as seamstresses. In 1866 Barbara Bodichon, Emily Davies and Jessie Boucherett drafted the first petition for the enfranchisement of women and the long campaign for the vote had begun.[34]

The first dress reformers: Bloomers, the Pre-Raphaelites and the Cimabue Browns

Given the elaboration of fashionable women's dress, it is not surprising that it was itself a focus for reform. Dress reform appears to have originated in the last years of the eighteenth century and was associated with the political ideals of the French Revolution. In its earliest manifestations it centred on trousered dress for women – an idea taken up by several groups of utopian socialists in the early nineteenth century. Alternative modes of dress were worn in a number of the utopian communities in the 1820s and 1830s, both in France and in the United States, their aim being on the one hand to signal the equal status of men and women and on the other to eliminate or minimise differences in class.

Dress reform, then, was being discussed in the United States before it was taken up by American feminists such as Elizabeth Cady Stanton and Amelia Jenks Bloomer, with whom it is chiefly associated today. The famous – or notorious – Bloomer costume, which they tried, unsuccessfully, to popularise, consisted of a jacket and short, full-skirted dress over oriental pantaloons which were loose but gathered at the ankle. With its low-brimmed hat and flowing sash the costume owed something to the generally Middle Eastern and specifically Turkish costume beloved by the Romantic poets and painters.

Despite its relative comfort, however, the Bloomer costume attracted such ridicule and horror that feminists felt compelled to abandon it, so damaging was it judged to be to the cause of the political and social emancipation of women. As one feminist wrote in 1888, to wear such clothes 'was to incur a social martyrdom out of all proportion to the relief obtained'.[35]

Nevertheless, it was from then on strongly associated in the popular mind with women's emancipation, and aroused deep-seated anxieties about the masculinisation of women. From the middle decades of the nineteenth century onwards, men attempted to deal with this perceived threat to their domination by denunciation, ridicule and even violence.

Opposite *In the nineteenth century there were many attempts to devise a form of trousered dress for women. These have come to be associated with Amelia Bloomer, an American dress reformer, but many radicals of both sexes tried to introduce alternative forms of dress for women and men, not always for the same reasons. They inspired music hall songs and jokes, and magazine cartoons.*

MUSICAL BOUQUET

THE BLOOMER VALSE; & THE BLOOMER REDOWA

DEDICATED TO Mrs COL. BLOOMER.

Punch become the vehicle for the average middle-class male's fear and loathing of 'strong minded women', and published endless cartoons throughout the second half of the century in which ugly, bespectacled and even moustached women are wearing the trousers both literally and figuratively.

Many women completely rejected the arguments of the reformers at every level, wishing neither for emancipation nor to be differently clad. Indeed, at a period when there was little else for women to do, much of their creativity could be displaced on to their toilettes, the elaboration of which may have partly to do with their being the focus of so much energy and attention.

The critique of fashion was not limited to feminists. The advance of medical knowledge in the nineteenth century meant that the Victorians were very conscious of health and hygiene, and all the more so because the environment in which they lived had to some extent deteriorated rather than improved. Public health was a major issue throughout the period in towns which were overcrowded, filthy and often less well provided with sewage disposal and clean drinking water than medieval settlements had been.

It was clear that gowns with long trains attracted dirt from muddy roads and pavements, and long hours were wasted in brushing and renovating these cumbersome garments. More serious objections were made to the constriction of the female body by tight-laced corsets and high heeled shoes. Medical objections to fashionable dress did not necessarily imply support for women's emancipation; on the contrary many medical men attacked the excesses, as they saw it, of fashion, for precisely the opposite reasons – that the distortion of the body that was involved would impair what for them was women's sole function: maternity.

There was a second source of alternative modes of dress – the Pre-Raphaelite movement, which had begun in the 1840s. The ideal of the Pre-Raphaelite artists – Dante Gabriel Rossetti, Edward Burne Jones, William Morris and others – was the painting of the Early Renaissance before the Italian painter Raphael (hence Pre-Raphaelite), and that distant period was also for them an ideal of a whole way of life opposed to the materialism of the industrial society in which they lived.

Dante Gabriel Rossetti's paintings of Elizabeth Siddall and Janey Morris show them in dresses free of crinolines or bustles, with wide armholes so that the arms could move freely, and without elaborate frills and trimmings. The Pre-Raphaelites rejected the crude aniline colours of the 1860s, preferring 'off' colours and half tints: salmon pink, sage green, indigo, deep amber – colours straight out of the textiles and embroideries that William Morris designed and his firm, Morris and Co., produced.

30

In 1867 Dante Gabriel Rossetti photographed William Morris's wife Janey in an early version of what became aesthetic dress. Not only has it loose sleeves and waist, but it seems to be worn without a corset.

Renouncing the frills, lace, beads, elaborate braiding called *passementerie*, appliqué and feathers with which fashionable women's dresses were festooned, the aesthetic dressers preferred simple embroidery or smocking, and sometimes touches of classical, oriental or East European peasant decoration. The absence of corsets was also an important feature of aesthetic dress. To wear a loose-waisted, corsetless ensemble was to court social disapproval. So intimately were dress and morals related that loose clothing was perceived as an infallible signal of moral looseness.

The aesthetic dressers also favoured a different style in female looks. Rejecting the submissive early Victorian look and the stronger and more voluptuous type of beauty which was coming into favour in the 1860s, they copied the frizzy auburn hair, pale faces and strong features found in many of Rossetti's paintings, at a time when red hair in particular was very much not the fashion.

Aesthetic dress was worn in the late 1870s by a circle whose leading figures were Mrs Humphrey Ward and Mrs Joseph Comyns Carr, wife of the director of the Grosvenor Gallery, a fashionable art gallery. Mrs Ward was a popular novelist, whose most famous novel, *Robert Elsmere*, was

NINCOMPOOPIANA.——THE MUTUAL ADMIRATION SOCIETY.

Our Gallant Colonel (who is not a Member thereof, to Mrs. Cimabue Brown, who is). "AND WHO 'S THIS YOUNG HERO THEY 'RE ALL SWARMING OVER NOW ?"

George du Maurier drew the male establishment's view of the aesthetic movement for **Punch***. This hostile depiction of raddled women with their effete escorts appeared in the issue for 14 February 1880.*

widely read in progressive circles. (Ironically, she herself was to become a committed anti-suffragist.) Her heroine Rose Leyburn goes through an aesthetic phase, during which she appears as:

a slim figure in aesthetic blue, a mass of reddish brown hair flying from her face . . . [her] skirts were cut with the most engaging naiveté, she was much adorned with amber beads and her red-brown hair had been tortured and frizzled to look as much like an aureole as possible . . . a damsel from the 'Earthly Paradise' [a poem by William Morris].[36]

George du Maurier lampooned Mrs Ward's circle as the 'Cimabue Browns' (presumably a reference to the Italian painter Cimabue) in a series of cartoons in *Punch*, and aesthetic dressers were often laughed at for being affected, hypersensitive and abnormally intense and thin. One novelist in the 1870s recorded an evening party in Gower Street, at which:

A young woman dressed as it seemed to me in nothing but an old-fashioned bathing gown and an amber necklace, whom I was asked to take to the supper room, returned to my enquiry of what I could get for her the lugubriously toned answer, 'I seldom eat.'[37]

32

The machine arrives

The elaboration of fashion would have been impossible without a revolution in the production and distribution of clothing. The Industrial Revolution had begun with textiles, and rapidly extended into other forms of production. In the long run, it removed from the home many of the tasks that had been performed within it, such as brewing, baking and, in fact, the making of clothes – much of which had been women's work.[38] Originally, tailors (men) made all clothing, but by the late seventeenth or early eighteenth century women mantua-makers (the mantua was a fitted formal dress) had taken over the making of most women's clothes, although items such as riding habits continued to be made by male tailors. Even in the eighteenth century, as today, garment-making establishments varied hugely in size, and even in method. In the early nineteenth century there is evidence that the 'complete garment method' (that is, one tailor making one whole garment or even suit of clothes) was already gradually being replaced by quicker methods. The radical, Francis Place, for example, who was a master tailor, was using a sectional method at this time. On the other hand, the complete garment method lasted right into the twentieth century.[39]

Tailoring had always been a skilled trade with a long apprenticeship (three years) during which the mysteries of cutting and other processes were transmitted. Each tailor kept his own pattern blocks and methods secret, as some still do today. Until 1796, when the first English tailoring book was published, there were no written works in the English language on the subject of cutting in this country, so that this, probably the most crucial process of the whole craft, was learnt by example.[40]

A deterioration in the conditions of work of the tailors occurred from the early nineteenth century, when overmanning and wage cuts hit the trade. The tailors were not the only group to be affected; but the new circumstances had broken the back of the traditional bespoke trade by 1850.

Ready-made clothes appeared in the eighteenth century, and were for sale in special 'show shops'. These shops in sea ports came to be known as 'slop shops', and by the early nineteenth century they and the garment making enterprises that supplied them had become well established. Two of the best known were E. Moses & Son Ltd of Aldgate and Minories, established in 1834, and H. D. Nicoll of Regent Street.

Both Moses and Nicoll dealt with middlemen contractors who farmed out the work to sweated outworkers. Nicoll's had originally been a show shop, and tailors had made stock on the premises. They were paid 14s [£22.22] for making a paletot, a loose, unfitted overcoat. Nicoll proposed paying them the lower rate of 9s [£14.22]. When they refused, he paid a

33

A stereoscopic photograph for home viewing of a poor dressmaker, of the 1850s–60s. Taken in a studio rather than in a genuine setting, it reflects real public concern at the time for the condition of such women.

middleman 7s 6d [£11.09], who in turn paid outworkers 5s [£7.93], out of which they had to find their own trimmings.[41]

Henry Mayhew, an investigative journalist, exposed these practices in his famous series of articles in the *Morning Chronicle* (1849–50). Conditions in the trade worsened, and this was associated with the entry of more women, and also Irish and Jewish immigrants. The exploitation of women and their concentration in this particular trade was one element in the process whereby women were gradually being squeezed out of many of the types of work in which they had formerly been prominent, so that by the 1840s, George Dodd, in his description of industry in London, commented:

A word or two respecting the employment of females in factories. The texture of English society is such that the number of reputable employments for females in the middle and humble ranks is very small. Most fathers and brothers are well aware of this; and women themselves, however desirous of contributing to their means of support, are cramped in their efforts by the limited range of avocations left open to them. The effect of this is such as never fails to result when the vineyard is too small for the labourers; the number of employments being few, so many females embark in them that the supply greatly exceeds the demand, and the value of female labour is thereby brought to a very low level.

Dodd records the employment of women in only a small number of factories – in certain parts of the tobacco industry, and in hat making, besides the garment industry. In 1851 it was recorded that there were 115 474 men as against 17 444 women employed in the whole clothing industry; but by 1911 the figures were 122 352 and 127 115 respectively.[42]

The conditions of employment of many of the seamstresses were appalling, and this was well known, and frequently written about by Friedrich Engels and many others. Mayhew's investigations contain numerous examples of the poverty of the needlewomen:

Never in all history was such a sight seen or such tales heard. There, in the dim haze of the large bare room . . . sat women and girls, some with babies sucking at their breasts – others in rags – and even these borrowed. . . .

'I am a shirt-maker, and make about three shirts a day, at 2½d [35p] a piece, every one of them having seven button-holes. I have to get up at six in the morning, and work till twelve at night to do that. I buy thread out of the price; and I cannot always get work. . . . I am now living with a young man. I am compelled to do so, because I could not support myself. . . . Sometimes we have been for two days with a bit of dry bread and cold water.'[43]

Many women were employed in making shirts and the underwear that came to be worn universally during the nineteenth century. (Prior to this, a shift was the only form of underwear worn.) Women's fine fashion garments were made in crowded workrooms above the imposing establishments in which customers would be received, and at the height of the social season (from April to July and again from October to December) most of these workers worked a fifteen-hour day. No 'lady' would dream

34

of buying ready-made clothes, other than accessories such as stockings or a shawl or mantle from the grand new emporiums or department stores.

Letters and diaries of the eighteenth and nineteenth centuries help us to understand the disadvantages of having all one's clothes made as well as the advantages. Clothes were not always carefully cut or made and the fit could cause problems. Until the nineteenth century knowledge of what was in fashion was also rather hit or miss, but by 1800 fashion plates and women's magazines were changing this, and were an indispensable feature of the diffusion of fashion in the century to come. Fashion plates were engraved and hand-coloured by a further group of underpaid female home workers and used to illustrate the new magazines such as the *English Woman's Domestic Magazine*, founded in 1853, and *The Queen*, which dates from 1861. Both of these were owned by Samuel Beeton, of cookery book fame, while *Harpers Bazaar* was launched in 1867.

The sewing machine was a further indispensable element in the garment revolution. Eventually patented by the American inventor Isaac Merrit Singer, the machine was not his idea alone and there had been several attempts to design and/or patent machines before his began to be manufactured *en masse* in 1851. Although it would appear that the earliest completely machine-made dresses (dating from 1860–5) were home made,[44] the factory production of clothes was the logical outcome of the invention of the sewing machine, and in the 1850s factories were springing up in which the machines were linked to a central shaft which provided steam power. Later the steam was replaced by gas and eventually by electricity.[45]

Once garments could be rapidly sewn up mechanically, a log jam was caused because the garment pieces were still being cut out by hand. John Barran of Leeds was able to get over this problem with the invention in 1860 of the band-knife, developed on the basis of the veneering band saw used for making finishes for wooden furniture. This knife could be used to slice through many layers of woollen material, thus enabling garments to be cut out in batches instead of one at a time. Finishing, hemming, tucking, buttonholes and many other processes continued to be done by hand, but during the 1870s and 1880s more and more machines were developed for felling (stitching down seams), band-stitching, collar padding, buttonholing and steam ironing.

In the mid-nineteenth century many reformers and those engaged in the garment industry believed that the coming of the machine would improve the condition of the workers. In the 1860s the Children's and Young Persons' Employment Commission was told that machinists' wages had risen and wages generally had gone up. On the other hand the first machines may have thrown many handworkers out of work, and the wage increases for the machinists may in any case have been temporary, associated with a rarity value that disappeared as machining became widespread. In addition, the use of the machine led in the long run to the demand for more and more handworkers – basters, pressers, fellers and cutters. The machine did not do away with the sweatshop either, but made the small workshop with just a few machines a viable proposition.[46]

The sewing machine also affected fashion itself, for it made possible far more ornamentations, such as are to be seen on the gowns of the 1860s onwards; the Aesthetic Movement may have been partly a response to this over-elaboration of dress. 'Sylvia' in her *How to Dress Well on a Shilling* [£1.30] *a Day*, was writing in the early 1870s: 'It is certain to be suspected that we owe much of the over-trimming now prevalent to the facilities offered by the sewing machines, which have become valued little friends in many a household.'[47]

Despite the emphasis on individual dressmaking for the 'lady of quality', part-made bodices for dresses were on sale by the 1830s.[48] Paper patterns were readily available, which must have made the productions of the individual dressmakers more successful. By 1875 the American pat-

Women's magazines provided fashion advice and paper patterns for bourgeois women and their dressmakers. This pattern for a 'Parisian' bodice (skirt not included), from the **English Woman's Domestic Magazine** *of 1858, would have been scaled up to full size.*

THE WORK-TABLE.

PARISIAN BASQUINE.

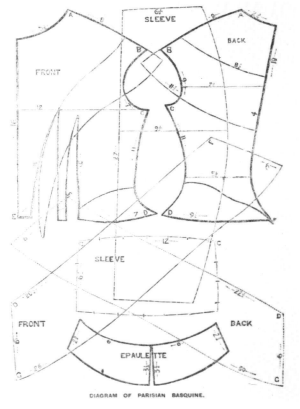

DIAGRAM OF PARISIAN BASQUINE.

tern company Buttericks had opened a shop in Regent Street from which they were selling between forty and sixty new designs each month. By 1880 Weldons were producing their own magazine, which carried patterns and detailed advice about fabrics. Patterns were sold throughout Britain via agencies in department stores or retail outlets. Buttericks by this time had several thousand agents in Britain.[49]

Another way in which fashion spread was through the department store. Moses and Nicoll had warehouses where their mass-produced clothes, mainly for men, might be purchased, but the department store was an altogether different affair. As with the sewing machine, there is no one inventor of the department store concept, and their origins have been traced to several developments in Britain, France and the United States. In all these countries retail stores with more than one department were springing up independently and more or less simultaneously in the 1830s. Bainbridges of Newcastle was one of the first, set up in 1838, with twenty-three departments by 1849. Bon Marché of Paris, Jolly of Bath, Kendal Milne of Manchester, were all in existence by the early 1830s followed closely by Lord and Taylor in New York and Marshall Field in Chicago. Jays, Marshall and Snelgrove and John Lewis, all of Oxford Street, opened in the 1840s and Dickins and Jones and Whiteleys of Bayswater were among the most fashionable in the 1870s.[50]

Probably the most famous and poetic description of such a department store is Émile Zola's *Au Bonheur des Dames* (1883), in which he charts the fortunes of a store modelled on Bon Marché. In his novel, which makes quite clear the devastation that the department store wrought on the surrounding small traders, and the exploitative conditions endured by the shop assistants, the overall effect is nevertheless of the phantasmagoria of the department store, a temple of consumerism, made to seem like an imaginary grand private house, with floorwalkers instead of butlers. What the department store sold was not just mere goods, but a dream of luxury and style.[51]

It was really as an adjunct to these stores that the women's clothing industry, the 'Light Clothing' industry as it was known, developed along more organised lines in the latter part of the nineteenth century. Dressmaking workrooms were attached to retail shops (not just the department stores). There:

to ensure full employment of their dressmakers when orders were scarce, dresses and other garments were made in advance of specific orders or sold ready made in the shops. Sometimes there would be a sale of these garments at a cheaper price which attracted less wealthy customers, and so produced a demand for a constant supply of cheaper garments, and the development of the 'rag-trade' image. However, this aspect of ready-made clothing was not synonymous with factory production as in fact it was the child of the service industries of dressmaking and bespoke tailoring.[52]

The department stores sold more and more of these new ready-to-wear clothes, at first concentrating on mourning wear, mantles and tailored clothes.

In 1866 Jay's was advertising 'fully sewn' dresses, and Sélincourt and Colman, another department store, was supplying ready-made clothing for women from 1869, including 'costumes' and other items of outerwear, made in London and Birmingham workshops. In 1870 Debenham and Freebody was offering five different qualities of clothing to their clients: made to measure in their high-class dressmaker salon; part-made; completely ready to wear; a dressmaking service which offered fabric and paper pattern; and a mail order service of all of these. They charged 10s 6d [£14] for making up a plain dress and 12s 6d [£10.72] for making up just the bodice of an evening dress.[53] By the 1870s the Public Record Office contained records of complete light-weight bustled back fashion dresses ready made for sale by a company called Rosa Salter, Commercial Road, London.[54]

Second-hand clothes

Mid-Victorian clothes were expected to last far longer than would even the most expensive clothes today. One reason for the continued use of hand sewing on expensive silk dresses was that the garments were normally 'turned' and/or remade into something different and machine-stitched seams would have been more difficult to unpick.

If the comparatively smart middle-class lady expected lengthy wear from her expensive clothes, those lower down the social scale could not expect to buy such clothes at all, or only second-hand. Fashionable clothing had been traditionally passed on by the lady of fashion to her personal lady's maid. Occasionally the maid would wear these hand-me-downs herself, but more likely she would sell them. The second-hand clothing business had flourished in the eighteenth century when it had centred on Monmouth Street, Seven Dials (Covent Garden), but it reached new heights in the 1850s, by which time its centre had moved to Rosemary Lane and Petticoat Lane in the East End.

In 1851 Mayhew described two Old Clothes Exchanges. One was run by Mr Isaac – the trade was dominated by Irish and Jewish merchants. Augustus Sala describes the Jewish women haggling for clothes at an Oxford Street auction at Debenhams; he uses what were for the times the standard anti-semitic description of greasy curls and hooked noses. At Isaac's Exchange some of the clothes were bought by the bale for export to Ireland, Belgium and Holland, others by retailers for resale either to wholesalers or directly to individual customers:

DUDLEY'S MART,
LONDON ROAD and FRASER STREET.
WHOLESALE PRICES.

Lined Satin, wadded & quilted, trimmed Russian fur, or to measure.

Lined Squirrel and other suitable Russian skins.

OLIVETTE, 31/6.   MARGUERETTE, 5 gs.

Manufactory for Ladies' Cloaks, Dolmans, &c., Lined Fur, Satin, or Silk, and Quilted.
Prices and Patterns on Application   Tailor-made in all Materials.

BRANCHES.

3, New Street, BIRMINGHAM; Eastgate Buildings, 3, Foregate Street, CHESTER; 174 & 176, Commercial Street, NEWPORT, Mon.; 40 & 42, George Street, LUTON; 49 & 51, Stafford Street, HANLEY; 24, King Street, SOUTH SHIELDS; Dudley House, Dalton Road, BARROW-IN-FURNESS; 23, Market Square, WIGAN; 47 & 49, Scotch Street, CARLISLE; Dudley Buildings, 45, High Row, DARLINGTON; Dudley Buildings, Tavern Street, IPSWICH.

By the 1880s, the ready-made clothes industry for women was flourishing: big companies had chains of outlets which offered the public elegant clothes at wholesale prices.

In another department . . . are assembled such traders as buy the old garments to dispose of them, either after a process of cleaning, or when they have been repaired and renovated. These buyers are generally shopkeepers, residing in the old clothes districts of Marylebone Lane, Holywell-Street, Monmouth Street, Union Street (Borough), Saffron Hill (Field Lane), Drury Lane, Shoreditch, the Waterloo Road and other places. . . .

In another part of the same market is carried on the *retail* old clothes trade to anyone – shopkeeper, artisan, clerk, costermonger, or gentleman.[55]

39

*Second-hand clothes dealers
went from house to house
swopping old clothes for new
crockery and plants. This
trade, in Victorian times, was
run largely by the poor for the
poor, as this illustration from
an article by Henry Mayhew
for the* **Morning Chronicle** *in
1849 shows.*

Direct purchasers came from the amorphous uncertain ranks of the genteel poor or upwardly mobile, the indeterminate classes of the new cities, 'the town mob or the underworld, the classless or the *déclassé*, the aspiring clerk or the impoverished professional man; 'the ready availability of second-hand finery greatly contributed to the well-dressed but socially confusing appearance of the London populace, a fact on which foreigners always commented'.[56]

Men's clothing was the most likely to be purchased second-hand. A second-hand frock coat might be purchased for anything between 2s 6d and 5s [£4–£8]. Even Nicoll's cheapest coat would cost at least 18s [£29] and second-hand bespoke was much superior in quality.[57]

There was an extensive export trade in second-hand men's clothing to Europe, South Africa and North and South America. It is said that one way typhus reached Canada in the late 1840s was through such imports.[58] Clothes were collected door to door, up and down the country. A coat was worth between 4d and 11d [54p–£1.50], and trousers 4d to 8d [54p–£1] at the mid-century.

London had a large industry devoted entirely to remaking ('translating' or 'clobbering') second-hand clothes. Dented top hats were cut down

in size and polished, holes in shoes were 'mended' with disguised card-
board or cheap leather patches, old coats were cut down, re-dyed and
patched up in all sorts of clever ways. Even rags were re-used – sold back
up to Yorkshire to recycle into the poorest 'shoddy cloth' for the slop trade
(the slop trade was the production of cheap ready-made clothes).

Women's wear also sold well, especially silk dresses, which were
cleaned with turpentine and resold at from 3s to 4s [£4.90–£6.50]. Even
more popular were the 'washing' cotton dresses. Underwear was bought
second-hand, but women seem to have been resistant to buying second-
hand corsets. Presumably these had to fit well, and would be difficult to
alter.

Clothing was widely distributed to the poor via nationally and locally
organised charities, particularly in rural areas without access to clothing
markets. To the poor, therefore, the lure of new clothes was very strong,
implying an escape from the penury and patronage to which most of
them remained condemned all their lives. While for the middle classes
fine fashions signified ostentation and the maintenance of the always
dangerously permeable class boundaries, to the aspiring working-class
personal adornment implied freedom and emancipation from the pinch
of want; and, if, as has been suggested,[59] many of our moral terms derive
from clothing metaphors, many of our expressions for impoverishment
and exhaustion likewise originate in the experience of not having nice
enough clothes – down at heel, threadbare, careworn and worn out.

At the Victorian high noon we find a surprising similarity between fashion and the clothing industry as it was then and as it is today. Enormous
differences in quality and methods of production, the association with
consumerism, exploited labour and kings of fashion, the persistence of
the sale of second-hand clothing: all these features of garment production and sale were in place then and, despite fluctuations, remain with us
as we reach the 1990s. The influence of exclusive designers continues, as
does the association of high fashion with social aspiration and alternative forms of dress with anti-establishment views.

As we have already seen, the manifest exploitation and luxury of the
trade, and the unhealthy and restrictive nature of many garments, were
already a cause for concern in the twenty years between 1860 and 1880.
Between 1880 and 1900 these concerns were intensified, and there was a
full scale, and bitterly contested movement for wholesale dress reform.

2

DOWN WITH FROU-FROU: AESTHETES, REFORMERS AND EMANCIPATED WOMEN 1890-1920

The Edwardian period from 1901 to 1910 – in France the *Belle Époque* – is usually pictured as one of elegance and graciousness. It is seen as the Indian summer of British world supremacy, and a time free of the rush and speed of modern life. Britain's Empire was at its zenith and stretched across the globe, while the fortunes that had been made during the Industrial Revolution were now supplying new generations with an income from investments for which many had never had to work. *Nouveaux riches* abounded. The ownership of land was still the passport to power and privilege, and the aristocracy retained its hold, but industrialists also bought estates and many gained titles as well. American heiresses crossed the Atlantic to marry dukes, and actresses and musical comedy stars – some of whom also married into the aristocracy – set the fashion as much as did society ladies.

High fashion continued to be extravagant and luxurious as befitted a leisured society. Styles had changed, however, and in 1900 elegant women no longer appeared small and submissive beside bearded Victorian patriarchs. Now they were tall, voluptuous and statuesque. Lucile, Lady Duff Gordon, one of the most important dress designers in Edwardian London, claimed that her mannequins were approaching 6 feet (1.8 metres) in height. The Edwardian society lady, with her jutting bosom and S-bend figure, floated across grassy lawns in frothy, high-necked gowns and huge hats. Lucile's designs were just as impractical in a different way as the bustles of the 1880s, for she designed dresses made of soft, easily damaged silk chiffons and crêpes, trimmed with yards of fine, hand-made lace. The Edwardian woman of fashion positively frothed

Opposite Actresses and musical comedy stars were the fashion models of the Edwardian period. In this photograph of 1905 the actress Miss Carol McComas wears the epitome of Edwardian frou-frou with extravagant hand-made trimmings and appliqué lace.

over with pastel femininity and 'frou-frou'. To dress fashionably was, moreover, a full-time occupation, as well as an expensive one. Lucile, in her memoirs, recalled that:

> To have worn the same dress at three functions in a season caused comment . . . very few women bother now [1932] to change their dresses five or six times a day, yet every Edwardian with any claims to being well dressed did so as a matter of course.[1]

The upkeep of the clothes worn by society and upper-middle-class women was also extremely labour intensive. The Marchioness of Bath recalled that out of forty-three servants at Longleat, the Thynne family seat, there were six laundry maids, two sewing maids and two lady's maids. The immense hairstyles alone, padded out for bulk and elaborately pinned up, required the attendance of a maid several times a day.[2]

The richest women still went to Paris for their clothes, and Paris styles set the fashions internationally, but there was, nonetheless, a flourishing London couture trade. Some establishments set themselves up in South Kensington, but the most successful tended to be located in Mayfair. There, firms such as Redfern, Worth, Lucile, Kate Reilly (who trained Madeleine Vionnet) and Reville and Rossiter (who trained Victor Stiebel) ministered to clients who included the future Queen Mary and Mrs Messel (Lord Snowdon's grandmother). Mrs Messel was one of Lucile's clients, but she also purchased from others of the many firms catering to this exclusive clientele – for example, Brighton Museum has a grey silk afternoon crêpe dress made for her by Mrs Hayward. The fashion pages of magazines such as *The Queen* reveal that at the turn of the century there

Lucile, Lady Duff Gordon, the British couturier, achieved international success. Her trade mark was daring chiffon gowns (and lingerie) in the neo-classical style, shown here in the couturiers' magazine **Les Modes** *of 1914.*

were many designers scattered over the smart districts of central London. Not all catered for those for whom money was no object. Madame Cooper and Madame Green, for example, described themselves as 'inexpensive for good dressmakers'.

The great department stores, then in their heyday, had couture salons of their own where clients could buy original Paris gowns or adapted versions of them. By this time workrooms attached to the fashion departments both undertook extensive alterations and made a wide range of fashionable clothing.

While women appeared more imposing, their male escorts seemed more youthful than their grandfathers had done. Although King Edward VII wore the pointed imperial beard, many young men about town were now clean shaven. They wore suits with short jackets and tight trousers, and, in summer, blazers and straw boaters.

Beneath the surface of luxury and lace, however, Edwardian society was deeply troubled. The glamorous Edwardian decade was in fact one of intense social strife. As well as the campaign for votes for women, which reached a violent climax, Ireland was in turmoil and there was serious industrial unrest between 1908 and 1913. However, the wealth that the Empire brought to Britain did benefit at least some members of the working class, and their standard of living as a whole was rising. The poorest sections of society, however, continued to live in squalor and misery.

The supreme confidence of the High Victorian age had given place by the 1890s to a sense of uncertainty. The economic depression of the last quarter of the nineteenth century by no means affected everyone directly, but gave rise to fears of German and American competition and to a narrow, chauvinistic insistence on British superiority. Yet from the 1880s onwards there were growing fears about the fitness of the British to shoulder the imperial burden, and many forms of dissidence in the arts, from the 'decadent' aestheticism of Oscar Wilde and Walter Pater,[3] to flourishing dress reform and socialist movements, and there was also, increasingly, militant feminism.

At the same time the social horizons of many were widening. By the end of the nineteenth century many middle-class women had followed the mid-century pioneers and were taking up paid employment in social work, domestic science and midwifery, while lower down the social scale more women were being employed as shop assistants, clerks and secretaries, both in the expanding public sector and in commerce and industry, and as teachers in elementary schools. Very few married women went out to work, although penury often compelled working class wives to take in washing or do sewing, or undertake other forms of homeworking such as finishing off small industrial goods. Such work, because it

45

was done in the home, did not offend the norms of respectability which increasingly influenced working-class families, nor did it appear in labour statistics, but it was certainly widespread.

Many young, unmarried women, meanwhile, were gaining greater freedom of movement and economic independence. The Fabian Society, for example, founded in 1884, had a high proportion of women members. The Fabians were non-revolutionary socialists who believed in the gradual evolution of British society towards socialism. Its members were drawn largely from intellectuals and white-collar workers. Its women members, too, were drawn from an aspiring class, many of whom had to fend for themselves and who hungered for education in order to be able to do so more effectively. That is not to say that women enjoyed the same independence as men. Their freedom was a relative affair. Before she married, Beatrice Webb, then Beatrice Potter, and later probably the most famous woman Fabian, was allowed to undertake investigative research for Charles Booth in the East End. She did not, however, receive payment for this, and she was also, as the only unmarried daughter, expected to look after her widowed father and run his household.

Fashions were no longer only for the wealthy. As the boundaries of class shifted, more sections of society were expressing their aspirations to social mobility in their dress, although differences in class position could still be easily deduced from the clothes worn.

Tailor-made or ready-to-wear clothing

In the 1890s, although women still wore tight corsets, the heavy, draped bustle was abandoned, and instead skirts were gored. The tailored suit, known as a 'tailor-made' or costume, introduced in the previous decade, became extremely popular. It was a fashion thought to have originated in England, with the tailoring firms of Redfern and Creed. In the 1890s and the first decade of the twentieth century, middle- and upper-class women were wearing these suits or the woollen and serge skirts, with light, soft, shirtwaist blouses, and for the first time were prepared to buy them 'off the peg'. These somewhat simplified garments could be, and were, mass produced, and although the cheaper models, worn by shop assistants, typists and so on, may not have been particularly well made, they at least looked smart and attractive. The novelist Arnold Bennett, however, in attendance at a talk at the Times Book Club given by H. G. Wells around 1910, observed that although the women present:

deemed themselves elegant . . . being far from the rostrum I had a good view of the back of their blouses, chemisettes and bodices. What an assortment of pretentious and ill-made toilettes! What

The frail vision of Edwardian femininity had rigid underpinnings, including extra long, flat-fronted corsets. These examples, advertised in **The Queen** newspaper in 1905, were made in Paris and sold in London at prices between 12s 11d and 3 guineas.

Tailor-made suits could be purchased at reasonable cost by mail order and were advertised in newspapers. In 1905 John Noble of Manchester stressed in the **Daily News** that 'the garments are Guaranteed Made Absolutely Without any Sweating of the Workers'.

disclosures of clumsy hooks-and-eyes and general creased carelessness! It would not do for me to behold the 'library public' in the mass too often![4]

But this type of costume was a boon, not only to the women of the middle classes, who found in it a practical and attractive form of dress for shopping and morning visits, but for the legions of young women now going out to work.

So, although this was a period of economic depression, the ready made clothing trade was able to expand to serve the typists and telephonists, the saleswomen of the city centres and the clerical workers of the growing state bureaucracy. These women were less well paid than the male clerks they often replaced, and the rigid office hierarchies kept them bunched at the bottom of the promotional ladder, or segregated in 'women's work' with few prospects of promotion. Usually their work was terminated if they married, and the very idea of a pregnant woman being seen at work was still deeply shocking – it was actually considered indecent. Yet there was a sense of the adventure of these new opportunities, however restricted; office workers at this time were pioneers, and were sometimes represented as holding advanced views. Olive Rayner's novel *The Typewriter Girl* (1897) portrays a perhaps atypical heroine, for this typist is a 'Girton girl' of good family. Limited means compel her to earn her living in a variety of office settings, and she even penetrates an anarchist commune. She also rides a bicycle, wearing rational dress.[5] Evidently, however, such a heroine was at least believable, although she was romanticised.

More typical was the secretary who recorded her memories for the *Observer* in 1987. She left school in 1911, and took a job in the City of London, for which she was paid 10s [£16] a week. Her 'uniform' for work was a long, navy blue serge skirt and a white blouse – although if you were daring, you might wear a pink one. 'To keep their sleeves clean, secretaries wore paper cuffs, which they changed each day. . . . Hats were *de rigueur* – felt in winter and straw in summer.'[6]

The woman clerical worker's life was not usually an easy or glamorous one, as George Gissing's novel *The Odd Women* (1893) demonstrates. His heroines could not afford fashionable clothes, yet their gentility forbade that they should dress like working-class women:

She set forth at half-past nine. With extreme care she had preserved an out-of-doors dress into the third summer: it did not look shabby. Her mantle was in its second year only; the original fawn colour had gone to an indeterminate grey. Her hat of brown straw was a possession for ever: it underwent new trimming, at an outlay of a few pence, when that became unavoidable. Yet Virginia could not have been judged anything but a lady. She wore her garments as only a lady can (the position and movement of the arms has much to do with this), and had the step never to be acquired by a person of vulgar instincts.[7]

48

For such women the tailor-made 'costume' was a relatively durable solution.

Although every gentleman still hoped to have his clothes made to measure by a tailor, ready-to-wear clothing was becoming more acceptable further up the social scale for men as well as for women. The economic depression may have meant that some men who in more prosperous times would have worn bespoke clothing might now be finding ready-to-wear an acceptable alternative. As the tailoring trade paper *Men's Wear* commented in 1892, the recession of the early 1900s 'might persuade some men who . . . very properly get their clothes made for them by a tailor [to] be tempted by a really good cloth made into ready-to-wear clothing in a large and detailed number of fittings'.[8]

The unskilled working class and what was referred to at the time as 'the residuum' (the very poorest and the unemployed) remained quite outside fashion. It was calculated by one researcher that 50 per cent of all adult male wage earners (approximately two and a half million workers) were bringing home less than 25s [£41] a week. A group of Fabian women investigating the disposable income of working-class families in Lambeth in 1909 declared that: 'clothing is, frankly, a mystery. . . . In the poorer budgets items for clothes appear at extraordinarily distant intervals, when, it is to be supposed, they can no longer be done without.' Working-class women, bringing up their families on 'round about a pound a week' [£32], spent more money on boots than on any other item of clothing, putting aside a shilling a week for the boot club [£1.60 today]:

The women seldom get new clothes. The men go to work and must be supplied, the children must be decent at school, but the mother has no need to appear in the light of day. If very badly equipped, she can shop in the evening in the walk, and no one will notice under her jacket and rather long skirt what she is wearing on her feet. Most of them have a hat, a jacket and a 'best' skirt to wear in the street. In the house a blouse and patched skirt under a sacking apron is the universal wear. . . . These women who look to be in the dull middle of middle age are young, it comes as a shock when the mind grasps it.[9]

The husbands of these women were in occupations such as bricklayer's labourer, plumber's labourer or builder's labourer, and some were unemployed. Even if he was better dressed than his wife, the working man's garments would consist only of a donkey jacket, trousers of corduroy or shoddy, and a flat cap and scarf.

Lady Bell, wife of a leading ironfounder in Middlesbrough, investigated conditions in the town in *At The Works* (1907). She found that wages varied considerably, and some families were quite comfortably off, especially if there were several wage earners in the family. Lady Bell observed that some of the workmen, who did not need such good clothes,

49

Salford second-hand clothing market in the 1890s. Some women are wearing traditional Lancashire shawls, but some are in the modern tailor-made suits.

were 'obviously much better off than many a clerk with the same amount'[10]. The poorest, on the other hand, obtained their clothes mostly from old clothes shops or through the tallyman (who supplied goods on credit), although the working man had to have a good flannel shirt and a Sunday best suit. As in Lambeth, the women had the worst clothes: 'A working girl said on one occasion that she thought the mark of a "real lady" was that she wore a short skirt and neat boots, this last representing to the working girl almost the unattainable'.[11] Many working people still had to rely on second- or even third-hand clothing, even for special occasions. In *Esther Waters*, published in 1895, George Moore described the apparel seen at a servants' ball:

It had been found impossible to restrict the ball to those who possessed or could obtain an evening suit, and plenty of check trousers and red neckties were hopping about . . . a young girl had borrowed her grandmother's wedding dress, and a young man wore a canary-coloured waistcoat and a blue . . . guardsman's coat of old time. These touches of fancy, and personal taste, divided the villagers from the household servants. . . . Cooks trailed black silk dresses adorned with wide collars and fastened with gold brooches containing portraits of their late husbands.[12]

The working class as a whole could experience sharp swings between penury and relative comfort – and such swings would also take place within a single working-class family at different times. When there were lots of young children to feed and clothe, or when the breadwinner was unemployed, then poverty stared the family daily in the face. In times of full employment, on the other hand, and once the children had grown up and were contributing to the family budget, then things were easier.

In some jobs, particularly in the dress and retailing trades, women had to look smart and wore reasonably fashionable clothes. Such was the

50

This poor family from Kirriemuir, in remote, rural Scotland, are wearing their best clothes – both bought and home-made – with ill-fitting boots. Photograph c. 1900.

importance of respectability that most working women wore sober colours – which were also, of course, more serviceable. Bedraggled finery was the hallmark of the woman who was no better than she should be. George Moore describes some of these women too – servant girls forced into prostitution:

Two young women came out of an eating-house, hanging on each other's arms, talking lazily, . . . poor and dissipated girls, dressed in vague clothes fixed with hazardous pins. The skirt on the outside was a soiled mauve and the bodice that went with it was a soiled chocolate. A broken yellow plume hung out of a battered hat. The skirt on the inside was a dim green, and little was left of the cotton velvet jacket but the cotton.[13]

So the Edwardian façade of luxury and glamour was ultimately deceptive.

Don't be a scorcher – reform and reaction

Central to the social struggle was the open conflict over the role of women. Apart from its more direct manifestations, the controversy often took a symbolic form and was expressed in fierce debates about appropriate forms of dress. This had a significance that actually outlasted the campaign for the vote, since it is hardly an exaggeration to say that the dramatic struggle between conventional styles of dress for women (and men) and the new 'anti-fashions', or various kinds of reform dress, determined the direction of twentieth-century mainstream fashions, particularly for women.

During the 1880s there was renewed interest in dress reform, the objectives of which were rather different from those of aesthetic dress, although there was considerable overlap, and, towards the end of the nineteenth century, sometimes a convergence. In the 1880s the German zoologist Dr Jaeger advanced with considerable success his view that men and women should wear only animal fibres, i.e. wool (the origin of the slogan 'wear wool next to the skin'), since vegetable fibres caused 'noxious exhalations'. Ideally this meant not only that wool clothing and undergarments (including the very successful combinations) should be worn, but that the interior of the home should also be furnished entirely in wool, down to the sheets on the beds. Jaeger's theory was, quite simply, scientifically wrong; yet it is significant that it was promoted precisely as *scientific.* For at this period 'science' was equated with everything modern and rational – hence '*rational* dress' – and a view developed that decoration of all kinds, but particularly in matters of dress, was irrational and therefore should be done away with. This was perhaps an understandable reaction to the fearful elaboration of women's clothes in the 1870s and 1880s, when a woman looked more like a cross between an armchair and a lampshade than a human being.

Nevertheless the stress on function and utility led to a neglect of the complex social meanings which dress conveys. From the point of view of dress reform, the pleasure that a beautiful garment can give was disregarded, or seemed suspect and unworthy, for there undoubtedly was a puritanical side to rational dress.[14]

There is a sense in which the movement for 'rational' dress was an attempt to *modernise* dress, particularly but not exclusively female dress,

52

and to devise a form of clothing suitable for the pace and demands of urban, industrial life in capitalist societies, where public life was becoming important in a new way, and where women in particular were moving into the public sphere.

Some women, by the last two decades of the nineteenth century, were determined to wear less constricting clothes. In 1881, Mrs King, author of *Women's Dress in Relation to Health*, formed, with Viscountess Harberton, the Rational Dress Society, later called the Rational Dress League. Its aims were as follows:

The Rational Dress Society protests against the introduction of any fashion in dress that either deforms the figure, impedes the movement of the body, or in any way tends to injure health. It protests against the wearing of tightly-fitting corsets, of high-heeled or narrow-toed boots and shoes; of heavily weighted skirts, as rendering healthy exercise almost impossible; and of all tie-down cloaks and other garments impeding the movement of the arms. It protests against crinolines or crinolettes of any kind as ugly and deforming. The object of the Rational Dress Society is to promote the adoption, according to individual taste and convenience, of a style of dress based upon considerations of health, comfort and beauty, and to deprecate constant changes of fashion that cannot be recommended on any of these grounds.[15]

In 1884 the views of the Rational Dress Society were given public exposure at the International Health Exhibition, nicknamed 'the Healtheries', at Kensington Town Hall.[16] Although much derided for its vegetarian restaurant and exhibits of a 'Rocky Mountain Travelling Costume', complete with Turkish trousers, this exhibition dealt with serious concerns such as health and urban sanitation. Lady Harberton's 'dual garments' or divided skirt, worn modestly under a full-length coat, aroused considerable interest, and in the following year Ada Ballin, in her book *The Science of Dress*, also advocated the divided skirt on the grounds that 'advantages may be gained by clothing each leg separately, as the passage of cold air which takes place beneath the petticoats is thereby avoided'.[17]

The issue of appropriate dress for women came to the fore at this time partly because a number of battles in the fight for the emancipation of women had already been won. As Viscountess Harberton pointed out in 1882:

Now that women are being gradually allowed to take their place in Society as rational beings, and are no longer looked upon as mere toys and slaves; and now that their livelihood is becoming more and more to be considered their own affair, the question of dress assumes proportions which it did not use to have.[18]

By the 1880s a number of academic girls' schools, and colleges for women at Oxford and Cambridge, were well established; and the expansion of women's education had a direct impact on women's dress. There was still considerable opposition to the education of girls from many

53

THE
RATIONAL DRESS GAZETTE.
Organ of the Rational Dress League.

No. 13	OCTOBER, 1899.	PRICE ONE PENNY.

The Objects of the Association are to foster and encourage reform in the dress of both sexes, but more particularly to promote the wearing by women of some form of bifurcated garment, especially for such active purposes as cycling, tennis, golf, and other athletic exercises, walking tours, house-work, and business purposes. Annual Subscription 2/6. Entrance Fee 1/-

Hon. Treasurer: VISCOUNTESS HARBERTON, 108, Cromwell Road, S.W.
Hon. Secretary: Mrs. F. J. HERON MAXWELL, 30, Ashley Gardens, S.W.
Assistant Secretary and Organiser: Miss EDITH M. VANCE, 64, Patshull Road, N.W.

Application for Forms of Membership, Rules, Patterns, &c., should be addressed to the Secretary. M.Ss. and Sketches for the Gazette are cordially invited and should be sent to Mrs. HARTUNG, 10, Guilford Street, W.C. Annual Subscription to the Gazette (for non-members) 1/6. Single copies 1d.

Rational Dress up-to-date, reproduced by kind permission of the Editor of the "Daily Telegraph."

*The **Rational Dress Gazette** was devoted to the discussion of reform dress. These three cycling outfits shown in October 1899 vary from the tailored style (right) to the more feminine versions (left and centre).*

quarters, and what the students should normally wear was a matter for anxious concern – how to steer a fine line between looking 'fast' or unladylike on the one hand and totally frumpish on the other, the balance being usually tipped in the direction of frumpishness. Victorian bourgeois culture seemed to have a real phobia about 'mannish women'. Perhaps the underlying cause of this was male hostility resulting from a double fear lest women should become economic competitors, and also lest they should cease to provide the domestic comforts to which men were accustomed. Some women also felt threatened by the 'New Woman' – because she questioned the terms on which women were permitted to participate in society, and demanded new and alarming economic and social freedoms, thus upsetting the leisured lady's apple cart.

With the expansion of education for girls, however, it came to seem unhealthy that they had so little physical exercise, and girls had already begun to play organised games and do formal gymnastics, eurhythmics and Swedish drill in the 1870s, or even earlier. In the last two decades of the nineteenth century adult women too were slowly beginning to participate in a whole range of active sports such as golf, swimming, rowing and cricket, but of widest social significance were lawn tennis and bicycling.

The newly developed game of lawn tennis enabled young men and women to meet and get to know one another in a relaxed, informal yet not entirely unsupervised setting. Middle-class tennis parties were the stage for flirtations and romance, and young women were therefore concerned to look elegant rather than efficient on and off the court. Kate Gielgud described typical tennis wear for women in the 1880s in her *Autobiography*:

Our tennis dress consisted of ankle length flannel or serge skirts closely pleated, and plain long-sleeved blouses with starched linen collars, and we wore wide leather belts and stiff brimmed boaters. Later the Huxley girls introduced us to stockinette jerseys, woollen and light, which left our necks free, though we were not allowed to roll up our sleeves.[19]

Betty Ryan, a Wimbledon tennis champion just before the First World War, recalled that when she and others wore corsets during their games of tennis these often became bloodstained, presumably because they cut into the players' flesh during their exertions.[20] The 'plimsoll' or flat rubber-soled canvas sports shoe, had been patented in 1876, and this made a more active game possible for women.

The 'New Woman' at the turn of the century typically wore a tailor-made suit. These students of St Hilda's College, Oxford, in the 1890s proudly display symbols of their largely scientific studies.

The development of the bicycle as a means of transport, and of bicycling as a leisure activity, had even more far-reaching consequences. The original velocipedes and penny-farthing bicycles had been dangerous vehicles, ridden mainly by athletic young men who adopted, for this pursuit, a special garb consisting of breeches, leggings, a Norfolk style jacket and a cap. Corah's Leicester hosiery and jersey factory devised a jersey bicycling suit for men in 1883, called the 'Fred Wood Champion Suit' after the Leicester cyclist who had become world champion in June of that year. (This firm also developed football sweaters for men.)

In 1884 the Rover safety bicycle, with two equal-sized wheels, and in 1887 the first pneumatic tyre were developed, and now bicycling could become a popular leisure activity, taken up enthusiastically by the urban and suburban middle classes, including large numbers of young women, and the craze even extended to some better-off working people as well, especially during the peak years of the craze, from 1895–7. Working-class cyclists were helped by the creation of the Clarion Clubs. Brainchild of Robert Blatchford, an ethical socialist and publisher of the socialist paper *The Clarion*, the Clubs formed groups to undertake cycling expeditions, and members were sometimes able to hire bicycles, or the Clubs purchased them in bulk at reduced rates. (The normal price of a bicycle was about £10 [£377 today].)[21]

Of course not all – or probably most – cyclists were radicals. The author's (Elizabeth Wilson's) grandmother Minnie Syms, whose family was solidly right wing, and who was not permitted to read Dickens until after she had married, was nevertheless allowed to go cycling unchaperoned, with her fiancé. In a letter, her eldest brother implores her, 'Don't be a scorcher', alluding to the fact that young women cyclists were considered rather 'fast'. Born in 1879, Minnie Syms was a lifelong Conservative and opponent of votes for women, so the fact that her cycling was taken for granted suggests its wide social acceptance. Nevertheless, there was a connection between bicycling, progressive thought and the emancipation of women, and this was condensed in the very public controversy that surrounded the costume women should adopt for this new activity.

No one could deny that women's ordinary dress was a hazard. As one woman wrote long afterwards:

My long skirt was a nuisance and even a danger. It is an unpleasant experience to be hurled on to stone setts and find that one's skirt has been so tightly wound round the pedal that one cannot even get up enough to unwind it.[22]

Controversy arose because women adapted men's jackets, shirts, coats, hats and eventually even trousers, or at least knickerbockers, as cycling wear. The scandal over women revealing their ankles and even their lower calves had passed by the mid 1860s, when special short-skirted, ankle-revealing croquet dresses had become socially acceptable, and by 1881, according to Arthur Lazenby Liberty (owner of the Liberty store in Regent Street), sportswomen had adopted men's tailored jackets, a white shirt with collar and tie and various kinds of masculine headgear. The rational, or reform dress worn by some of the most advanced women bicyclists, however, was more shocking.

Only a small minority of mostly privileged women actually wore any full-scale form of 'rational dress' for bicycling in Britain (although it seems to have been more popular in France and Germany). Surviving examples (for example, the pair at the Gallery of English Costume at Platt Hall, Manchester) are rare collectors' items. But it was widely discussed, both in magazines for a general readership, and in the cycling press (*Cyclist* and *The Lady Cyclist*, for example). In 1893 Miss Tessie Reynolds rode a man's bicycle from Brighton, her home town, to London and back, dressed in rationals. *Cycling* magazine – presumably representing the views of a mixed readership – abhorred the costume, particularly its 'scantiness'. To us the costume appears, if anything, overdressed and cumbersome, but these garments emphasised not just the legs but even more unmentionable parts of the female anatomy. Many women as well as men found rationals indecent, while others opposed them on the grounds that they would hinder the general 'cause' of cycling. *The Lady Cyclist*, however, applauded the intrepid Miss Reynolds, and thereafter the controversy raged through its pages.[23] Most women, however, if they wore breeches at all, hid them modestly under a skirt the flap of which could be buttoned safely out of the way, or else wore the less provocative divided skirt, or just their usual clothes.

Women who did flout convention by wearing the contentious breeches risked public affront. Viscountess Harberton herself was refused admittance to the coffee room of the Hautboy Hotel, Ockham, Surrey, in 1898, because she was wearing breeches, and had to go instead into the common bar parlour. A court case resulted, because members of the Cyclists' Touring Club were guaranteed hospitality at the hotel, and the Viscountess was a member of the Club, which meant that the owner of the hotel, Mrs Martha Jane Sprague, was in breach of contract. Mrs Sprague, however, actually won the case. In the heated debate which ensued in the pages of *The Lady Cyclist*, supporters of rational dress were in the majority, so it could be said that Viscountess Harberton had won the argument.[24]

When *The Lady Cyclist* fulminated against fashionable attire it enunciated some of the main arguments in favour of dress reform:

A rare photograph of Viscountess Harberton in her personal version of rational dress, c. 1890. She was the leading campaigner for the promotion of 'bi-furcated garments' for over twenty years.

Fainting, hysteria, indigestion, anorexia, lassitude, diminished vitality and a host of other sufferings, arise from interference with the circulation of the blood and the prevention of the full play of the breathing organs. These conditions of a living death will never be removed until the corsets, banded skirts and petticoats, irrational footgear and other errors in clothing are abandoned.[25]

The language used here – 'irrational', 'errors' – reminds us of the supposedly scientific and rationalistic basis of dress reform, but health and science were not the only reasons for hostility to the fashionable dress of the period. Dress reform attracted diverse groups of women and men who shared a number of overlapping yet varied beliefs and values. The extravagant frivolity, as many felt, of feminine fashion seemed to stand for all the worst aspects of the economic and social system, yet was easier to attack than capitalism itself.

There was outrage, for example, at the cruelty to animals and birds whose pelts and feathers adorned the woman of fashion. At first this came mainly from naturalists, but was taken up by humanitarians. Traders continued to circumvent such restrictions as were placed on the import of feathers and birds, and in 1895 the Duchess of York tactlessly wore an aigrette (feathers as a hat trimming) at an RSPCA prize giving; but by 1906 Queen Alexandra had announced that she would no longer wear wild birds' feathers, and in 1911 Queen Mary eliminated all plumed millinery from her wardrobe before the royal visit to India (source of the egret and other fashionable plumage). Many attempts to pass legislation that would prohibit the hunting and trading of birds for their feathers failed, but the Importation of Plumage (Prohibition) Act finally became law in 1921, passed, *The Times* felt, largely as a result of 'popular agitation, and to that extent the Act is in accord with popular feeling'[26]. But by that time fashions had changed, and women no longer wished to wear hats weighed down with tail feathers, wings and even whole birds.

Most women who cycled in the 1890s wore the conventional full-length skirt. It was a struggle to maintain decorum when mounting and dismounting.

Aesthetic reformers

Aesthetic dress continued to attract adherents. Oscar Wilde was an advocate of dress reform, but his views on dress also incorporated aesthetic views and he was insistent on the importance of beauty in dress as in everything else. Wilde himself wore breeches in a variety of forms; he was lampooned in a Little Lord Fauntleroy Van Dyke suit of black velvet with a loose, low collar, and was described in a 'brown suit with innumerable little buttons that gave it the appearance of a glorified page's costume'[27]. By 1883, he had given up breeches in favour of trousers, and had also had his long hair cut shorter, but he continued to dress in flamboyant and provocative style.

59

In 1884 he gave a lecture on dress in which he argued that clothes should be hung from the shoulder rather than from the waist. He wished, as did all dress reformers, to do away with the bustles, high heels and corsets of contemporary women's dress, suggesting instead that they wear Turkish trousers, and believed that it would be better for both sexes to wear garments designed along the lines of ancient classical, Mesopotamian or Egyptian dress.

His wife Constance also dressed in the aesthetic fashion. On one occasion she is described as wearing 'a Greek costume of cowslip yellow and apple-leaf green'. This observer evidently found aesthetic dress attractive and described how Constance Wilde's hair, 'a thick mass of ruddy brown, was wonderfully set off by bands of yellow ribbon supporting the knot of hair on the nape of the neck and crossing the wavy tresses above her brow.'[28] A friend, by contrast, deplored her style: 'She dressed for the part in limp white muslin with *no* bustle, saffron coloured silk swathed about her shoulders, a huge cartwheel Gainsborough hat, white and bright yellow stockings and shoes – she looked too hopeless.'[29]

Constance Wilde attended meetings on rational dress, and is described at one of these in 1886, as she rose to propose a motion, dressed in 'cinnamon coloured cashmere trousers and a cape with the ends turned under to form sleeves', while in 1888, 'she addressed an audience of women at the Somerville club on the subject, "Clothed and in our right minds". The lecture was reported in the *Rational Dress Society Gazette* for January 1889.'[30]

The socialist artists William Morris and Walter Crane, and other members of the Arts and Crafts Movement, hated the aesthetic impoverishment, as they saw it, of the nineteenth-century urban environment, and this included dress. While some dress reformers seemed to be attempting to modernise dress, others wished rather to renounce many aspects of industrialism altogether and to return to an earlier rural way of life. Many in the Arts and Crafts Movement tended to look towards Guilds of Handicraft (along mediaeval lines) rather than to trade unions as instruments of social change, while William Morris himself, although he was a socialist, held conservative views about women's place. In his utopian novel *News From Nowhere*, published in 1890, his narrator travels forward in time to a London of 1962 in which women – and men – would be wearing aesthetic dress:

[The women] were decently veiled with drapery, and not bundled up with millinery . . . they were clothed like women, not upholstered like armchairs, as most women of our time are. In short, their dress was somewhat between that of the ancient classical costume and the simpler forms of the fourteenth century garments, though it was clearly not an imitation of either.[31]

While the women in Morris's imagined 1962 wear archaic dress, Hammond, a patriarchal figure whom the narrator meets in this future environment, wears a Norfolk jacket, breeches and stockings – in other words, he wears a costume very similar to male reform dress of the 1890s. But Hammond is no feminist:

'But what about this woman question?' [the narrator enquires]. 'I saw at the Guest House that the women were waiting on the men: that seems a little like reaction, doesn't it?'

'Does it?' said the old man; 'perhaps you think housekeeping an unimportant occupation, not deserving of respect. I believe that was the opinion of the "advanced" women of the nineteenth century, and their male backers. . . . Don't you know that it is a great pleasure to a clever woman to manage a house skilfully, and to do it so that all the house-mates about her look pleased, and are grateful to her? And then, you know, everybody likes to be ordered about by a pretty woman.'[32]

Even in the advanced, bohemian circles of the socialist groupings and the Arts and Crafts Movement there was often at best an ambivalence or uncertainty as to women's rightful place, yet participation in the movement did bring women some advantages:

In many ways May Morris [the daughter of William Morris] typified the advantages and disadvantages of women in design. Like her self-effacing domestic role, her interest in embroidery was completely within the bounds of the patriarchal status quo, but she was enabled by opportunities that stemmed from the Arts and Craft Movement to become a teacher, writer, lecturer, craftswoman and designer of embroidery, jewellery, wallpaper and bookbinding. As head of the Embroidery Department for Morris and Company, she was an employer of women, creating a well-organised workshop staffed with highly skilled assistants, some of whom she taught herself. In fact, women were central to the activities of May Morris, who taught them, wrote books for them, employed them and sold goods to them. She founded the Women's Guild in 1907.[33]

Jessie Newbery, wife of the head of the Glasgow School of Art, was deeply involved with the work of architect Charles Rennie Mackintosh. She dressed in a completely personal style inspired by peasant and Renaissance art. Here she is wearing a wool cape with her own embroidered decoration over a 'Carpaccio dress', c. 1905.

Aesthetic dress continued into the 1890s. Jessie Rowat, who attended Glasgow School of Art, and married its principal Francis Newbery in 1889, devised for herself a style as timeless as that of Mrs Comyns Carr. For her wedding she designed and had made up a dress based on that worn by St Ursula in the series of paintings by Carpaccio in the Accademia in Venice, which depict incidents in the life of the saint. Soon after her marriage a second, similar dress was made, this time of fine, green corded silk, with white chiffon slashed insets in the sleeves and a square neck edged with black pearls, the whole dress lined with white alpaca. Because this dress was outside contemporary fashions, she was able to wear it for many years, the Glasgow papers describing it variously as a 'Carpaccio dress', a *robe de style* or a 'picture gown'. She seems to have designed all her own and her children's dresses. Some of these were made up by a visiting dressmaker, who used a machine, but Jessie Newbery herself always sewed by hand and often used saddle stitch to emphasise the construction of the garment. Her clothes (which she continued to design until her death in 1948) had no tailoring darts, nor did the skirts have waistbands; instead they were suspended from a silk 'Liberty'-type bodice. Dresses might be gathered and tied at the waist and she went in for layered clothing – the skirt with its bodice was worn under a loose tunic, the sides of which were left open and fastened with unusual or exotic buttons or embroidered bobbles.[34]

In 1894 Jessie began teaching embroidery at the Glasgow School of Art, where she was joined by Ann Macbeth. Embroidery was an important feature of aesthetic dress, but it had a more than decorative significance for these women. Ann Macbeth was a suffrage bannermaker, and, like Jessie herself, a member of the WSPU (the Women's Social and Political Union, the militant wing of the suffrage movement, founded by Emmeline Pankhurst in 1903). In 1911 she and Margaret Swanson wrote *Education Needlecraft*, in which they set forth their belief that embroidery should be for all. In particular they believed that to teach children in elementary schools this traditional craft was actually revolutionary, and they 'desired above all things to dress the elementary schoolchild in beautiful raiment'[35].

Dorelia John, originally Dorothy, who lived with the painter Augustus John, was another who rejected conventional dress altogether. She came from south London, but under the influence of John and of his sister Gwen John, also a painter, she transformed herself into a kind of exotic gipsy. From the first few years of the century right up until her death in the 1960s she wore simple, round-necked dresses with loosely gathered, full-length skirts with a slightly dropped waistline. This fashion was to influence later generations of Bohemian young women in the Chelsea of the period between the wars, when peasant dirndl skirts expressed a reaction against the jazzy, angular mainstream fashions. Like Jessie Newbery, Dorelia shopped at Liberty's for fine materials from which she made her clothes. The John children were also clad in bizarre garments, often to their disgust and embarrassment.

An article in the *Strand* magazine in 1891, written by a woman student who had studied at the Royal Academy schools, sums up the convergent aims of all the dress reformers:

Architecture and decorative design are taught in the schools, but dress which has existed since the world began, has no guiding laws, and sways from the severely ugly and matter of fact to the wildest extravagances of form and colour. . . . To be beautiful [dress] should be the expression of a beautiful mind, a beautiful body and of perfect health and ease and of natural delight in movement. Also it should have no association with pain. . . . What womanly woman would wear real astrakhan on her jacket . . . or the corpses of gulls, doves, humming birds, swallows etc. in her hair? . . . Our garments should be garments with a meaning and a purpose. We should never contradict nature's simple lines by false protuberances or exaggerations. To be beautiful, clothes should by their shape express the

At this aesthetic wedding, c. 1890, the two little bridesmaids are wearing the Liberty-style smocks, favoured by the Healthy and Artistic Dress Union, while the seven older bridesmaids wear loose, draped aesthetic-style dresses.

figure underneath; any cutting about of material to contradict the natural lines of the shape must be wrong.[36]

All forms of alternative dress continued to meet with extreme hostility. Mrs Eric Pritchard, for example, who wrote on fashion for the *Ladies Realm*, launched a vitriolic attack on all aspects of dress reform in her book *The Cult of Chiffon*, published in 1902. In this curious work she caricatures both the masculine or 'athletic' woman, who is 'wonderfully devoid of humour', yet 'very self satisfied in the matter of clothes' and also that other 'terrible type' to be found in 'studios in Bohemia': the artistic type. 'She has a strong tendency towards soft draperies in artistic shadings . . . ignores corsets, and is ever stretching out a scraggy neck in search of information.' According to Mrs Pritchard, she 'is not nearly so much to the fore today as she was before the invention of the Cimabue Browns' although 'let me think – I am not sure she has not had a resurrection as a socialist woman. Anyhow, she is aggressive . . . her ideas are limited to dead shades and washed out tints which somehow look muddy and only possess the virtue of matching the poor lady's complexion.'[37]

Aesthetic and reform dress, however, were already influencing mainstream fashion. In a sense they were themselves a fashion, and their

63

assimilation to conventional modes was assisted by Arthur Lazenby Liberty, whose department store in Regent Street opened in 1875. Liberty specialised in the provision of oriental, Arts and Crafts and Morris textiles and household furnishings. The shop also sold Celtic-based designs. The success of the store encouraged Liberty to extend his business into women's clothes. In 1884 he opened his 'Historic and Artistic Costume Dress Studio' under the direction of the interior designer E. A. Godwin.

Clearly by that time the vogue for aesthetic dress had spread beyond its original Arts and Crafts and 'simple life' usage into a wider circle of upper- and upper-middle-class devotees, and was thus commercially viable. While artistic innovators such as Jessie Newbery and Dorelia John bought materials at Liberty which they made up, or had made up, into dresses of their own design, less original or daring women bought the garments ready made from Liberty, who also sold a range of styles, for women and children, from reproduction classical Greek costumes in Arabian cotton, and embroidered and smocked peasant dress in thin Umrista cashmere, to tea gowns in wool, silk or velvet. Tea gowns − a modified and fashionable version of the unwaisted aesthetic garment − were increasingly worn informally at home by women of fashion, and were made by many fashionable dressmakers.[38]

One Liberty customer was Mrs Katherine Sophia Farebrother, wife of a Salisbury solicitor. While she enjoyed watercolour painting, she was no aesthete, and usually shopped at Dickins and Jones for conventionally fashionable clothes. However, of the twenty or so of her dresses in the collection at Brighton Museum, one is a gently modified Liberty S-bend dress of about 1900, but cut with 1630s-style sleeves. In heavy, deep red velvet, it is decorated on the bodice with deep pink silk and matching ivy leaf embroidery.

Liberty's children's clothes, modelled closely on the rural and regency styles in Kate Greenaway's book illustrations, quickly became popular with high society mothers, and even royalty took up certain aspects of aesthetic dress. Mrs Clara Frances Lloyd, who worked in the embroidery room at Liberty's, recalled that smocking became fashionable as a result 'of Princess Mary having dressed her boys in smocks'[39]; during the period she worked at Liberty's, smocking was one of the specialities of the firm.

Smocking was one of the crafts that had been revived under the auspices of the Arts and Crafts Movement; just as it was dying out in the countryside (it had traditionally been used on the smocks worn by male farm labourers) it began − around 1875 − to be used on women's tennis costumes, later on tea gowns and blouses, and particularly, as Mrs Lloyd remembered, on children's clothes. According to a magazine of the period, *The Women's World*, the revival owed much to Constance Wilde, and the 'artistic modistes had to send their delicate Liberty silk down to humble cottages in Sussex and Dorsetshire where a few conservative rustics still adhere to the old smock frock'.[40]

In 1890 the Healthy and Artistic Dress Union was formed. Its journal, *Aglaia*, and the *Rational Dress Gazette*, disseminated both the aesthetic dress and reform dress philosophies, which were in any case increasingly fused together. Sir Arthur Lazenby Liberty contributed an article to *Aglaia* in 1894, stating clearly that his aim was to: 'promote improvements in

By the 1880s the two strands of the dress reform movement, aesthetic and rational, had merged to form the Healthy and Artistic Dress Union. The cover of their journal **Aglaia** for spring 1894 has an Arts and Crafts-inspired drawing by Henry Holland.

dress that would make it consistent with health, comfort and graceful appearance, but [dress] should not obviously depart from the conventional mode'.[41]

Poiret and orientalism

By 1910, although the Paris couturiers might not have admitted it, a major inspiration for fashion change was drawn from the philosophies behind the aesthetic and dress reform movements of the European middle classes. The most innovative, exciting and influential couturier was Paul Poiret.

After a conventional training at the houses of Worth and Doucet, Poiret opened on his own in 1906. By 1908 his designs were beginning to revolutionise the whole physical appearance and posture of the fashionable woman. He created 'sheath' dresses, which fell straight in a tube from shoulder to hem (just as Oscar Wilde would have wished), and neo-classical adaptations of the aesthetic chiton (the tunic of the ancient Greeks). These *Directoire* fashions were so called after the Directory period in France,[42] which preceded the Regency period in Britain, and they looked back to the slender, high-waisted fashions of those times. The new designs, launched at his fashion house in the rue Pasquier in 1906, first appeared publicly in the album *Les Choses de Paul Poiret*, illustrated by Paul Iribe and published in 1908. Poiret and Iribe subsequently quarrelled, and in 1911 Poiret invited another artist, Georges Lepape, to produce a new series of drawings. Later, Lepape's son was to claim that 'at least four' of the designs had actually been created by Madame Lepape, specifically the daring prototype trousered outfits.[43]

Poiret himself, however, is likely to have been well aware of the campaigns for trousered dress for women. In addition, he was familiar with Persian, Indian, Japanese, North African and European peasant textiles and dress. He would also have seen the fabrics and dresses in the Paris branch of Liberty's, opened in the 1880s. His oriental beturbanned Odalisque models, in their turquoise, yellow, red and pink silks, appeared just as Diaghilev, director of the *Ballets Russes*, arrived in Paris in 1909.

The newness of the *Ballets Russes* – their music, designs, choreography and sets – inaugurated an aesthetic revolution. It was not just the brilliant, clashing colours of which Leon Bakst and other Diaghilev artists made use, but the pervasive mood of orientalism and the exotic which thrilled audiences and influenced not only fashion but also the fashionable interior. Purple, orange, jade green and black now became popular colours for decoration, while rooms were furnished with ottomans and soft silk tasselled cushions. Orientalism also justified divided skirts or harem trousers, and these were first introduced by Poiret in 1913, together with his lampshade tunic. This was a very short 'crinoline' worn over a long straight skirt or even loose trousers. Such an outfit bore a startling resemblance to the one worn by Amelia Bloomer so shockingly seventy years previously. Thus, ironically, Paris had at last sanctioned as the latest fashion what had once seemed outlandish and horrifying.

Other designers were beginning to share Poiret's feeling for a less constricted, freer, looser, lighter style of dressing. But it was Poiret above all who for the first time catapulted many of the ideals of the dress reform and aesthetic dress movements into the world of high fashion. The Poiret woman wore soft Liberty-type silks, trimmed with bold oriental embroidery, or printed with dynamic wood block prints designed by Raoul Dufy, the Fauve painter, from 1911. Instead of the old rigid corsets Poiret made fashionable lighter and more flexible if longer undergarments – although he did also introduce the hobble skirt.

A weekend fête in the gardens of Blenheim Palace in May 1911. The ladies wear watered-down versions of Paul Poiret's **Directoire** *line of 1908.*

The Venetian designer Mariano Fortuny went even further than Poiret in designing a revolutionary aesthetic garment. His 'Delphos' robe was patented in 1909, and was inspired by the statue of the charioteer at Delphi. It was a pleated silk tube with openings for head and arms and the sleeves, short or long. The silk was elaborately and minutely pleated in a process which is still not fully understood today, and dyed in wonderful colours. It was a completely timeless garment, and Fortuny continued to

67

produce it for forty years. For the great French novelist Marcel Proust (the chronicler above all others of this period of aesthetic creativity):

these Fortuny gowns, faithfully antique but markedly original, brought before the eye . . . that Venice saturated with oriental splendour . . . evocative as they were of the sunlight and the . . . fragmented, mysterious and complementary colour.[44]

On the other hand, Proust disliked the Poiret style:

In place of the beautiful dresses [of earlier years], Graeco-Saxon tunics, pleated . . . or sometimes in the directoire style, accentuated Liberty chiffons sprinkled with flowers like wallpaper . . . passed before me in a desultory, haphazard, meaningless fashion, containing in themselves no beauty.[45]

But he was clearly in a minority. By the outbreak of the First World War, Poiret's designs had greatly altered the way women felt they should look.

Sweating: women workers in the fashion trade

Yet although Poiret's designs paved the way for freer styles for all women, his exotic adaptations of aesthetic dress did not move fashion far enough away from luxury and frivolity to satisfy committed feminists. In 1908, the very year that Poiret launched his successful Oriental style, the first weekly newspaper aimed at working-class women in Britain published an article on 'Dress for the woman worker'. It announced the manufacture of a 'Workers' Dress – both cheap and artistic. It was to be made in two or three different styles out of plain, good material (of the homespun type) in various colours . . . with a little embroidery on the bodice.' The article concludes:

Fashion will not always rule despotically. As the great upward movement of womanhood broadens and the dawn of woman's consciousness of mighty power grows clear, it will be pleasing to watch its influence on the ladies' papers, and see how long their snobbish twaddle and rag-trade announcements endure.[46]

The manufacture of fashionable clothing remained grounded in poverty and exploitation, particularly the exploitation of women workers. Women's work in the tailoring trade had originally grown out of a family system (when the whole family, including children, had worked under the direction of the male head of the family) and this was one reason why women workers were so badly paid. It was assumed – often wrongly – that women did not need a subsistence wage, because their wage was only an addition to their husband's 'family wage'. Many male workers, however, in tailoring and other trades, were earning well below subsistence wages towards the end of the nineteenth century; and in any case, many women had no working husband:

Of the 82 000 people engaged in the clothing trades in 1891 returned as heads of households, 30 000 were women. Miss Vines, a factory inspector, for example, described one family of three adults and two children who were entirely dependent on the earnings of the mother, who worked at home on 'trouser finishing' – putting in pockets and linings and sewing on buttons, soaping and pressing the seams and felling the legs of the trousers. One pair of trousers took between two and three hours to finish for between 2½d [35p] and 3½d [49p] per pair. And in addition 'she had to find her own trimmings, thread, cotton and also soap for irons, and lost half an hour to an hour daily in fetching and returning the work'.[47]

Messrs. Lotery's factory, with its rows of young machinists working in cramped conditions, was featured in the **Tailor and Cutter** *for 11 April 1907 as a model works.*

During the last years of the nineteenth century the incidence of sweated labour was increasing. This was at one time thought to have been due to depressed conditions in the trade, but it seems rather that both sweating – which meant primarily very low wages and poor conditions of work, and outwork – and the contracting out of work, whether to small workshops or to workers in the home, were 'a feature of the rapid growth of the tailoring trade and [of] its partial mechanisation'.[48]

This coincided with the arrival of large numbers of Jewish refugees in flight from pogroms in Russia and Poland. By 1901 there were more than 1300 Jewish workshops in the London garment trade. Increasing numbers of women also were entering paid work. British male workers tended to blame both these groups, disadvantaged as they were, for the depression of wages and conditions. In fact, Jewish workshop masters usually paid better wages than their Gentile counterparts. Nevertheless, so far as the public was concerned, theirs was the responsibility for the sweatshop. Partly for this reason, an Aliens Act was passed in 1905 which reduced immigration substantially.

Often the conditions in the Jewish workshops were frightful, although they did vary and, in any case, were no worse than general conditions in the trade. A Factory Act was passed in 1901 requiring the principal manufacturer to keep a list of all his outwork contractors and their employees, but this, the first serious measure against sweated work, was widely evaded. In London especially, the existence of many small workshops made the job of even checking, let alone improving conditions and wages, extremely difficult. In 1887–8, Beatrice Potter discovered only 21 out of 1015 workshops that employed 25 or more hands, while 758 employed fewer than 10.[49]

The seasonal nature of the work and irregular hours hampered recruitment to trade unions. Many of the immigrant workers preferred the Jewish Friendly Societies, of which there were 176 in London in 1901, to the unions; in 1892 it had been estimated that of 300 000 Jewish immigrant workers in London, only 1000 to 2000 were members of Jewish trade unions. Yet among some of these workers there was a strong tradition of anarchism, socialism and militancy.

In Leeds, out of 51 clothing factories only one was Jewish, and workers in this north of England clothing centre tended to be organised into larger workshops. In Manchester, in 1893, 252 clothing workshops employed 1960 Jewish workers and 134 others. Under these different conditions there was a higher rate of trade unionism among the Leeds Jewish workforce. Yet conditions for the workers appear to have been little better in Leeds than in London, and despite the larger size of workshops and factories in that city, sweating was common there too; in 1888 the medical journal *The Lancet* ran an exposé of the insanitary conditions of the workers, injurious to health.[50] Although women's wages were higher in Leeds than in London, they were still below subsistence. One young woman at John Barran's – the biggest clothing manufacturer in Leeds – was taken on at the age of fifteen at 6s [£13.50] a week, and four years later, in 1893, she had progressed to the magnificent sum of 11s [£19.50]. (Subsistence was reckoned by Cadbury at 16s [£28.50] a week for a woman, 25s [£44.50] for a man.)[51]

In the early years of the twentieth century reformers and radicals, perhaps particularly women, were much preoccupied with the question of sweating. Women such as Clementina Black campaigned and undertook surveys of women workers, and in 1906 the *Daily News*, which was owned by the philanthropic Cadbury family, organised an Anti-Sweating

Exhibition, which was attended by 30 000 visitors. As a result the National Anti-Sweating League was formed, a Select Committee set up, and in 1909 the Trades Board Act, the first of its kind, was passed. It probably had little impact on sweating. Indeed it is possible that it even further institutionalised low pay by setting different minimum rates for men and for women.[52]

The tailored wear was mostly cut and sewn by male workers. Women made buttonholes and trimmings, and the often elaborately trimmed blouses worn with the tailor-made. The majority were extremely badly paid, but Clementina Black's survey of married women workers revealed that there were some skilled workers who could earn what was for the period quite a respectable amount: 'There exist also very great differences of rate between one employer and another; for practically the same work women may be receiving 2s 3d or 3s 3d [£5.45] a dozen, and sometimes more work is demanded by the worse paying employer.'[53]

Clementina Black also found that there were different ways of being employed. Some women attempted to employ others; some worked on their own for private customers; however, the majority did homework for 'fairly large firms'. Most of the women visited were sewing blouses in materials ranging from 'cheap silk' to 'fine lawn and nainsook'; some with relatively simple tucks and 'insertions' of lace, others with much more elaborate embroidery. The more elaborate work did not necessarily attract a higher rate of pay, sometimes the reverse.

Quite apart from the sweated workshops, there was extensive employment of seamstresses in the workrooms of the department stores, where they altered and made up models. One such worker, Ann Cheriton, was employed for several years at the turn of the century by Swan and Edgar (a department store at Piccadilly Circus, closed down in the 1970s). Along with six or seven other young women she worked as a bodice hand for 12s 6d [£23] a week, later 15s [£27.60] and then 17s 6d [£32]. There was no holiday pay and they had to live at home, for this was not a subsistence wage in London.[54] Like Clara Frances Lloyd, who worked at Liberty during the First World War, Ann Cheriton took an early train to work in order to take advantage of the 4d [38p] 'workmen's' return. The hours were long – 9.00 a.m. to 7.00 p.m. at Swan and Edgar, and 8.30 to 6.30 at Liberty's – and both did elaborate hand sewing in workrooms which were divided into numerous sections – skirt rooms, sleeve rooms, tailoring rooms and embroidery rooms. At Liberty's good lunches were provided at the reasonable price of 1s 6d [£1.71] per week, and there was a week's paid holiday. These improved conditions of work by comparison with Swan and Edgar fifteen years earlier probably reflect the improvements in pay and conditions that occurred as a result of the war.[55]

The First World War and after

A mannequin, probably a shop assistant, models an afternoon dress for a customer in the gown department of Morgan Squires, the Leicester department store, c. 1905.

Fashion continued to develop during the First World War, even if some of the major French designers closed their premises for the duration. Women's role had changed so much that there was now nothing too untoward in their participation in the war effort as nurses or ambulance drivers behind the lines in France – a number of ex-suffragettes came into their own here; while some working-class women were able to earn more in the munitions factories or in heavy industry than they had ever earned before. There they replaced the men who had gone to the front to fight. Their employment was referred to as 'dilution', because they were paid less than the men had been, and were to be employed 'for the duration' only.

Not all women fared better during the war, and Sylvia Pankhurst helped those in the East End who were left penniless or surviving on a tiny army allowance while their young men or husbands were away. The

72

majority of women, however, although they did not gain equal pay, were able to enjoy a higher standard of living, and younger women were able to spend some money on smarter clothes and accessories. Significantly for the future of fashion, the women in factories and working on the land sometimes wore practical boiler suits or jodhpurs, which began to break down the taboo against trousers for women. By the end of the war, women's clothes were looser-waisted, with shorter skirts, and simple round necklines had replaced the old stiff, high collars.

Yet it would be a mistake to see the war as the main cause of the great changes that appeared to come about in the 1920s, symbolised by short skirts, short hair, make-up, smoking and free and easy manners and morals. The belief that the 1920s was the great age of emancipation for women is one of the best-known clichés of fashion and social history. It has been the aim of this chapter to demonstrate that it was in the years leading up to the First World War that the basis was being laid, in fashion as well as, more directly, in political and economic ways, for the changes that appeared much more generally in the 1920s. These prewar years were years of significant social innovation and change notwithstanding the tremendous opposition to women's emancipation. It is true that before the war all sexes and ages, but particularly women and girls, were still normally wearing too many stuffy, restrictive clothes. Vera Brittain described her school wear in 1911 as consisting of:

woollen combinations, black cashmere stockings, 'liberty' bodice, dark stockinette knickers, flannel petticoat and often, in addition, a long-sleeved, high-necked, knitted woollen 'spencer'.

At school, on the top of this conglomeration of drapery, we wore green flannel blouses in the winter and white flannel blouses in the summer, with long navy-blue skirts, linked to the blouses by elastic belts which continually slipped up or down, leaving exposed an unsightly hiatus of blouse-tape or safety-pinned shirt-band. . . . For cricket and tennis matches, even in the baking summer of 1911, we still wore the flowing skirts and high-necked blouses, with our heavy hair tied into pigtails.[56]

but more and more women were rebelling against such voluminous, hot, unhealthy clothing.

At the time, both the supporters and the opponents of dress reform saw the movement as the expression of total opposition to high fashion. In retrospect, ironically, we can see that in the end many of the ideas of the wearers of rational dress, socialist gowns, aesthetic modes and 'vegetarian drawers' were incorporated into the mainstream, their ideas contributing towards the radicalisation of women's dress. In the 1920s it was men who were perceived as imprisoned in unhygienic, restrictive and outmoded clothing.

73

3

HEALTH AND BEAUTY OFF THE PEG 1920-39

*I*n a characteristic advertising image of the years between the wars a young man and woman advance with confidence into a sunburst – towards the horizon of the future. For us, images such as this have a certain poignancy, for the young men and women on their hiking expeditions or in their sports cars, on the beaches or in the sun-tranced suburbs, look towards a bright future that has become our troubled past.

The consumerist side of the twenties and thirties was often expressed in designs that prefigured a utopian future. The streamlined simplicity of some factories and houses suggested the world of 'modernity' – clean, white and scientific. Dresses, tea sets and motor cars were designed to appear jazzy, youthful and new.

This new Britain of arterial roads and Art Deco sofas was largely confined to the south and the Midlands where new light industries created jobs. Meanwhile the north stagnated in the gloom of unemployment. In a famous passage, J. B. Priestley summed up the contrasting Englands he had found on a tour of the country in 1934. There was the old, rural, almost feudal England which still existed in the south-west; there was the industrial north, much of which was now laid waste and derelict; and there was the new south:

The third England . . . was the new postwar England, belonging far more to the age itself than to this particular island. America, I suppose was its real birthplace. This is the England of filling stations and factories that look like exhibition buildings, of giant cinemas and dance-halls and cafés, bungalows with tiny garages, cocktail bars, Woolworths, motor-coaches, wireless, hiking, factory girls looking like actresses, greyhound racing and dirt tracks, swimming pools, and everything given away for cigarette coupons . . . periodicals about film stars . . . swimming costumes and tennis racquets and dancing

Opposite *The Women's League of Health and Beauty aimed to improve the health of ordinary women and to promote peace, and their campaign for publicity included displays and marches. This photograph shows their annual event in Hyde Park in May 1935.*

shoes. . . . You need money in this England, but you do not need much money. It is a large-scale, mass production job, with cut prices. You could almost accept Woolworths as its symbol. Its cheapness is both its strength and its weakness. It is its strength because being cheap it is accessible; it nearly achieves the famous equality of opportunity.[1]

But its weakness, Priestley thought, was that it lacked spontaneity, and depended upon the advertising man rather than making use of the inventiveness and talent of the working class. What Priestley observed was the way in which technology was now creating the preconditions for mass cultural movements associated with new leisure pursuits: the radio, the dance halls and the cinema drew large popular audiences, and they were an international phenomenon.

One aspect of the new pursuits was their emphasis on health: sports, dancing and beauty culture all emphasised the body beautiful. The cult of the perfect physique was linked to the politics of the time. It was progressive in looking towards the eradication of poverty and disease. In the Soviet Union, for example, painting and sculpture glorified the healthy, muscled peasant or worker, the strong and radiant mother.

Yet the identification of the perfect human being as a blonde Aryan was a sinister aspect of the Nazi cult. The belief in the perfectability of the Aryan race also fed into the then popular ideas of eugenics, the 'science' of 'race improvement', which seems inescapably racist to us today; in the first forty years of the century it captured the interest and imagination of a surprising number of politicians, intellectuals and artists right across the political spectrum: for example, the poet W. B. Yeats, who had Fascist leanings; some of the Fabians; and several prominent British scientists who were members of the Communist Party.

The whole obsession with the body beautiful was thus profoundly ambiguous. It celebrated human potential, yet encouraged widespread beliefs in the superiority of the white races, as well as promoting stereotypes of beauty, particularly in women.

We no longer share the conviction, expressed so widely in popular culture then, that progress through science and planning is inevitable. And indeed, we might argue that for a significant minority there was little real progress between the wars. Perhaps partly by way of compensation the image of progress was displaced; the illustrations, music, modes and styles gave men and women a feeling of modernity and progress which often bore little relationship to the quality of their lives.

What we see in the 1920s and 1930s is a changing popular – or commercial – culture with fashion as one of its most important elements. What this culture created was in some respects an illusion of freedom, democracy and emancipation. The majority were better off than their parents and grandparents had been, but real wealth was still concentrated in few hands, and the élite still dominated the social scene in the sense that the popular imagery of a desirable way of life was based on the way this élite lived.

Mass consumerism was possible because, although unemployment was high, the spending power of those who remained in work actually increased. Even at the height of the slump, when many workers experienced wage cuts, the cost of living was falling even more rapidly. By 1939 it was 11 per cent lower than in 1924, while average wage rates were 3½ per cent higher.

A substantial section of the population, however, continued to live in grinding poverty. The poverty and ill health of women was particularly marked – many could not afford to feed their children properly, still less to eat adequately themselves. A survey of women's health undertaken by Margery Spring Rice in 1938 for the Women's Health Enquiry Committee revealed the shocking results of years of neglect by successive governments. Women's health had actually deteriorated since the end of the First World War. The body of this report consists of example after example of malnutrition, illness and appalling housing conditions. Typical, for example, was:

a woman in Derby who lives in a house in a slum court entered through an archway in a slum street. . . . She has no facilities for cleanliness at all. . . . At the end of the court is the row of tub lavatories shared with the other cottages. The corporation clears the tubs twice a week. She gets water from a tap at the end of the yard. There is no sink in the house. This woman is twenty-four, she has three children under five and is in very bad health. She has never been to the 'Talkies'.[2]

The majority of the 1250 women interviewed suffered from chronic ill health. Clothing is barely mentioned in the report, apart from the telling remark: 'Even if [the housewife] could raise the money to send the washing out – she hasn't got the second set of clothes or bed coverings which this necessitates.'

For families such as these, new clothes were sometimes available through the clothing club or the tallyman, by mail order or from the Co-operative societies. They were more likely to have to make do with altered and second-hand clothes. These were often provided by welfare workers, sometimes in humiliating circumstances – handed out in school classrooms, for example:

They were not pretty dresses but sacklike garments in dull colours.

I have no idea how the other kids felt. I only know my shame and mortification lasted a very long time, for only the children whose parents were very poor indeed were called out and one was thus labelled before the whole class.[3]

The lives of many women did improve between the wars. The vote was an important symbolic victory, although perhaps more important in day-

In the twenties new fashion was still beyond the reach of many people. Maud Bunker of London wears her 'best' coat, handed down through two elder sisters. She 'translated' the fur hem into a roll collar in the late 1920s.

to-day terms was a series of legislative changes in the 1920s which gave women greater equality in respect of divorce and child custody. Women were now more readily admitted to the professions and the civil service, although a marriage bar operated in the latter and in teaching. Equal pay had yet to be achieved.

Working-class women were exploited and ignored, driven out of their wartime jobs when male workers returned, and forced in many cases back into domestic service, although in the south-east and parts of the Midlands the growth of factory work did provide an alternative. For them as for middle-class women, however, marriage remained by far the most acceptable destiny – but while marriage could still be a life of leisure for the upper-middle-class woman, for the poor it was inevitably a life of drudgery:

It is often heartbreaking to see how rapidly a pretty, attractive girl grows old and drab after a few years of marriage. She loses her looks and ceases to take pride in her appearance; minor ailments are neglected . . . the needs of the husband and childen are inevitably the first consideration and the mother has seldom anyone to notice her fatigue or her ailments. . . .

People who lightly censure the woman gossiping on her doorstep, untidy and even slatternly as she may seem, often fail to realise how completely she is tied to her own small home, and how few opportunities she has of escaping from the wear and tear of family life at close quarters. The cinema has done something to bring mental peace and refreshment, but it costs more money than she can often afford; wireless is beyond the means of many homes.[4]

There was an increase in salaried workers from just under 600 000 to 750 000 between 1920 and 1938.[5] This growing lower middle class migrated to the suburbs that began to stretch out around the large cities in the 1930s. In those often monotonous roads and cul-de-sacs, women struggled to create a genteel lifestyle with the aid of a few basic electrical appliances – although even a Hoover was a luxury then – and a 'daily help' instead of a live-in maid. The lives of these suburban wives, too, were often of isolation and drudgery, but at least they would be more likely to have the comfort of the wireless and the occasional trip to the shops or the movies.

Suburban life was hedged about with restraints, restrictions and minute markers of social difference:

The fear of losing caste was nowhere more apparent than in the matter of dress which was regulated by a whole series of modesty rules, and provided the middle class with a rich vocabulary of pejoratives; you could tell a lady-killer by his coloured socks, and a socialist by his fuzzy hair and pullover, a man in baggy trousers was by definition a 'crank', a woman with 'potatoes' [holes] in the heels [of her stockings] was by definition a 'slut'.[6]

Women's clothes had to be 'dainty' and 'becoming' and women dressed to be quiet and ladylike – anything sexually suggestive would have seemed terribly vulgar in the suburbs. Working women had to be even more careful, with 'nothing to call attention to appearance'. 'Discretion in dress is sure to be noticed by almost every class of employer.'[7]

It is therefore inaccurate to see the women of the 1920s as having somehow achieved emancipation; yet the standard interpretation of the fashions and customs of the 1920s is precisely this: to translate short skirts, cosmetics and cigarette smoking directly into 'freedom' for women. As in the 1960s, the situation was actually more complex and more contradictory. The popular meaning of 'emancipation' for women had shifted away from the ideas of social and political rights that had been so important before 1914. Social emancipation – the freedom to drink, to smoke, even to make love, to dispense forever with chaperones – served as a substitute for possibly more solid economic freedoms, and was in any case an option only for those few women who *were* socially and economically independent. For the majority, sexual freedom was limited or non-existent; many working-class unmarried girls were allowed out only one or two evenings a week, and even then had often to be home by 9.30 or 10 o'clock.

The ideas of the sexologist Havelock Ellis and even of Sigmund Freud, the inventor of psychoanalysis, were nevertheless beginning to influence avant-garde middle-class circles. Contraception was no longer a taboo subject. The birth rate was very low in the thirties, and 'Registrar General Class III, clerical or lower-middle-class occupations, had the lowest fertility rate of any social class'.[8] There were many 'only children' in the suburbs.

Disillusionment and uncertainty surrounded the whole subject of sexuality. Two of the most famous bestsellers of the 1920s feature 'liberated' heroines – but in Margaret Kennedy's *The Constant Nymph* (1926) the heroine dies before she has actually committed adultery, while Iris Storm, heroine of Michael Arlen's *The Green Hat* (1924), commits suicide, unable to cope with the knowledge that she has 'a pagan body and a Chislehurst mind'.

Iris Storm's clothes express the ambivalence even of the sophisticated towards a free female sexuality. She is first seen wearing a dress patterned with a design of miniature elephants, a sophisticated motif originally designed by the French painter Raoul Dufy. Yet the miniaturisation of wild animals is equally a feature of nursery design. It was therefore a brilliant stroke on the part of the author to pick a design that symbolised *simultaneously* both the worldliness and immaturity of his heroine.

Iris Storm was partly based on the society beauty Nancy Cunard, who was far less trammelled by convention than her fictional counterpart. Yet she too was a troubled and contradictory character. With her slender,

79

Elephant textile design, 1924, by the Fauve painter Raoul Dufy who created hundreds of sophisticated designs for the top silk manufacturer Bianchini-Ferier of Lyons between 1912 and 1928.

androgynous looks and sleek boyish head, she seems to have epitomised the twenties for Evelyn Waugh and Aldous Huxley who based heroines on her, and Cecil Beaton and Man Ray who photographed her.[9] Although boyish, however, she and her fictional analogues were ardently hetero-sexual. They might, nonetheless, identify with what was perceived as the 'male' attitude towards love. Like Nancy Cunard, Agnes Smedley, the American revolutionary and journalist who spent years in China reporting on Mao Zedong's campaigns, took 'sex like a man' (Smedley's own words) and yet also wanted 'a real man'.[10]

Nancy Cunard appears in Aldous Huxley's *Point Counter Point* (1926) as a heartbreaker who searches for rough sex in the arms of a virile Italian she has picked up in the street. D. H. Lawrence's *Lady Chatterley's Lover* (1928) was also about the quest for the truly potent lover. Yet whether as wife, as career woman or as sexual adventuress, the emancipated woman of the twenties was portrayed, whether truthfully or not, as ultimately unhappy and unfulfilled.

Suntan, cosmetics and the naked leg

Fashions of the 1920s emphasised the modern aspect of popular culture, yet managed to suggest the sexual ambiguities as well. Above all, like everything else, the human body had to be modernised. The expansive curves and fussy outlines of the nineteenth century were banished, and indeed the style-setters loathed everything Victorian; the slender, the sleek and the rigorous were in.

Women's clothes were much more relaxed and more casual than they had been in the Edwardian period. Soft blouses and jumpers were worn, and women emerged into peacetime still looking romantic, but now increasingly girlish instead of matronly. A few women had their hair bobbed, but long hair was still the prevailing mode, while hats with large brims added to the romantic look. But within a few years women longed to be small breasted, long legged and tubular in shape: the *'garçonne'* had arrived.

Key features of the *'garçonne'* look were short skirts and hair, the helmet-like cloche hat, long earrings and Peter Pan collar. This last item seems to have originated with Colette, whose first novel, *Claudine à L'École* (1900), had featured a provocative schoolgirl. The book was dramatised, and the part of Claudine was taken by Polaire, a music hall actress and Colette's great friend. Both women were to be seen in prewar Paris wearing the Claudine outfit, with the collar.

Women in the twenties began to cut their hair shorter and shorter with the shingle, the bingle, and, in 1926, the Eton crop. They cultivated a slim figure, while brilliantly rouged lips and mascaraed eyes smouldered from beneath the cloche, which almost entirely hid the cropped hair, save for the fringe and perhaps a single, brilliantined kiss curl lying like a comma against the cheek.

Most dramatic of all, of course, was the way in which legs were revealed – for the first time, literally, in centuries. We now take the female leg so much for granted that it is quite difficult to grasp the extent of the shock that this new nakedness produced. For, as the controversy over rational cycling dress had indicated, once fashion (or anti-fashion) for women revealed that woman is bifurcated, it also acknowledged her sexual parts.

In fact, skirts rose to the knees for only a few years in the mid-twenties. Handkerchief point, or uneven hems, bias cut, fuller skirts and pleats modified the starkly tubular silhouette of 1925–7. Then, in 1929 Patou abruptly lowered his hems, ushering in the new, slinky and sinuous silhouette that was to be the hallmark of the 1930s. Once Patou had lowered the hemline, dresses remained at calf length for most of the 1930s, with long gowns once more fashionable for evening wear and for formal occasions, such as (in England) Ascot, presentations at Court and the Henley Royal Regatta. Styles were more romantic, and the narrow svelte look continued until about 1938, when Paris began to introduce tighter waists and fuller skirts, styles which prefigured what was to come after 1945.

A lunchtime fashion parade for 'business girls' at Gamages department store in London in June 1925. The model in her mass-produced woollen bathing suit represents everyday reality rather than fashion plate glamour.

Even at the time this was recognised as a Victorian revival. At the request of King George VI, Cecil Beaton took a series of photographs of Queen Elizabeth in lavish Norman Hartnell crinolines, the poses and settings in deliberate imitation of the Winterhalter portraits of European queens and princesses of the 1860s in their crinolined Worth concoctions. Marshall and Snelgrove were selling hooped petticoats in 1938, to create the crinoline effect.

During most of the 1930s, the styles, although less daring, were arguably more sophisticated than the garçonne look, which with its short skirts, bobbed hair and button-strap shoes often created a childish, Christopher Robin effect in the mid-twenties. On the other hand the use of make-up, although still usually discreet, cut across the little boy look. Powder and eyelash tint might now be used, and eyelids gleaming with vaseline added to the 'Vamp' look popularised by the Hollywood film star Theda Bara. By the end of the 1920s lipstick and rouge were even acceptable for younger working-class women (when they could afford them). Middle-class women were perhaps the last to succumb to cosmetics.

This new fashion for cosmetics was made respectable by the movies. Max Factor was a Hollywood firm; Elizabeth Arden and Helena Rubinstein were both founded by independent women who saw themselves as pioneers for women's freedom. These and numerous other firms, such as Yardley in Britain, developed a mass industry and maintained, through their advertisements, a relentless emphasis on the beautification of women's appearance. The idea that every woman could become beautiful if she used their products was part of the 'scientific' vision of progress and perfectability of the times.

The new crazes for dancing and music also came from across the Atlantic, and had a direct impact on the way women, especially, came to look. Jazz and ragtime had already been known before the war, but only in the 1920s did they achieve social respectability as well as huge popularity. By the 1920s, 'the shimmy was shaking suburbia'. The new dances 'demanded a new freedom of movement which was not possible in old-fashioned corsets'.[11] The rugs were rolled back in suburban lounges as young couples danced to their phonograph records; for the youth of the working class, dance halls began to appear – to cater to their desire for music, fun and movement.

Sport continued to influence fashion. Suzanne Lenglen, the supreme woman tennis star of the 1920s, who was dressed on and off court by the Paris designer Jean Patou, introduced the shorter skirt, short sleeves and collarless neckline to Wimbledon in the early 1920s, although stockings were not abandoned until a decade later. (Photographs of Lenglen in play, however, show that the tops of the stockings and the bare thigh above must have been intermittently visible.) Fashionable women began to wear trousers for a wider range of sports, including ski-ing and hiking, and the bolder ones took to beach pyjamas.

With improved transport, the countryside was also more accessible for city dwellers. Weekend 'rambling clubs' for office workers were formed – the ramblers using the new suburban bus routes to take them to the starting points of long country walks. In 1923, London Transport published guide books to the north and south of the Thames, thus publicising and, they hoped, popularising the new tube extensions that were pushing out into 'Metroland'.

In the late 1920s the more strenuous 'hiking' came into fashion. Whereas a ramble had been a day's outing, hiking was a proper (though inexpensive) holiday spent exploring the countryside for which special sporty clothes and sometimes even shorts were worn. Apparently the word hiking came from the United States, but the concept was German in origin. Also from Germany came the idea of the Youth Hostel, and in the 1930s the British Youth Hostels Association was founded. The Association provided cheap hospitality (1s [£1] per night). Breakfast cost a further shilling. Hiking became even more popular during the thirties, possibly because by that time more workers were getting a week if not a fortnight's paid holiday. Many new clubs organised hiking expeditions, and there were Hikers' Leagues, sponsored by provincial newspapers – especially popular in the industrial Midlands and the north.[12]

Bicycling continued to be popular. Winifred Holtby wrote of 'the silent swoop of cycling clubs in close-locked flight down the country roads'; and many families could now afford a week instead of simply a day by the seaside.

Holtby, a feminist writer of the period, argued that these new social customs did signify real improvements in the lives of the young and that the clothes they wore symbolised those improvements:

The psychology of clothes is not unimportant. Nowadays, thanks to the true democracy of the talkies, twopenny fashion journals and inexpensive stores, it is possible for one fashion to affect a whole hemisphere with no distinction of class and little of pocket. . . . The postwar fashion for short skirts, bare knees, straight, simple chemise-like dresses, shorts and pyjamas for sports and summer wear, cropped hair and serviceable shoes is waging a defensive war against [the] powerful movement to reclothe the female form in . . . frills and flounces, to emphasise the difference between men and women.[13]

This was written in 1934, when fashions, as the writer noted with alarm, had changed again; but the leisure clothes to which she referred were indeed part of a new fashion aesthetic which persisted in the thirties. One Birmingham dress manufacturing firm advertised several hiking outfits in 1932; one was a drill suit, priced at 11s 6d [£12.30], another was in grey flannel with tailored jacket and matching shorts, 'perfect for summer or winter walks', costing 15s 9d [£16.40].[14]

The fashion for the suntan was one of the most enduring to emerge from the cult of sport and the open air. Sunbathing had originally been encouraged in Germany as a cure for deficiency diseases. It was also popular in California, and was brought back to Europe by the expatriate Americans who were now colonising Paris, the Venice Lido and the Côte d'Azur. Only the rich, and bohemians and intellectuals, travelled regularly abroad, but the concept of foreign holidays gave sunbathing social cachet, and it was, in addition, rapidly popularised in the late 1920s by fashion leaders such as Gabrielle 'Coco' Chanel. Cecil Beaton described one European society beauty as having a skin tanned to the colour of iodine.[15] It is difficult for us today to grasp how revolutionary this change was, for the suntan has become one of the most wearisome clichés of fashion, but in the 1920s its effect was dramatic; hitherto women had gone to great lengths to protect their skin from the sun, a brown skin had been considered to be the hideous result of manual labour and the consequent exposure to the elements. So another aspect of the new physical and social freedom for women was that they no longer had to encumber themselves with lotions, veils and parasols.

Interestingly, it appears that already doctors in the 1920s were warning of the dangers of prolonged exposure to the sun because this 'weakened the resistance of the skin to infection'.[16] In general, however, sunshine was associated with health rather than disease.

No one seems to have linked the fashion for a sun-darkened skin with the appearance of blacks (mostly Afro-Americans) – at that time referred to as negroes – in fashionable circles. Usually they attended society functions as musicians and entertainers, and their proximity to white womanhood could cause dismay and outrage. For example, a British daily newspaper reported with horror that at an upper-class swimming party held at St George's Baths in London, a negro band had been placed at close quarters to young white women in bathing costumes.[17]

The nightclub singer Josephine Baker became the toast of Parisian avant-garde society and mingled with the artists and socialites who were having such a strong influence on design and style, but she was very much an exception. On the whole, black men and women were only ever tolerated in Europe as exotic curiosities, as stylistic appendages in some cases. Ducharne, for example, who produced some of the most beautiful materials for Parisian haute couture in the twenties, used to ride round Paris in a white Rolls Royce driven by a black chauffeur.[18] Even at the height of the Harlem Renaissance in the 1920s, when a vital black literary, artistic and musical culture flourished in New York City, the vast majority of black people in the USA encountered extreme exploitation and oppression. In Britain this took the form of an unthinking acceptance of the British Empire by most of the population.

Cubist artists such as Picasso, Braque and Brancusi made use of African motifs in their work and were particularly interested in African sculpture, which, like their own work, was not 'realistic' in the manner that had been so dominant in European art. Their work influenced some dress designers, notably Elsa Schiaparelli. In 1928 she was designing knitted sweaters which featured her own version of motifs from Congolese art. Others were more indirectly influenced, using Cubist black and beige and watered down 'jazz' prints and embroidery. In 1924 Chanel designed the costumes for Diaghilev's *Le Train Bleu*, working with the Cubist sculptor Henri Laurens, who designed the set. The ballet featured bathers, tennis players, golfers and bright young things on the Côte d'Azur. Chanel was also friendly with Picasso and Juan Gris.[19]

Schiaparelli genuinely admired and respected African art. So did Nancy Cunard, who habitually wore an armful of heavy African bracelets in materials such as ebony and ivory. (She also wore clothes designed by the Cubist artist Sonia Delaunay.) Nancy Cunard had a black American lover for some years, and worked politically for the cause of the American negro.

However, the incorporation of African motifs into fashion and design did not normally imply an acceptance of non-European cultures as equal. On the contrary, for the most part these exotic cultures were rendered

Sonia Delaunay, the Orphic Cubist artist, drew inspiration for her paintings, textiles and dress designs from Cubist solar disc themes, coupled with the vibrant use of light and colour. In the mid 1920s she designed and sold textiles and even cut, ready-to-sew clothes. Her bold patterns inspired couturiers such as Patou and Chanel. This photograph shows a 1923 design.

'primitive' by comparison with 'modern', scientific Europe and America. The barbaric – whether in the form of jazz syncopation or the vogue for ancient Egyptian motifs which followed upon the discovery in 1922 of the Pharaoh Tutankhamen's tomb in Luxor – merely added a superficial frisson of stylistic daring to fashionable lives.

Although neutral colours were the height of chic, the Paris designers also worked with the most exotic Arabian Nights materials, particularly for evening wear. Maison Ducharne, for example, produced purple or orange crêpes, admired by Colette, which featured large, drooping poppies brocaded in gold, and another series of designs based on the Alhambra, with swallows flying behind the Moorish arches amongst the clouds. Yet these materials were so delicately made that although they shimmered and sparkled they never looked vulgar.

The simple Look: Vionnet, Patou, Chanel

In the 1920s as Poiret's star waned (although he was still producing some beautiful clothes) new designers appeared: Chanel, Patou and Vionnet. One of the most serious weaknesses of fashion history is the tendency to attribute to individuals what were actually general fashion tendencies, and thus to obscure our vision of the way in which fashion evolves.[20] Nevertheless, the major designers were genuine innovators.

Madeleine Vionnet had been trained in London at the dressmaking and tailoring firm of Kate Reilly, and in Paris at Callot Soeurs, and by Madame Gerber and Jacques Doucet before opening her own house in 1914. Like Poiret, she claimed to have done away with the old tight-laced corsets, but she is most famous for her bias cut. 'You must dress a body in fabric, not construct a dress,' was her guiding principle. The cut of her dresses, on the cross of the material, was often a complex operation, but the end result was of fluid simplicity, especially when she used plain crêpe and satin that draped well on the body. Henceforward a dress could be slipped on over the head. As Christian Dior pointed out, the bias cut did away with the old static fashions. She closed her house in 1939, but in her heyday she employed a workforce of 1000, for whom she built a modern American factory building at the rear of her mansion in the avenue Montaigne; this factory included a ventilation system that changed the air every three minutes, and a dispensary with a dental clinic attached.[21]

Jean Patou's designs epitomised the twenties – sportswear, and its adaptation for daily life, was his forte – and he combined neutral colours, for example navy blue and white, into sparkling ensembles. He

The fluidity of Madeleine Vionnet's couture clothes was achieved by her mastery of bias cutting. The evening dress on the left, c. 1933, is made of expensive gold silk satin reversing to green crêpe; the one on the right, of 1938, has a transparent skirt of silver lamé and grey tulle over a narrow underdress and was worn by the Duchess of Windsor.

enticed American customers by showing his designs on tall American models, opened boutiques at smart seaside resorts, and his beachwear was the first to feature his name logo, JP, on an outside pocket.

Chanel invented a style that persisted right into the sixties and still influences fashion today. To the revolutionary shapes introduced initially by Poiret she brought the sobriety of masculine materials and colours. Her first designs, just before the First World War, were for women's hats, but soon she began to design relaxed, simple sweaters for women in stockinette jersey. Despite the brief British vogue for jerseys in the 1880s, inspired by Lily Langtry, jersey was normally a porridge-coloured material associated with men's underwear. Its use for women's fashion wear signalled an enormous change and the start of casual 'sweater dressing'. In the twenties Chanel worked with fine wool jersey especially manufactured for her by the French textile company Rodier. Chanel was later to popularise country or work wear materials such as tweed, and she adapted masculine garments, for example the trench coat and the sailor suit, for women. She is said to have invented the 'little black dress', simply cut and almost unadorned, the perfect setting for the svelte beauty of its wearer, or equally for the 'costume' jewellery made of uncut emeralds and rubies which Chanel also made fashionable.

Cecil Beaton dubbed the fashion aesthetic that Chanel and Patou created the 'poor look'. A version of the little black dress, perhaps with a white Peter Pan collar, could be worn by duchess and shop girl alike, as could the grey or navy suit, or the simple wrap-over or edge-to-edge coat in black or beige. The edge-to-edge coat lacked a fastening so although 'simple' it was not very comfortable for ordinary women as it had to be held together – clutched in one hand – in cold or windy weather.

The simpler fashions for men and women in the 1920s, which blurred class difference, have been accounted for as an expression of 'democracy'. Clearly this is an over-simplification in the sense that Chanel's

Coco Chanel in a 1929 version of her own model jersey wool suit, which was copied at every level of the international ready-to-wear industry.

models were hand made from the most expensive materials and a mass-produced garment could never achieve the same effect. The explanation, however, is not referring to actual garments so much as to the visual image created by the new styles. At this abstract level – the level at which fashion acts as a representation or symbol of this or that aspect of a social mood – the fashions of Chanel and Patou, whether made up in precious *crêpe de Chine* or cheap rayon, did suggest both modernity and the democracy of urban society. The notion of democracy was something of a myth in France in the 1920s for women did not even have the vote; but what twenties styles purveyed was precisely a *myth* of equality and liberation. Despite the vast differences in the quality of the actual clothes, the myth had its own potency, and may even have contributed to a subjective feeling of emancipation for women, while physically the lightness and comfort of the actual clothes must have made a real difference to women who wore them, whatever their price.

This Chanel look-alike suit was produced by Matita in 1927. By this time the British ready-to-wear fashion industry was producing fashionable middle-class couture designs which were copies of haute couture clothes.

Most potently of all, however, the new fashions suggested youth. Henceforward to be fashionable was to look young. Many older women never wore the new fashions because they disapproved of short skirts. Queen Mary, the present Queen's grandmother, is perhaps the most famous British example of a woman who adhered to the pre-1914 long coat and skirt for the rest of her life. Women of the slums are sometimes to be seen in photographs and drawings still dressed in Edwardian-style blouses, long skirts and pinnies. Presumably they could afford no new clothes at all, or only out-of-date second-hand ones. For them even the symbols of emancipation were unavailable.

America dictates

Paris was the most important fashion centre throughout the interwar period and the main source of new ideas. In 1928, an American economist calculated that the Paris clothing industry employed 300 000 men and women, and that 'a quarter of Paris is . . . involved in apparel for women'. The twenty-five largest couture houses were producing between 500 and 1000 original models or designs each year.[22]

The nature of the Paris couture industry was changing. Although the salons still catered mainly for the private individual customer, a number of couturiers were turning their attention to wider markets, particularly in the United States. The economic crisis inaugurated by the Wall Street crash of 1929 had a profound effect. No American buyers came over to Paris in 1931, and in the early 1930s the Paris couture houses were laying off staff and cutting wages. The United States put up tariff barriers, and the American customers upon whom the Paris couture trade already increasingly depended did not return until the mid-thirties.

In the long run this led to the further rationalisation of the industry and to the development of new profit-making schemes. For example, toiles (canvas, linen or calico copies of models) began to be made and sold for copying purposes – with New York's Seventh Avenue garment district primarily in mind – and couturiers began to market cheaper designs (later called boutique ranges). Lucien Lelong, an established Paris designer, started a boutique business in the 1920s. The models from his exclusive couture house cost between 50 and 100 guineas, which at today's prices would be £460 to £1890. In his boutique, models known as 'Lelong Éditions' were ready made and sold at between £10 and £20 [£180–£200], so even these fashions were far from inexpensive.[23] Although to begin with many of his colleagues rather despised this move, they later copied it, and bags, jewellery and other accessories were added to the items for sale.

Following Paris: the British fashion industry in the thirties

Vionnet, Chanel and Patou created a simple fashion aesthetic which gave impetus to the mass production of fashionable clothes, for their garments could much more easily be copied *en masse* than the prewar styles. British fashion was produced at many different levels. Society women went to Paris for their clothes; British haute couture was seen as second best, but in the 1930s designers such as Victor Stiebel, Hardy Amies, Digby Morton at Lachasse and the Anglo-American Charles James enjoyed a period of development and success, although on a relatively small scale. They capitalised on the reputation of British tailoring, high-quality materials, especially wool, and classic styles. Norman Hartnell, who dressed Queen Elizabeth (now the Queen Mother) in the 1930s, at first showed his clothes in Paris in an attempt to overcome the prejudice against London-based couturiers. By 1939 he was employing 400 staff and selling dresses at approximately 45 guineas [£950].[24]

For upper-middle-class women who could not afford the originals, Paris fashions were reinterpreted in the design rooms of the large department stores, by upmarket dressmakers and by wholesale manufacturers who produced 'wholesale couture'[25] – firms such as Jaeger, Cresta, Matita, Deréta and Dorville. Deréta was started by the Ritter family. They adopted American sizing (much more precise than British) in 1927. The company did not employ a designer. Instead, Lou Ritter, son of the original Ritter, used to bring model garments back from Vienna, and David Mostyn, a tailor who worked for the firm for many years, described how they were copied. (Viennese models were preferred as being better made than French.) The manager and chief cutter would construct a replica, and Mostyn would sew it, altering it as he went. Between them they created a prototype that could then be put into production. Teams of three workers – presser, machinist and tailor – made up the garments once they had been cut out, and fellers and finishers were employed to complete the handwork on the more expensive garments. Outworkers were employed to make up the cheaper ranges. Approximately fifty models were designed in the manner described each season, to be reproduced in bulk. At first Ritter's used labels supplied by the stores that retailed their garments, but in 1936 they introduced their own brand name and began to advertise in *Vogue*.[26]

Olive O'Neill, who started Dorville, 'left art school in her native Southport under a cloud because she insisted on mixing colours like royal blue and turquoise, rose pink and orange in her fashion designs'.[27] She began as a designer for a small Southport shop, but soon joined a London

An early linen and lace dress by the British designer Edward Molyneux from **Vogue**, *1922. With salons in Paris and London, he was internationally successful by the early 1930s.*

dorville models.

★ This gay Tartan swing-back jacket is worn over a sophisticated tailored navy-blue woollen dress, the sash echoing the jacket's merry mood. Dorville models are at the leading London Stores and fashion houses, and at fine shops in every city. Please write for a copy of the new Spring Catalogue. Rose and Blum[?]an, Dorville House, 24[?]6, Margaret Street, London, W.1.

The British ready-to-wear industry was firmly established as a source of well-made clothes by 1937 when Dorville advertised this spring dress and jacket in **Vogue***.*

firm, set up a factory to make the designs under her own supervision, and later she too adapted the American sizing system for the firm.

In the vast majority of dressmaking firms there was no designer as such. On the rare occasions when the title was used, it was combined with another role – for example, isolated advertisements appeared in trade journals for a 'designer manager'. In 1930 the *Garment Manufacturer and Fabric Review* stated that:

The term 'designer' has in recent years come into general use in this country to describe the work of the person responsible for the technical side of garment production. Until we adopted the American word we were content with the older term, pattern-cutter.[28]

and F. R. Morris in his *Ladies' Garment-cutting and Making* (1935), also describes the role of designer as a largely managerial and technical one.[29]

Although the firm of Rhona Roy sent their designers to Paris regularly, and some manufacturers purchased models or toiles from the French couture establishements, most designs came either from fashion journals produced specifically for the trade or from the copying of actual garments in the manner described by David Mostyn. Pirating was rife and almost impossible to control. Margery Allingham even used it as the basis of a murder mystery in 1938:

Val [the designer] . . . was standing in the fitting room . . . when Georgia [her client] dropped the bomb.

'Val, my angel,' she said. . . . 'It's breathtaking! It's *you*. It's *me*. But my pet, it's not *new*. I saw it last night at the Dudley club . . . I can even prove it unfortunately. There's a photograph of the Blaxill woman wearing it in one of the morning papers . . . .'

There was no doubt that the incident was a major catastrophe. . . .

'It's a leakage – you can't stop it in any show where designs are secret. It's an infuriating thing.'[30]

The Americans and Germans in particular appear to have employed individuals or teams who memorised the garments they saw at the Paris shows and then returned at once to their hotel rooms to make the accurate sketches which were dispatched to the manufacturers or model houses. These copies became the department store models which the cheaper end of the trade then in turn copied more crudely – although many design managers registered their own versions of the couture originals at the Public Record Office in order to prevent the copying of these copies.

Surviving garments in museum collections demonstrate that many of them were dressmaker-made. Worthing Museum possesses the account book of a local village dressmaker, Miss E. M. Haffenden of Goring, covering the period 1911 to 1929. She made clothes for 'the Vicarage' and the local nurse, and charged, for example, 18s 6d [£16.95] in 1922 for the fabric and making up of a lady's pinstripe suit.

Yet local dressmakers such as this were a declining group. In 1932 the Board of Trade published an *Industrial Survey of the Lancashire Area.* This reported that factory competition had become so overwhelming to small dressmakers that:

a frock which can be made up for 1s [55p] to 3s [£1.65] according to style, could not be made by a dressmaker for less than 25s [£13.75]. Actually factory-made dresses can often be sold in the shops for less than the cost of the cloth brought in retail stores. This has brought ready-made frocks within the reach of the majority of women and has compelled numbers of local dressmakers to go out of business.[31]

It appears that many women who had once been dressmakers branched out into the sale of ready-made garments in small shops, sometimes known as 'Madam shops'. Some were smart boutiques in a town centre; others might be little more than a shop front for what remained essentially a single dressmaker enterprise. Some offered their own exclusive designs, and undertook alterations on the premises, as did the department stores. (The purchase of the more expensive ready-made designs still normally included the option of having them altered for a better fit, or even of having minor details added to your own specification.) There were also 'guinea gown' shops. These sold cheap special outfits, or evening dresses and cheaper mass-produced clothes (1 guinea in 1932, £11.95 today).

In many of the 'Madam' shops a limited range of clothing only would be displayed, in order to give an impression of exclusiveness. The proprietors might buy a small number of styles from manufacturers who were themselves small scale, making only limited numbers of any one design. The middleman or wholesaler could supply a small shop with dresses and outfits from a number of different manufacturers, so although the shops were small, their stock might be quite varied. This compared favourably with the multiple stores which at this time were selling a very limited range of styles.[32]

A rare collection of the stock from such a shop at the lower end of the market survives at the Lock Museum in Willenhall, near Birmingham. From 1920 to 1960 this shop was a 'General and Fancy Drapers – specialists in ladies' underwear, blouses, etc'. It was run by Edith and Flora Hodson. They sold dresses, pastel rayon jersey slips and camiknickers – these would probably have been purchased by better off local women; and cotton overalls, serviceable stockings, and Edwardian-style combinations and heavy cotton 'stays' (corsets) which were more likely to have been bought by older women and by those who worked in the local lock factories and earned less than £1 [£18] a week. Customers chose from stock or from the wholesalers' catalogues, and Edith travelled on the bus

*There is the world of difference between these two 'Madam' shops of the twenties: Madame Wright's of Cheltenham (**below**) still open today, sold top-class French and British ready-to-wear, whereas Sovereign Gowns (**right**) sold only the cheapest.*

to Birmingham to collect the goods, or ordered them from Manchester or Leicester.

The museum houses boxes and boxes of unsold stock, complete with tickets (evidently the sisters were not the most efficient businesswomen), and these give a clear picture of the quality, style and price of a wide range of mass-produced clothing at this level. Almost all the dresses are made from rayon or cotton, although a very few are silk, and they are clearly intended as 'best' afternoon or Sunday outfits, with a few dance dresses. They are machine stitched with cheap though decorative accessories, watered-down 'jazz' designs and on the whole drab colours. The smartest and most expensive are the Chanel copy jersey suits in wool or rayon, made by St Margarets of Leicester (subsequently renamed

Corah). In the 1920s prices started at 2s 6d or 3s 6d [£2.12–£3] for a Bell overall, went to 6s 11d [£6] for a printed rayon dress, and up to 38s 6d [£32.75] for a wool jersey suit.

All the smaller establishments had to compete on the one hand with home dressmaking, on the other with the expanding chain stores and the department stores. Home dressmaking was becoming widespread. Because styles were simpler, home-made garments could look more professional, and home dressmakers were aided by the wider availability of simple technology: very cheap paper patterns, and the Singer sewing machine, which (decorated with ancient Egyptian motifs after the discovery of Tutankhamen's tomb) was by now a familiar item in many working-class homes. Home-made clothes lacked the status of the ready-made, and many women probably made their own (and/or their children's) out of economic necessity rather than for the love of it.

A general interest in fashion was catered to by the spread of women's magazines. At this time you could borrow a copy of *Vogue* from the public library. More significantly, the thirties saw the lift-off of the mass circulation women's magazines. *Woman's Own* was founded in 1932, and *Woman*, launched in 1937, had half a million readers by the end of that year. This was nothing like the mass readership of the 1950s, their period of peak popularity. Mary Grieve, who edited *Woman* from the beginning until the 1960s, pointed out that this was partly because the living standards of most readers was still too low for mass advertising on the scale developed later, and that most readers, for example, would not have had a telephone or been able to take a daily bath.

Mary Grieve regarded herself as a feminist and as 'left of centre', and for her there was no conflict between feminism and *Woman*.[33] The new magazines and the new consumerism were widely perceived as agents of progress; they would bring a higher standard of living to the woman in the street – or rather in the suburban home. Other, slightly more downmarket magazines such as *Mab's Fashions*, *Women's Companion*, *Woman and Home* and *Harmsworth Fashions* offered free dressmaking patterns, indeed their fashion pages showed no ready-made garments at all, these appearing only in the advertisements.

One of the most significant trends between the wars was the expansion of the retail chain stores. Marks and Spencer and C & A sold cheap, mass-produced clothes, and the Co-operative Societies' dividend schemes enabled holders to save for family clothes. Some branches of the Co-op also ran clothing club schemes. In 1938 the Co-ops were selling one-third of the total supply of women's and children's wear, mostly staple items such as women's underwear and overalls. When, in the 1920s, they tried to introduce fashion lines, they lost money.

Marks and Spencer on the other hand benefited in the 1930s from economies of scale and special arrangements with manufacturers such as Corah of Leicester to introduce cheaper garments which were designed to be 'in fashion' – simple but quite stylish blouses and summer dresses, for example, bearing in mind their price range which stopped at 5s [£5.25]. Another company mass-producing reasonably priced garments for the 'Guinea Gown' market was Marley Gowns. They were turning out 10 000 fashion dresses a week in 1939. Cresta, at the top end of ready to wear, sold dresses made up from screenprints designed by artists including Patrick Heron.

Cheap mass-produced fashion was mainly for the young working woman, and perhaps for the lower-middle-class suburban housewife. Some mill- and office-workers in Bolton were interviewed about their clothes in 1939, but out of eleven, only two appear to have bought ready-made garments, while seven made their own dresses and costumes (although not coats) and two patronised a dressmaker. One of the women who made her own clothes said that were she better off she would buy them ready-made. None had extensive wardrobes; they spoke of a need for three dresses a year, plus one or two jumpers and skirts, and they would consider spending £2 or £3 on a dress [£40–£60];[34] even the poorest woman had to wear a hat out of doors.

The young office-worker was seen as the vanguard for the new mass fashion market. These were young women 'trying to dress like a duchess on seventy shillings a week'.[35] The maintenance of a smart appearance was, for them, a source of anxiety as much as pleasure: ' ''Oh . . . blow! Another ladder!'' Miss Jones hits her Remington savagely and swears that she will never again buy good stockings. That's what comes of wearing her best pair of non-stop silk on a weekday.'[36]

One journalist investigating the plight of homeless women in London in the 1920s found that even many young women in hostels and rooming houses attempted a smart appearance: 'The outcast, until she gives up hope, tries at all costs after ''silk'' hosiery.'[37] One young woman:

was in the regulation get up of the moment – as supplied by weekly instalments of one shilling by the local tallyman – a close fitting black coat, with grey fur collar and a helmet hat, cut and style extraordinarily good, the quality pure shoddy.[38]

Stockings seem to have been particularly the focus of attention, partly because it was such a novelty to have to expose your legs. What had always been part of your underwear was suddenly outerwear, visible to all, and while silk stockings were expensive, cheaper substitutes were not really satisfactory.

That cheap stockings existed at all was due to the development of rayon, which led to changes in all underwear, not just stockings. In the

SPRING & SUMMER 1932

By 1932 fashionably styled dresses had reached the mass market through wholesale companies such as Good Style, of Birmingham.

1920s, despite the simplicity of outerwear, most women still wore a vest, brassiere, long, boned or elasticated corset, suspenders and *Directoire* knickers (with legs gathered on elastic just above the knee). In the 1930s, however, bias cut underwear and new designs such as camiknickers and 'French' cut knickers began to be introduced to the public at large.

Upper- and middle-class women had these designs made up in silk. In London the best ones were made by a Russian émigrée, who had opened a boutique from which she sold her silk and lace appliqué lingerie. Lady Holman, a diplomatic wife, had several sets, including one short slip, now in the collection at Brighton Museum, which features a hunt, with horses leaping over hedges, appliquéd in black lace on eau-de-Nil silk.

The new style underwear became available to some of the less well off because it could now be copied in synthetic materials. Serious attempts had been made to develop substitutes for silk from wood pulp cellulose in the late nineteenth century. But the breakthrough came in the interwar period, and particularly in the thirties, when rayon was successfully developed on a commercial scale. Fine rayon jersey, in particular, also called celanese, made the production of low cost fashion stockings, underwear and summer dresses much more feasible.

In the early postwar years women's stockings were still made of cotton (lisle) or wool; only the rich and fashionable had silk ones, and sometimes even these were of cotton or wool above the knee. By 1927 200 000 000 lb (90 720 000 kg)[39] of rayon was produced in Britain – three times the quantity of silk – yet rayon or artificial ('art') silk, as it was called, had a low reputation. By this time rayon stockings had supplanted the old-fashioned lisle for young women, but rayon hose were easily recognised as such because they laddered easily and were very shiny; they were a poor imitation of silk stockings, but cost only one quarter the price of silk. Even so, the typist on £3 10s [£63] a week might be tempted by the cheaper silk ones found in markets such as Berwick Street, Soho:

A glorious colour is given to Berwick Street by thousands of silk stockings. Every shade of sunburn is there, from the boiled shrimp to the colour of a brunette spending a holiday in Jamaica. . . .

'Now miss, four and six a pair, any colour! The very same you pay ten shilling for anywhere else. . . .'

Her hands dive into silk stockings. . . . Ah: the right smart shade, the right subtle tint: not that cheap pink, or that common reddy brown.[40]

Rayon jumpers, too, cost only half as much as woollen ones, and home- and factory-knitted rayon sweaters were popular with both middle-class and working-class customers. On the whole, though, cus-

In 1929, in an attempt to improve its low quality image, the rayon industry held the British Artificial Silk Exhibition at Olympia in London – with only limited success at first. However, by the late 1930s, rayon had become accepted even in the middle market range of ready-to-wear.

tomers purchased rayon because it was the best they could afford and was modestly fashionable, but there is evidence that most women of all classes would have chosen silk for preference.

Rayon fabrics were continually improved in the thirties. In 1936 the firm of Courtaulds spent £135 000 on advertising and attempted to introduce a whole series of seductive names for the fabric: Delysia, Silkella and Courgette (before the latter had been heard of as a vegetable in Britain). English couturiers were occasionally persuaded to use rayon; for example the House of Reville devoted an entire collection in 1930 to rayon and cotton mixtures, in an unsuccessful attempt to save their fortunes.[41] By the late 1930s the quality of rayon fabric had clearly improved and was used by middle- and even top-quality ready-to-wear companies. Courtaulds had great success with it at this time and advertised successfully with Harrods in *Vogue* to launch their new, fashion-conscious image.

The Hollywood look

One development in fashion peculiar to the 1930s was the influence of Hollywood, and the marketing of special 'film fashions'. Paris was the main influence on Hollywood design; Chanel designed the costumes for Gloria Swanson in *Tonight or Never*, although these were regarded as too understated in California; Schiaparelli designed for Mae West. The film industry also developed its own designers, Adrian, Orry-Kelly and Travis Banton being some of the best known at this period, and Hollywood styles did have their own accent and allure.

In the silent film era – the 1920s – female stars tended to be represented either as vamps (Theda Bara) or as exaggeratedly girlish and innocent (Mary Pickford). German Expressionist melodrama, with its intense chiaroscuro (light and shade) effects, dominated movie style, although even then Louise Brooks presented an alternative image in many of her films as the ordinary city girl-in-the-street who sported the *garçonne* look. (She also starred in two of the most famous Expressionist movies, G. W. Pabst's *Pandora's Box* and *The Diary of a Lost Girl.*)

In the 1930s a new generation of stars such as Katharine Hepburn and Carole Lombard, starring in realistic comedy films, introduced the more down-to-earth ideals of the sporty girl and the girl next door. There was thus a reversal of what was happening in fashion: if one saw the fashions of the 1920s as simple, practical and *sportif* (as Winifred Holtby obviously did), then this was a very different image from that of Theda Bara with her kohl-shadowed eyes and dark lips. In the 1930s the breezy Katharine Hepburn seemed a far cry from the *svelte* Parisian fashions of that time. This contrast should not be taken too far, however, since Jean Harlow, Marlene Dietrich and Greta Garbo represented potent images of exotic or sultry sexuality on screen.

Mass culture was producing a whole variety of ways for women to look, and in the thirties this became part and parcel of the Hollywood industry. With the advent of sound, and greater realism, the women in the audiences who watched the 'talkies' in their millions could identify with the stars, and learn from them how to dress, how to wear make-up, how to style their hair, how to smoke a cigarette, even how to kiss.

Aware of this, Samuel Goldwyn deliberately embarked upon a strategy of attracting women to his cinemas. In an interview in *Colliers Magazine* in April 1931 he predicted that they would go to the movies, 'one, to see the pictures and stars; and two, to see the latest in clothes'.[42] Women's film magazines such as *Women's Filmfair*, first published in 1934, and *Film Fashionland*, gave women advice on how to copy the beauty routines, dress and manners of their favourite stars. In the first issue of *Filmfair*, Ena Glen advised readers: 'It should be every woman's aim to pick out a star personality resembling her own face, figure or temperament, and be inspired by it. Choosing clothes will then become an easy and fascinating business.'[43]

The obvious next step, commercially, was actually to make the fashions seen on film available to ordinary women. Many magazines,

99

including *Film Fashionland*, provided a postal service offering some ready-made screen styles, and paper patterns for others. Thus, any woman could make a garment for just a few shillings in the conviction that its design was based upon a glamorous Hollywood model. Some stores even had cinema departments, where they sold film fashion models ready-made.

Don't "Filmfair Fashions" look attractive in this effective display arranged by Messrs Lewis's at their Birmingham stores? The mannequin in the foreground is wearing the Margaret Sullavan picture frock.

LOOK FOR THIS LABEL IN EVERY FROCK

THIS IS A GENUINE
filmfair fashion
Sponsored by WOMAN'S FILMFAIR

As part of the Hollywood publicity machine, both women's magazines and film-goers' magazines featured fashion and beauty hints from the stars. Film Fare *magazine even offered a line of 'film star' dresses in 1936.*

In 1935 the trade periodical *Commercial Trade and Industry* reported a British plan, originated by Mrs Marianne Horn, wardrobe supervisor to the Gaumont British Picture Corporation, to market copies of dresses worn by the Gaumont stars. The dresses were to be advertised and put on sale at the time when the films were distributed, so there was a very direct tie-in. There was an emphasis on these fashions as British, and it was hoped to sell 15 000 a week, at around 2 guineas [£44], although the magazine commented sceptically that: 'Most of the dresses seem far too exaggerated in style to make any general appeal to the woman of limited means'.[44]

After 1934 the Hollywood Hays Code of Censorship created stringent rules regulating the presentation of sex and nudity on screen. Eroticism, therefore, was all the more likely to be the creation of an atmosphere, a visual magnetism on the part of the star, in which her dress played an important part. The Hollywood film did much to popularise the sleek slithery curves made possible by the Vionnet bias cut, especially when the material used was satin, the shine of which accentuated the flat yet sinuously seductive lines of the body.[45]

Even if Hollywood pitched its appeal primarily at women, young men also identified with the more realistic screen heroes – or anti-heroes – of the talkies: Edward G. Robinson in *Little Caesar* (1930), James Cagney in *Public Enemy* (1931), and George Raft in *Scarface* (1932). A reporter on the *Islington and Holloway Press* visited 'Islington's most notorious café' in 1934, where he observed some of the local tearaways:

They acted all the time. . . . Movie mad . . . clothing 'the latest worn', ridiculous styles and with a horrible 'cut price' appearance about it . . . the conversation . . . mostly in American accents. . . . Nearly every youth, with a very long overcoat and a round black hat on the rear of his head, was to himself a 'Chicago nut'.[46]

Cogs and levers: workers in the 1930s fashion industry

Between the wars mass production methods were increasingly attractive to large-scale garment manufacturers. Yet one survey in the 1930s revealed that in London at least the majority of establishments were still employing less than ten workers. There was great variety in size of firm and methods of working which coexisted in this rather chaotic industry. A 1942 Board of Trade survey – which must have reflected the situation as it existed just before the outbreak of war – estimated that of 842 firms in the women's tailoring trades 1 per cent were using the conveyor belt system (complete mechanisation), 40 per cent the sectional system (whereby individual workers concentrated on one part or section of a garment, making sleeves or collars all day) and 50 per cent the complete garment method (one skilled worker making up a whole garment); for 807 dress, blouse and overall manufacturers the figures were 2 per cent, 18 per cent and 72 per cent.[47]

Government legislation from 1934 onwards encouraged the spread of clothing factories to the 'special areas' (depressed areas of Britain) by giving financial assistance to relocate there. Clothing factories traditionally, however, employed women rather than men, save in the overseeing and other more responsible positions, so that this initiative had little impact on male unemployment in the north of England.

The Midlands were to some extent protected from the slump by a long tradition of clothing manufacture. Leicester, for example, had a tradition

101

of hosiery and knitwear making that went back several hundred years, and this was maintained and even expanded in the 1930s. J. B. Priestley described one of the factories specialising in this kind of work:

> There were enormous rooms filled with women and girls, who worked with small machines at long tables. . . . There is still far more hand labour than machine work. . . . In these factories . . . you saw long rows of sewing machines worked by electric power but guided by hand. . . . I was left with a dazed impression of miles and miles of stockings, underclothes, knitted dresses and the like, with bright acres of femininity at work on them. I remember a cutting machine that went through a thick soft pile of material for men's pants like a knife going through cheese. But that seemed the most dashing whole-sale process on view, for after that an immense amount of hand work, merely eked out with electric power, appeared to be expended on the garments.
>
> [Yet] in these factories they are using some elaborate new system of organising and tabulating their production [with the result that although] . . . the human element in labour appears still to be dominant . . . this human element has been woven into a gigantic system of minute subdivision of labour until the whole place is really an enormous machine in which the workers are simply cogs and levers.[48]

As a justification for the boring nature of the work, the manager of this factory resorted to the old cliché that the women preferred routine and monotonous jobs because then they could dream about film stars while turning out their hundreds of pairs of men's underpants.

Men's clothes . . . and the Reform movement spreads

The new simplicity of women's wear in the 1920s lent itself to mass production, but although men's clothes were mass produced, the styles now seemed restrictive by comparison with feminine fashions. Indeed a strange reversal had occurred. Whereas in the 1890s women's over-elaborate clothes had seemed to unfit the wearers for modern life, while men had appeared suitably dressed for the formality and public importance of their daily routine in city and suburb, by the 1920s it was men who appeared stuck in clothes that the reformers regarded as stiff, old-fashioned and unhygienic. They were still wearing long johns and vests with sleeves, or combinations, although these garments were now more likely to be made of cotton than of wool; they wore shirts with stiff collars, waistcoats and thick suits, even in summer; professional men, politicians and city workers still normally wore their uniform of black coat and pinstriped trousers. Lounge suits or tweeds were popular; but it was only in the Fair Isle sweaters (popularised by the Prince of Wales), plus fours (adapted from reform dress) and the wide-legged flannels for sportswear that middle-class men achieved a casual look that could compare with that of young women.

This young spinner, in a Courtauld's factory in Coventry in the 1920s, was able to afford a fashionable look, covered here with a printed cotton overall which was almost a uniform for working at home or in the factory.

Working-class men's clothes were also stiff and awkward; the poorest and the unemployed had just the rough trousers, jacket and flat cap so familiar in photographs of the hunger marches and the depressed areas, although every man would struggle to own a best Sunday suit of black and if possible a bowler hat or a Homburg, although these might have to be pawned during the week. There were also sub-cultural styles in slum areas, such as that adopted by the Islington 'Chicago nuts', referred to earlier.

Between these extremes, the mass manufacture of men's clothes was also extended and streamlined. Burtons and John Collier the 'Fifty Shilling tailor' flourished, selling cheap made-to-measure clothing (made up after one fitting) to the growing ranks of white-collar workers.

Given that menswear remained so conventional and stuffy, it was not surprising that dress reformers transferred their attention from women's wear to that of men. There was a Sensible Dress Society and a Hygienic Dress League. Nothing is known about their activities, but we do know something about the Men's Dress Reform Party, which was active from 1929 to 1937.[49] Its steering committee consisted of a number of distinguished people, including the painter W. R. Sickert, Dean Inge of St Paul's, Ernest Thesiger, a well-known actor, Guy Kendall, headmaster of University College School, and Dr Caleb W. Saleeby, chairman of the Sunlight League. Dr J. C. Flugel, psychoanalyst and author of an influential theoretical work on dress (it has a eugenic flavour to the present-day reader), was also associated with the group.

An Oscar Wilde collar and loose tie, shorts, bathing trunks and lighter materials were some of the major innovations advocated by the Men's Dress Reform Party. Health and hygiene were motivating forces; and the leading light was Dr Alfred Charles Jordan, a radiologist of international reputation.

The Men's Dress Reform Party was a small and shortlived organisation. The Women's League of Health and Beauty was much larger, longer lasting (it still exists) and more influential. It was formed by Mollie Stack, who had originally trained in movement and exercise with one of the prewar pioneers of exercise for health and beauty, Mrs Josef Conn. After experience of teaching dance and exercise to children and to adults with disabilities, she founded the League in 1930. In a sense it represented the popular culmination in Britain of the great interest in health and hygiene which had begun in the second half of the nineteenth century.

In 1931 Mollie Stack's *Building the Body Beautiful*, which set out her system, was published. Various publicity efforts – a march to Hyde Park and a display at the Albert Hall – generated enormous interest and by

1933 League membership had leapt to 30 000. Mollie Stack saw her work as bringing women together in the interest not simply of health and beauty but also in the cause of Peace, and her own words sum up the ideals of the movement, in many ways so typical of its period:

I see a goal further ahead than Health and Beauty, in the ordinary sense, and that is Peace, and further on stands Love – universal Love and service. Human Health and Beauty are but the stepping stones to that ideal. . . . Health represents peace and harmonious balance in the innermost tissues of mind and body. Beauty seems to me to represent this idea carried out by every individual, by humanity universally.[50]

The League was typical of its period in its utopian vision of a world cleansed of ill health and ugliness by scientific and spiritual knowledge, and of the perfect human body as an embodiment of this knowledge and progress – the ideal we discussed earlier as having such divergent possibilities.

Fashion between the wars is perhaps best understood as the spearhead of consumerism, which was at last reaching at least some sections of the working class. Comfort, style and cleanliness were beginning to be within the grasp of many, although millions were still deprived of them. And, in the last analysis, short skirts and short hair had more to do with convenience than with sexual liberation, still less with economic equality, which was as elusive as ever for women in the Jazz Age and the Age of Dictators. Paradoxically, it was during the Second World War that women were to make economic advances, and it was also during this period that the state direction of resources was to extend to the state supervision of style.

4

$\mathcal{R}$ATIONED FASHION
1939-50

The period from September 1939, when the Second World War broke out, to October 1951, when the Conservative Government was returned to power, falls neatly into two halves. The war ended in 1945 and in Britain the first majority Labour Government was elected on a programme of radical reform. What the wartime and the postwar halves of the decade had in common was planning; and planning extended even to clothes.

The war and the war effort involved the Home Front to an extent never experienced before. To begin with, Britain was alone and vulnerable, and what soon became the Coalition Government was faced with an enormous task: life in Britain had to go on at the same time as the forces had to be supplied with arms, vehicles and uniforms. Before the outbreak of war, Britain had been crucially dependent on overseas supplies of food and raw materials; now the food had to be produced at home, and the raw materials directed where they were most urgently needed. Everyone suddenly had a role to play and everyone had to pull together. This total involvement of the Home Front meant a shared sense of struggle and community.

Immediately after war broke out the French writer Simone de Beauvoir noted in Paris: 'Bought a copy of *Marie-Claire*. The word war is never mentioned once, and yet the issue is perfectly slanted for present conditions.'[1]

In the first phase of the war, neither Britain nor France really suffered from shortages. In Germany, on the other hand, Frau Scholtz-Klink, head of the Nazi Women's Bureau, announced that 'German women must now

Opposite During the war mothers with young children struggled with food and clothing shortages. This airman's wife is serving tea to her large family.

deny themselves luxury and enjoyment'. Hilde Marchant of the *Daily Express* was ready with a riposte:

I would have liked to take [Frau Scholtz-Klink] with me on a . . . shopping tour of the West End. I would have argued that the women I saw buying crazy new hats to begin the war in, will put up a more determined resistance in the winter months ahead of us than Frau Scholtz-Klink's German ideal, who begins war in a mackintosh and flat shoes. . . .

The war begins in Autumn; that is no reason why we shouldn't buy our new winter clothes. There is no shortage of anything in London's shops. The new fashions are gay; the hats even crazier than ever. . . . [And] the women who were trying them on were having a grand fling. But for the blackout curtains over the shop windows, it would have been like any ordinary autumn buying.[2]

The situation described by Hilde Marchant could not last long. In the summer of 1940 the Germans overran France and occupied Paris. French industry of every kind was at once turned towards the benefit of the Third Reich. Adolf Hitler wanted to have the Paris haute couture industry moved wholesale to Germany, there to create a magnificent new luxury export trade. Lucien Lelong, head of the Chambre Syndicale de l'Haute Couture, was taken to Berlin to see the extent of the German fashion industry. On his return to Paris he explained to the Nazi authorities that it would be impossible to move the workrooms and designers to Berlin and Vienna. The industry, he argued, needed the atmosphere and talent native to the city of Paris and nowhere else. Thus Lucien Lelong is said to have 'saved' French couture. He managed to negotiate a special allowance of 'points' for material for the couture trade, and obtained permission for haute couture clothes to remain outside the rationing system that the Germans had imposed.

Designers who were not French nationals, such as Elsa Schiaparelli, Molyneux and Mainbocher, had left soon after the outbreak of war, and Jacques Heim, who was Jewish, went into hiding. Chanel closed her house, but spent the war with a lover who was a German officer, and was an ardent supporter of the collaborationist Vichy regime. Gradually, however, many other houses re-opened and remained open throughout the war, among them Lelong, who employed Christian Dior and Pierre Balmain, Marcel Rochas, Jeanne Lanvin, the house of Patou, Robert Piguet and Nina Ricci. Lelong was employing about 400 workers in 1942.[3] The clientele, however, changed dramatically. None came from overseas; a much smaller number of the traditional French clients remained; they were joined by the wives and mistresses of German officers and of the French collaborationist politicians and by 'les dames du marché noir' – women associated with black market profiteering. Some of these women made fortunes out of selling abandoned Jewish property to the Nazis.

For some of those who continued in business this must have been an

108

uncomfortable time. Balmain and Dior watched their unwelcome new clients maliciously, and Dior remarked that they would be shot after the Liberation.[4] Madame Grès got into trouble with the Nazis when she sent models down the catwalk in the red, white and blue of the Tricolour (the French national flag).[5] Perhaps, though, the heroism attributed to those who continued in business has been exaggerated; and the French couture industry has also not been able to escape the taint of collaboration, a pervasive and shameful feature of French life under the Nazi occupation.

Even under Nazi occupation during the Second World War Paris couture styles continued to evolve. These elaborate full-skirted designs shown in the **Album de Modes de Figaro,** *1943, would have been unthinkable in Britain.*

The clothes produced in these abnormal circumstances continued to evolve, but not surprisingly diverged more and more from what was being worn in Britain and the United States. Nobody outside France realised this for several years, and indeed the extravagance of French haute couture under the Nazi occupation was remote from the lives of most Frenchwomen, who struggled with shortages of all kinds.

In Britain, too, daily life was transformed. Although Britain was fortunate by comparison with most other countries involved in the war, suffering neither occupation nor fighting on her soil, the mass bombing of the blitz, which began in 1940, was hard to endure, and for the first three years of the war there were more civilian than forces casualties, about 43 000.[6] Once the blitz began, women had little time to be fashionable.

An air raid warning might sound at any time – while you were shopping, travelling, working or in the bath. There was no time to waste in dressing up, and as time went on there was little to dress up in. Survival was the overwhelming priority. Pearl Binder, the author Lou Taylor's mother, comments that 'no one was sluttish, or depressed', but the energy expended on keeping going at all costs, in the shelters, in the forces and in the factories, left little time for leisure pursuits of any kind. Quite apart from the casualties, bombing made many homeless. Shortages soon became acute. By 1941, the British were spending 20 per cent less on food, 43 per cent less on household goods and 38 per cent less on clothes.[7]

It was also in 1941 that the shortage of labour became fully apparent: two million were needed for the forces, and for munitions and manufacturing. Accordingly, on 8 December 1941, all unmarried women and childless widows aged between twenty and thirty years of age were called up, and soon afterwards nineteen-year-olds as well.[8] Many women with children worked too, and many more, mostly middle-class women, undertook voluntary war work. The myth has grown up that this was a time of emancipation for women, when collective provision – of meals and childcare in particular – diminished the domestic burden, while women gained social and economic independence as war workers or, even more excitingly, in the armed forces. There was never, however, a total mobilisation of women, and women were still probably more likely to be reliant on family than on government provision for domestic assistance. The government could never really decide whether it thought mothers ought to be engaged in war work or not.[9] And, while women replaced men in 'male' jobs, they did not receive equal pay; 'in January 1944, women in metalwork and engineering earned on average £3 10s [£54] a week, as compared with £7 [£108] for men'.[10]

Doing without: wartime chic

At the beginning of the war women were still wearing fashions influenced by Paris, and the twice yearly couture shows in the capital of fashion continued until February 1940. With the war fully under way everything changed. Informality was inevitable. Hardly anyone dressed for dinner any more. In November 1942 *Picture Post* described the gaiety of London's expensive night clubs and restaurants, but even here:

Among the women who are still dressing up for the evening, we have seen marked signs of clothes rationing. We saw a gay young thing wearing what amounted to a silver lamé tennis dress, because her coupons had not allowed her enough material for sleeves, and a soignée woman in an evening dress made out of pink striped mattress ticking.

Opposite *Ordinary recruits to the Women's Services were issued with mass-produced and often ill-fitting uniforms. Wealthier officers bought their own, made-to-measure uniforms from companies such as Moss Bros, advertising here in* Vogue *in 1943.*

Thousands of women of all classes were in uniform. The rich bought theirs from the best London stores and tailors and even had them made to measure. Austin Reed, for example, advertised in *Vogue* in January 1942 that:

Women who know what they are about, take the ordering of a uniform seriously . . . behind our uniform department is a background of expert cutting and expert knowledge of women's tailoring. They come to us too because we pride ourselves on the dispatch with which we can turn them out all correct in accordance with regulations.

(In the United States the uniforms for the women's forces were specifically designed to look fashionable, so as to attract women into the services.[11])

The military uniform strongly influenced the fashions of the war period, and this converged with the simplicity of 1930s-style coats and skirts to create the 'classic' suit of the period – its universal shape the short, narrow skirt and tailored fitted jacket. The jacket had a tighter waist than would be usual today. One surviving example of this style, a non-Utility model made by a small Hampshire tailor, is beautifully finished, with a silk crepe lining, and is well cut. It appears, however, to be made from material more usually reserved for a man's suit, and instead of a zip the skirt has a row of poppers to comply with Utility regulations.

Hats also became military in style. When Princess Elizabeth (now the Queen) joined the ATS (the women's section of the army), her peaked cap triggered a fashion of hats similar in shape. The peasant scarf, tied simply under the chin, was also given the royal seal of approval by the Princess. Another fashion in headgear was the 'glamour band', a scarf worn twisted round the head and tied in a roll at the front, completely covering the hair save for a curl rolled up at the front. This had developed as regulation wear in some factories, since, owing to the Hollywood fashion for long, rolling curls (for example the Veronica Lake style of 1943) horrific accidents had sometimes occurred when women's hair got caught in machinery – women were literally scalped. The glamour band was worn outside as well as inside the factory, but was predominantly a working-class fashion, although hats in a similar shape were also made. For middle-class women, a hat was still almost essential out of doors. Middle-class women were also reluctant to sink to the level of going without stockings and wore ankle socks instead. Another working-class custom was to wear a suit jacket over a summer frock.

As in the First World War many women grew accustomed to wearing trousers and dungarees at work, although one ex-landgirl remembered that when a group of them entered the local pub in their corduroy jodhpurs there was some hostility from the locals. She attributed this to

Women were prepared to wear overalls such as these because they were practical and didn't require coupons; soon dungarees, trousers and siren suits became acceptable wear both for work and for leisure.

the presence of women *en masse*, however, rather than to the actual garments they were wearing.[12] Theodora Fitzgibbon, who had been a fashion model in the late thirties, recalled that it was still not usual for civilian women to wear trousers, although she herself wore old jodhpurs and a riding jacket in London in order to keep warm.[13] The upper-class novelist Nancy Mitford describes one of her more raffish characters as wearing 'trousers with the air of one still flouting the conventions, ignorant that every suburban shopgirl was doing the same'.[14] While Nancy Mitford may well have been overstating the case, some women do seem to have worn their absent husbands' trousers, as they were or cut down to fit, but it seems unlikely that the more conventional woman would have contemplated such a step. On the other hand the usefulness of 'slacks', as they were called, was much discussed in the pages of *Vogue*. As with cosmetics in the interwar years, middle-class women were the last to accept trousers as appropriate, but it was probably during the Second World War that women's trousers began to make the cross-over from being only for sportswear and work to being considered suitable for ordinary daily life.

Wartime wedding photographs seldom show brides in white. More often the bride wears her best tailored suit or afternoon frock, but perched on her head is an elaborate hat, the last remaining indicator of a pent-up longing for glamour. When brides did manage a white wedding the dress was usually short, made of rayon or cotton and very simple, or else a borrowed, second-hand gown from prewar days. Mrs Margaret Taylor, the author Lou Taylor's mother-in-law, an iron-moulder's wife from Falkirk in central Scotland who took in dressmaking to earn extra cash, remembers making a wedding dress for the bride of a local doctor. The bridegroom brought a pair of white cotton curtains back from Italy when he returned on leave, and Mrs Taylor made them into a full-length dress.

Vogue made a virtue out of the necessity of the new austerity:

The new look: it's a look of simplicity. . . . Dressiness is démodé. It looks wrong to look wealthy. Understatement has a chic denied to over-emphasis. . . . The 'too-good-to-be-true' look which only a personal maid can produce is absent – because the maid is absent – on munitions.[15]

Norman Hartnell echoed this view:

Clothes in London today are clothes for the connoisseur, perfect in cut, in workmanship and in fit . . . lines are slim and elegant; no woman would like to think she was using more fabric nor the labour of man than is needed, when both are wanted for the war effort. Hence a complete lack of extravagance. Colours chosen are always interchangeable throughout the wardrobe, so then a woman busy on war work does not have to change all her accessories from one occasion to another. A coat must go equally well with, say, two dresses and one suit, and so must bag, belt and gloves.[16]

The fashionable London store Fortnum and Mason advertised in *Vogue* in October 1941 the 'New Models for Old' department. This was a remodelling service, especially opened to deal with wartime conditions:

We have just opened a re-modelling section. There, we copy new models from materials which are at present hanging in your wardrobe. Ask to see our portfolio of sketches and new ideas. It's astonishing what rejuvenation can be wrought by using a little creative ingenuity.

    Suit or long coat turned and remodelled: 12 guineas [£195]
    Special quotation for renovations: from 3 guineas [£49]

Class differences undoubtedly persisted in wartime Britain. There was no dramatic move towards 'democratic' clothing, nor was there fundamental equality. Nancy Weir, for example, who had been a cook in service with upper-class families before the war, found herself running a workers' canteen in St John's Wood, London. There she was assisted by rich women from the class she had formerly served. While she ran the canteen as a full-time worker, however, the society women put in a couple of hours a day on a voluntary basis.[17]

Similarly, if you were rich, you still had both the time and the money to have your hair done in the-basement bomb-shelter salon at the Dorchester Hotel. Even after the introduction of clothes rationing, some women could evidently afford the by now much more expensive couture models, although a made-to-measure coat and skirt cost £42 [£645] as against the prewar price of 14 guineas [£225], a nightdress £14 [£215] instead of a little over £1 [£16].[18] In January 1942 *Vogue* reported that Lady Stanley of Alderley, a member of the *Vogue* staff, had 'found it well worth while to spend eighteen coupons on [a] warm . . . wool tweed suit, from Lachasse, with collar and cuffs of black velvet'.

Nonetheless, there was a common experience of shortages as the war continued. Women of all classes had to get by as best they could and resorted to any number of ingenious expedients. Curtains and furnishing materials, for example, were never rationed, and were often converted into perfectly acceptable dresses; alternatively the unworn parts of two or three garments could be converted into one 'new' outfit. Adult clothes were often cut down for children, while jumpers were unravelled and reknitted. Mrs Margaret Taylor, the Falkirk dressmaker, had to cut up a man's overcoat in heavy black wool cloth to make a suit for a woman to wear to a funeral on one occasion, and she herself did not buy any new clothes during the war, relying entirely on second-hand clothes and home dressmaking. Blankets were made into coats, silk maps into dresses and dressing gowns (there are some interesting examples at Worthing Museum), blackout material was made into skirts and knickers, and parachute silk was sometimes secretly made into underwear. (This was not strictly speaking legal.)

One woman who was in her teens during the war remembers how universal was the patriotism of 'doing without':

In spite of being . . . mad on fashion, I never remember using the 'black market' or even coming across it. And I never bought coupons until after the war in Petticoat Lane. . . . It's a mistake to think that better-off people went on buying things as usual; *they didn't*. . . . The better off people were the most [patriotic] – they could do it easily as they had other things to fall back on! . . . It would have looked odd to have a lot of new clothes. Except in London there were no dress agencies or old clothes shops that 'ladies' could use, but the upper crust bought and sold through the classified ads. in *The Times* and the *Telegraph*.[19]

Some male historians have assumed that men simply gave up on clothes for the duration, relieved that they no longer had to bother; in fact, it appears that men often left the handling of their clothing coupons to their wives or mothers, or even treated them as 'beer money'; an open

Because of shortages, women used any fabric they could lay their hands on. This dressing gown was made from a printed silk wall map of northern Indo-China.

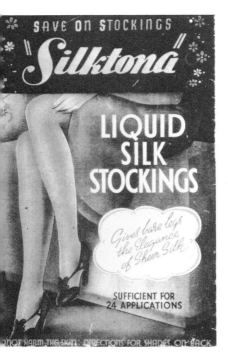

Stockings were such a luxury during the war that young women took to wearing socks, or dyed their legs with liquid make-up. Rayon and silk stockings were rare, nylon unobtainable.

trade in clothing coupons developed with coupons changing hands for about 2s 6d [£1.86] each.[20]

Presumably some women also felt relief at not having to bother, just as, no doubt, a good many men wanted to go on looking smart. At least, though, men did not have to worry about cosmetics, which were now well established as female necessities, but rapidly became scarce luxuries. Crude substitutes were available, and basic ingredients could sometimes be obtained as medicines. One woman has described how she and her friends contrived to make themselves glamorous in spite of everything:

Our one aim in life seemed to concern our faces and hair. Pond's cold cream was slapped on by the potful to rid our skins of real and imagined grime. A touch of vaseline on our eyelids gave our eyes an irresistible look when going to a dance – or so we thought. A beauty spot would be marked on with a black eyebrow pencil, like the one Margaret Lockwood, the film star, had on her chin.[21]

Women even painted their legs with a special lotion to imitate stockings, and used the ubiquitous eyebrow pencil to draw a 'seam' down the back.

Coupons and Utility

There was a commitment by the Coalition Government to the fair distribution of scarce but essential goods such as food, clothing and furniture. To this end a comprehensive rationing scheme was introduced, which operated much more strictly and fairly than anything attempted during the First World War; so much so that the poorer sections of the population were better fed during the war than they had been in the 1930s.

Clothes rationing was first considered in June 1940, and actually introduced in June 1941. Ironically the scheme of coupons for clothes and food was copied from the Germans. Initially the allowance was 66 coupons a year, but in spring 1942, because of growing shortages, this was cut down to 60 for fifteen months, approximately 48 coupons a year.[22]

Vogue had joined the government in campaigning for rationing and an end to extravagance in clothing, and the October 1941 editorial told its readers: 'Rationing is fair. Nothing counts in comparison with victory. We may not grin, but we can bear it. Ingenuity within the spirit of the regulations is legitimate. It is fair to coax two dresses out of one length.' Lady Stanley of Alderley, besides the 18 coupons she spent on her Lachasse suit, used 4 on a new blouse, 3 on gloves, 10 on shoes and 8 on stockings, to make a total of 43. Mrs Anne Parker remembers that:

It was a matter of pride to keep within the coupon allowance: in fact most older women gave all their coupons to young relatives – schoolboys, etc. . . . It was possible to manage quite well. One could buy about one coat, one blouse, one pair of shoes, and a few stockings per year. The next year it would be

RATIONING
of Clothing, Cloth, Footwear
from June 1, 1941

Rationing has been introduced, not to deprive you of your real needs, but to make more certain that you get your share of the country's goods—to get fair shares with everybody else.

When the shops re-open you will be able to buy cloth, clothes, footwear and knitting wool *only if you bring your Food Ration Book with you*. The shopkeeper will detach the required number of coupons from the unused margarine page. Each margarine coupon counts as one coupon towards the purchase of clothing or footwear. You will have a total of 66 coupons to last you for a year; so go sparingly. You can buy *where* you like and *when* you like without registering.

NUMBER OF COUPONS NEEDED

Men and Boys	Adult	Child	Women and Girls	Adult	Child
Unlined mackintosh or cape ..	9	7	Lined mackintoshes, or coats (over 28 in. in length) ..	14	11
Other mackintoshes, or raincoat, or overcoat	16	11	Jacket, or short coat (under 28 in. in length)	11	8
Coat, or jacket, or blazer or like garment	13	8	Dress, or gown, or frock—woollen	11	8
Waistcoat, or pull-over, or cardigan, or jersey ..	5	3	Dress, or gown, or frock—other material	7	5
Trousers (other than fustian or corduroy)	8	6	Gym tunic, or girl's skirt with bodice	8	6
Fustian or corduroy trousers ..	5	5	Blouse, or sports shirt, or cardigan, or jumper	5	3
Shorts	5	3	Skirt, or divided skirt	7	5
Overalls, or dungarees or like garment	6	4	Overalls, or dungarees or like garment	6	4
Dressing-gown or bathing-gown	8	6	Apron, or pinafore	3	2
Night-shirt or pair of pyjamas ..	8	6	Pyjamas	8	6
Shirt, or combinations—woollen	8	6	Nightdress	6	5
Shirt, or combinations—other material	5	4	Petticoat, or slip, or combination, or cami-knickers	4	3
Pants, or vest, or bathing costume, or child's blouse	4	2	Other undergarments, including corsets	3	2
Pair of socks or stockings ..	3	1	Pair of stockings	2	1
Collar, or tie, or pair of cuffs ..	1	1	Pair of socks (ankle length) ..	1	1
Two handkerchiefs	1	1	Collar, or tie, or pair of cuffs ..	1	1
Scarf, or pair of gloves or mittens	2	2	Two handkerchiefs	1	1
Pair of slippers or goloshes ..	4	2	Scarf, or pair of gloves or mittens or muff	2	2
Pair of boots or shoes ..	7	3	Pair of slippers, boots or shoes ..	5	3
Pair of leggings, gaiters or spats	3	2			

CLOTH. Coupons needed per yard depend on the width. For example, a yard of woollen cloth 36 inches wide requires 3 coupons. The same amount of cotton or other cloth needs 2 coupons. KNITTING WOOL. 1 coupon for two ounces.

THESE GOODS MAY BE BOUGHT *WITHOUT* COUPONS

¶Children's clothing of sizes generally suitable for infants less than 4 years old. ¶Boiler suits and workmen's bib and brace overalls ¶Hats and caps. ¶Sewing thread. ¶Mending wool and mending silk. ¶Boot and shoe laces. ¶Tapes, braids, ribbons and other fabrics of 3 inches or less in width. ¶Elastic. ¶Lace and lace net. ¶Sanitary towels. ¶Braces, suspenders and garters. ¶Hard haberdashery. ¶Clogs. ¶Black-out cloth dyed black. ¶All second-hand articles.

Special Notice to Retailers

Retailers will be allowed to get fresh stocks of cloth up to and including June 28th, of other rationed goods up to and including June 21st, WITHOUT SURRENDERING COUPONS. After those dates they will be able to obtain fresh stocks only by turning in their customers' coupons. Steps have been taken, in the interests of the smaller retailers, to limit during these periods the quantity of goods which can be supplied by a wholesaler or manufacturer to any one retailer however large his orders. *Further information can be obtained from your Trade Organisations.*

ISSUED BY THE BOARD OF TRADE

*The aim of the Board of Trade legislation was to provide reasonably priced clothes for the whole population. On 3 June 1941 the **Daily Express**, and other national newspapers, carried the details.*

This beautifully cut, pale brown wool check suit was the second of the thirty-four garments designed by the Board of Trade's Utility scheme of 1942 by members of the Incorporated Society of London Fashion Designers. Manufacturers' copies from such prototypes were of varied success.

one wool suit, two jumpers, one pair of shoes and one summer dress. . . . I don't remember clothes being so awful, the real awfulness was not being able to get hot water bottles or washers for the plug or parts for Hoovers.[23]

Perhaps even more important than rationing itself was the equally far-reaching and ambitious Utility scheme, which applied to a range of household items such as furniture as well as to clothes. The scheme aimed to regulate the distribution of cloth to manufacturers and the setting of prices at a level within the reach of ordinary wage earners.

The Utility scheme had to comply with the general austerity restrictions introduced in the spring of 1942. These austerity restrictions came in as a series of Making Up of Civilian Clothing (Restriction) Orders, and applied to all clothes produced for the home market. The goal was to make further savings of labour and materials by simplifying the garment styles. To this end trimmings such as embroidery and other ornamental stitching were banned; the use of scarce materials, in particular steel and rubber, was forbidden, except that elastic might be used in women's underwear and in children's clothes, and for industrial garments. Styles were also restricted in order to economise on cloth and cut: the number of buttons, use of pleats, the widths of sleeve, skirt and hem were curtailed, and men's trouser turn-ups were eliminated, the latter deeply resented. At the same time, patterns were often meticulously and cleverly cut, with inserted panels to form pleats and tiny hems, or even none at all. The Victoria and Albert Museum owns an attractive prototype model for a three-piece suit. The herringbone material is positioned so as to provide a pattern contrast, while the underblouse is not hemmed, but just uses the selvedge. Finally, in order to encourage long production runs, a limit was set on the number of basic designs to be made by any one firm in a given year: six styles of women's underwear and fifty dress styles. These austerity restrictions applied to all clothes, not just to the Utility range.[24]

All clothes in the Utility scheme had to be in wide demand (that is to say, they were basic, necessary garments, not fashion fads or extreme designs). They had to be economical of labour, pass tests for good coupon value, shrinkage, colour fastness and waterproofness (where appropriate). Provided that their production did not misuse labour or materials, the Board of Trade would also approve cloth of the cheapest quality.

In May 1942 the Apparel and Textiles order gave the Board of Trade wide powers to control the supply of cloth, the main aim being to reduce the variety of cloth available to manufacturers. This again enabled long runs of material to be woven. Furthermore, the control of cloth made accurate price control possible.

Strict specifications regarding cotton and rayon, relating to type and fineness of yarn, closeness of weave, weight of cotton per yard, and type of finish were imposed. In the case of rayon, the number of threads in the warp and in the selvedge and the allowance for shrinkage, were all determined by decree. Because of the variety in types of raw materials and machines, the specifications for wool were less rigid, being limited to maximum and minimum prices. Colours, made from a restricted stock of precious vat dyes, were deliberately bright – rich pinks, greens, reds, blues and browns – while patterns were small to avoid wastage when matching up seams. The Utility scheme favoured rayon, both during the war and afterwards, until its demise in 1952. Utility fabrics were free of purchase tax; non-Utility fabrics paid a tax of 66⅔ per cent. Even so, by 1942–3 the British rayon industry was operating on a 15 per cent cut in output.[25]

In order to secure supplies of cloth a manufacturer had to undertake that two-thirds of the firm's output would be Utility. At first the scheme covered 50 per cent of all clothing manufactured, but at its height this rose to 85 per cent.

The price of all Utility clothes was set by the Board of Trade. Prices were controlled at each stage of production and distribution. A manufacturer was permitted to charge only the cost of production plus a 5 per cent mark-up, and ceiling prices were set for each garment type. There were also two quality levels within the Utility range: at the lower level the maximum price was set at two-thirds the maximum price of the better quality.

Not so classless: Utility

It would be easy to assume that these restrictions inhibited and stifled the fashion industry, but their effect appears to have been beneficial. Frederick Starke credited the inventors of the Utility scheme with an important and enduring influence on the development of the fashion industry. He pointed out that the restrictions compelled manufacturers to take more care in their choice of materials, and to pay more heed to standards of garment making, and that customers, who now purchased clothes infrequently, became more discriminating and demanded long-wearing, well-made garments.[26]

Even more important, perhaps, than Utility was the Concentration Scheme. This, also begun in 1942, permitted a limited number only of existing clothing factories to continue producing. This meant that some manufacturers had to combine with others, and that newcomers could not enter the field. This eliminated some manufacturers at the bottom end of the market who in prewar years had produced cheap, badly made clothes. All in all, the new regulations led to greater stability and efficiency. Methods used for the mass production of uniforms were extended

119

to the further mechanisation of the industry as a whole. At the same time workers in the factories that did remain were classified under Essential Works Orders – they could now neither leave their jobs nor be dismissed. Pay and conditions were regulated, and, as in the First World War, in general these improved as compared with the 1930s.[27]

Utility clothing was made at every price level from couture to mail order. From May 1941, the top ready-to-wear and model houses, together with lingerie and knitwear companies – Braemar, Mary Black, Travella, Healthguard, Marlbeck, Motoluxe, Matita, Gossard, Utility Berketex, Wetherall, Peter Scott, Two Steeples, Valstar, Silhouette de luxe, Deréta, Windsmoor, Frederick Starke and Morley knitwear – took out joint advertising pages in *Vogue* to show, patriotically, their link with Utility; and, more specifically, that they were still in production. The struggles of British ready-to-wear companies to keep operating at all during the war have barely been acknowledged; yet it was an heroic enterprise.

Utility regulations applied to every level of the British fashion industry. Even top quality ready-to-wear companies such as Windsmoor, advertising here in Vogue *in July 1942, had to limit their range and quality.*

Firms 'designated' by the Board of Trade to produce Utility clothing were given a priority in retaining their skilled staff. This enabled them to continue to produce good-quality clothes at prices that were not exorbitant. In January 1942 *Vogue* featured an advertisement from Harrods for a 100 per cent camel-hair coat at 17 guineas [£273] and eighteen coupons. Deréta felt obliged to reassure its customers that:

You will be interested to learn that Deréta are now producing a completely new line of inexpensive coats made with government controlled Utility cloth. This does not mean, of course, that the original line of classic Deréta models has been discontinued. Stocks will be definitely limited; but the purchaser of a Deréta classic will have made an investment she is never tired of in style and workmanship.

Lower priced lines were also advertised at 83s 11d [£64] and fifteen coupons in 'fresh spring colours'. Other typical prices in advertisements in the spring of 1942 were: a Deréta coat at 83s 11d [£64] plus fifteen coupons; a Jaeger suit, 97s 4d [£74] and eighteen coupons; a Spectator dress, 62s 10d [£54] and twelve coupons; tweed trousers, 27s 10d [£21] plus eight coupons; and a cotton wind jacket at 47s 10d [£37].

At the bottom end of the market, mail order catalogues such as Kays, the Co-operative Society and the wholesale companies of London, Manchester and Birmingham, such as Vedonis, featured mainly Utility but also a few non-Utility garments. Fabrics show a high proportion of rayon and cotton, and prices are lower than the Deréta and other models which

At the cheapest end of the market, Utility clothes were skimpily made, often of poor quality rayon. Kays' mail order catalogue for 1943 described their rayon fabric as 'fibro spun' to make it seem glamorous.

were purchased over the counter. The designs are simple and stylish at first glance, with few buttons, no fancy trimmings and short sleeves; they appear to resemble closely the couture prototypes. But there was an enormous difference in quality between those and the mass-produced imitations, such as those suriviving at the Lock Museum at Willenhall. There, three poor-quality rayon jersey day dresses from the Vedonis wholesale company in Birmingham can still be seen. They have short sleeves, niggardly and fraying seams, false pleats and thin tie belts. Although they appear to copy quite closely a Utility prototype of 1942, they are mean and skimpy and of inferior quality cloth, although bright in colour. Other surviving examples in museum collections are more successful; Brighton Museum has a red tartan skirt, cleverly cut with vertical tucks which successfully create an illusion of deep pleats.

Life without Paris

The absence of style leadership from Paris created an unprecedented situation. The whole international organisation of mass-produced clothing for women was built around the designers' and buyers' seasonal visits to the French capital. The professional forecasting services such as Tobé of New York and the professional trade magazines in the USA such as *Fairchild's Monthly* were also closely linked to Paris. They provided the ready-to-wear companies with precise and accurate details on seasonal change in cut, hemlines, choice of fabric, trimmings and accessories. Suddenly all this disappeared.

The American fashion industry hoped to fill the void, and in fact aimed to replace France as the world fashion leader after the war. In America as in Britain, restrictive legislation under the L85 Act of 1942 placed limits on what could be done, but American designers seized the opportunity to produce attractive model suits and softly draped afternoon dresses. They excelled in easy-to-wear casual clothes, which could also be easily mass produced, and the industry was feeling extremely optimistic. The New York Dress Institute boldly declared in 1944 that: 'like the skyscrapers that dare to soar eighty stories high, New York fashions have the assurance to challenge the world. . . . There is an AUTHORITY to New York fashions, because the most exciting city on earth accepts them. New York at present is "out in the lead".'[28]

In the absence of style leadership from Paris, British ready-to-wear looked to New York, as well as to its own London designers for inspiration. Eric Newby, whose father was in the wholesale trade, remembers designs being filched from any available copies of American *Vogue*.[29]

British haute couture also took a step forward as a result of the war. As

*For design ideas, British manufacturers looked to the USA rather than Paris during the war, and copied from American **Vogue** when they could get hold of it. This rayon 'slack suit', advertised in October 1944, epitomises the chic yet casual styles from the US.*

Hardy Amies wrote in 1954: 'The whole idea of an established and organised haute couture in London [was] very new. Its biggest impetus to organise itself came with the encouragement of export during the last war.'[30] The Incorporated Society of London Fashion Designers was set up in 1942, established with two aims: to co-ordinate couture efforts to help in designing for the home market; and to help the government in its export drive for much-needed dollars. In other words, it took a world war to force British couturiers to work together – something the French had been doing for nearly a hundred years.

In 1941 (and again in 1946) the Board of Trade asked top British fashion and textile designers to produce export collections for North and South America. Fabrics were designed for the Ascher silk firm by foremost artists, among them Graham Sutherland, Henry Moore and Ben Nicholson. Hartnell, Molyneux, Amies and others designed the clothes. Fabric manufacturers donated their material free of charge, and the government granted concessions which made possible this development of

123

fashion exports. *Vogue* reported that the clothes were to be shown in Buenos Aires, Rio de Janeiro, Montevideo and São Paulo, and called it a 'co-operative collection'.

The British couture houses continued to show seasonal fashion collections in London, but on a much-reduced scale. They showed only twelve models instead of the hundred-plus of prewar shows.[31]

The British haute couture designers were closely involved with the Utility scheme.[32] The Board of Trade asked them to pool their efforts to produce prototype Utility designs for mass production. Thirty-two basic designs were selected and first seen publicly and featured in the fashion magazines in March 1942. (Samples were donated to the Victoria and Albert Museum, where they can still be seen.) Some attractive designs were produced which were made up into dresses by couturiers. Jacqmar produced a range of propaganda scarves, one of which used the Fougasse 'Careless talk costs lives' poster designs against gossip or casual conversation which might give away vital war secrets. It featured lip and finger motifs; other motifs were based on the 'Dig for Victory' campaign. Courtaulds even produced a jacquard woven rayon fabric which featured a portrait of Winston Churchill, the Prime Minister, giving his famous 'V' for victory sign.[33] The input of the top couturiers was an important feature of the Utility scheme, and was instrumental in achieving for it an enthusiastic response from the press.

The idea that the whole realm of taste was a *woman's* realm was rather typical of this period. So was the view that women might be encouraged into good taste by means of government intervention – that the state could and should educate women's taste. The educationalist John Newsom was to give this view forceful expression after the war when in his *The Education of Girls*, published in 1948, he argued that:

> Our standards of design, and therefore our very continuance as a great commercial nation, will depend on our education of the consumer to the point where she [sic] rejects the functionally futile and aesthetically inept and demands what is fitting and beautiful. . . . Woman as purchaser holds the future standard of living of this country in her hands.[34]

There was something offensively patronising about the view that women needed education in taste and quality – after all, if women had bought cheap, badly-designed goods before the war, this was surely because they were too poor to afford anything else, while the failure of taste was the manufacturer's rather than the customer's. But this condescending attitude towards ordinary women hints at the still widespread and rigid distinction made between who was a 'lady' and who was not. If working-class women were to have more to spend in the postwar planned society, the fear was that they would spend it on vulgar design.

124

This is not to detract from the Utility scheme, which was admirable in its intentions. In theory, one of the most important aspects of the scheme was to improve and extend good design so that it would be within the reach of all women. However, the initial reaction of the media was one of suspicion. Unfortunately, Hugh Dalton, President of the Board of Trade at the time, introduced the scheme on the radio as a scheme to produce 'standard' clothes, and the word put people off. Once the clothes were seen, the reaction of the women's press, at least, was much more favourable. In order to generate favourable publicity the Board of Trade sponsored a fashion show in September 1942. After a press showing of the clothes, the reporter from the monthly *Woman and Beauty* wrote: 'We came out walking on air. . . . How the word Utility ever crept into the description of these goods we can never imagine for they are smart, well cut, beautifully made and with a wide choice of materials, styles and colour.' *Vogue* reported that the clothes had 'a basic design of perfect proportion and line for which haute couture has always been famed. Now the women in the street, the government clerk and the busy housewife will all have an equal chance to buy beautifully designed clothes, suitable to their lives and incomes.'[35]

The favourable reaction was not surprising, since the fashion journalists were shown the couture prototypes. Anne Scott James was particularly enthusiastic when she explained the Utility scheme to readers of *Picture Post* in March 1942 under the headline 'They cut out luxury and defeat the profiteer'. She announced that:

a designer can turn out as many models as he likes, providing he sticks to specified fabrics and controlled prices. The fabrics are not as good as those of expensive prewar clothes. Trimmings are simple, [with] good cut, finish and colour schemes. Colours are good and varied, and in spite of dye shortages, dyers have contrived to preserve the subtlety of their shades. I have seen Utility clothes in particularly good blues, greens and raspberry reds.[36]

In 1943 she wrote in *Picture Post* of the 'marvellously low Utility prices'.

After the end of the war, some fashion journalists changed their tune and became intensely critical of Utility. With the exception of Alison Settle in the *Observer*, however, these criticisms appear to have come from the rightwing press – the *Daily Express* and *Daily Mail* for example – and, of course, by this time the Labour Government was in power and party politics and hostility to 'socialism' had superseded the wartime ethic of national unity. Any criticisms should therefore be placed in this context.

The views of the women who wore the clothes seem to have varied widely. To some Utility may have been a code word for cheap, whatever the actual quality. In 1942 Mass Observation found that most of their respondents were in favour of the scheme, but concluded that this was because they saw it as forwarding the war effort rather than because they liked the actual garments. A survey of 2500 persons carried out by Social Survey for the Board of Trade in 1950, however – five years after the end of the war – demonstrated that there was still a strong constituency for government controls in the area of clothing. Fifty-seven per cent were in favour of quality control, with only 14 per cent against; 83 per cent were in favour of prices fixed by the government; while 49 per cent were in favour of 'more standardisation' with 39 per cent opposing this.[37]

In particular, there seems to have been an improvement in the quality of underwear as a result of the Utility scheme: the cotton vests and knickers were of a far higher standard than in prewar days, and were purchased by all social classes. On the other hand, one of the Mass Observation surveys, undertaken in 1944, revealed that women were much more critical of corsets and stockings than of anything else. The reason for the special dislike of these items of underwear may have been that ill-fitting stockings and corsets are qualitatively more uncomfortable than dresses or suits. Stockings that twist or a corset that pinches can be a source of constant irritation, even torment, while a sagging skirt or dreary dress is a more intermittent cause of distress.[38]

Even in 1943 an item in *The Times* suggested that 'the accumulation of large stocks of low grade utility cloth and suits has shown public prefer-

Practicality, warmth and durability were the essential qualities for clothing in war-time Britain. Under Utility control, mass-produced underwear actually improved in quality.

ence for better wearing materials'.[39] By 1944 only 66 per cent of cloth produced was Utility as opposed to 80 per cent in 1942; and a new range of more expensive cloth was added at the beginning of 1945.

Make Do and Mend

Just as the private growing of vegetables had been glamorised into the 'Dig for Victory' campaign, so now the government thought up the 'Make Do and Mend' campaign, personified by 'Mrs Sew and Sew'.[40] This was to encourage personal initiative to fill the gap left by the disappearance of so many daily items that had been taken for granted before the war – not only clothes, but bed linen and children's soft toys, for example.

The campaign was featured in the whole range of women's magazines and was aimed at all social levels. To the more privileged readers of *Vogue* detailed instructions on thrift and methods of remaking clothes may have been genuinely helpful; for working-class women such advice was redundant. The idea, however, that these women needed to be educated merely represents a new version of the longstanding attitude of the reforming middle classes towards the 'lower orders'. In the nineteenth and early twentieth century poor women were often perceived as feckless, inadequate and unskilled in domestic crafts. The belief that the wives of working men needed to be educated into the domestic role was a persistent one (as John Newsom's views on education demonstrated).

The pamphlet put out by the Ministry of Information as part of the Make Do and Mend campaign, *The Housewife's Guide to Making and Mending* (price 3d) is a basic guide to the care and preservation of clothes. As well as instructing the reader how to make a slip and knicker set out of a long evening slip, or a new coat out of two old ones, it gives detailed instructions on how to mend and clean clothes, turn sheets sides to middle and so on. 'Thrift is the fashion' is the message. There is a section on corsets: 'Now that rubber is so scarce, your corset is one of your most precious possessions.' This reminds us of the extent to which all women still wore these foundation garments, regarding them as an essential part of life.

It is hard, though, to believe that most ordinary working-class women would ever have owned a long evening slip that could be turned into camiknickers or a lingerie set, or, for that matter, that they had owned two coats that could be turned into one. It is therefore rather difficult to judge the impact of the campaign, but at least some women seem to have felt that working people would have known all there was to know about making do without any help from the government. For them the old stand-bys remained the same as they had always been: second-hand (and now coupon free) clothing, home made, and the cheapest mail order or small shop outlets. As one woman said:

Who had the time to make one pretty 'new' dress out of three? I mean, really, every one of my friends was involved in war work in some way. . . . We hardly got enough sleep, what with the air raids *and* the piles of work they gave us. Those poor Land Army girls; women, city women had never dreamed work as hard as that was possible. . . . When we had the money and the coupons we bought a new dress or pair of shoes. What a waste of time making pretty dresses. . . . I'd have been ashamed always to look smart and pretty myself. . . . They weren't telling us anything new.[41]

The story of the British Home Front during the Second World War is one of unselfconscious and fairly stoical bravery, endurance and good humour. But the war years took their toll. *One Fine Day*, a novel by Mollie Panter Downes, captures the mood at the end of the war. Laura, the main character, is going grey, and is surrounded by the visible signs of shabbiness and decay as her gentrified way of life crumbles about her:

'Your hands, Laura darling!' [her mother said]. 'They used to be so pretty. . . . It worries me to death thinking of you struggling along here with the housework and cooking and the child. . . . My darling, you're looking dreadfully fagged out. . . . So far as I can see, you spend the entire day doing the work of an unpaid domestic servant.'[42]

For a rare dinner party, Laura brings out her old red chiffon, 'feeling slightly foolish as she tripped over her long skirts and assisted a flowing chiffon sleeve out of the sink'.[43]

'Not in the public interest': the New Look

The war was over − but victory euphoria rapidly melted away, and the curious and contradictory atmosphere of the second half of the decade was brilliantly symbolised in the new fashions that soon appeared: what became known as the New Look.

In August 1944, the liberation of Paris revealed to an astonished fashion world the styles that had developed during the occupation. Lee Miller, the war photographer and former model, sent a report back to American *Vogue*, describing attractive girls in what appeared as a bizarre silhouette, with full skirts and tiny waists. 'They were top heavy, with built-up, Pompadour-front hair-dos and waving tresses, weighed to the ground with clumsy, fancy, thick-soled wedge shoes.'[44]

The designer drawings she sent back so deeply shocked the American authorities that censors tried to prevent their publication. They declared them not to be in the public interest while America was sending aid to France in the shape of clothing and blankets and while American soldiers were dying in Europe. When they were published, Edna Woolman Chase,

Elizabeth, Empress of Austria, with diamond stars in her hair, painted by Franz Winterhalter in 1865. Her ball dress of star-spangled tulle is by Charles Worth, the founding father of Paris haute couture.

Left These expensive French silk afternoon dresses (1865–7) show the practical versatility of fashionable clothing, even for the rich. The grey dress has a second, low-cut evening bodice to match the skirt. The rust dress was up-dated with a bustle in the 1870s.

Above The height of Paris fashion for 1883, with close-fitting princess line, hour-glass bodices and heavy bustled skirts for all weathers. The suit in the centre has the tailored look which had evolved slowly since the mid-1860s. Illustration from *Journal des Modes*, Paris, 1883.

131

Right 'Jacqueline' – a medieval-inspired dress from a Liberty's catalogue for 1905 – showing the 'couture aesthetic' look. This was an adaptation of the radical aesthetic styles of the late 1870s which were worn without conventional corsets or elaborate trimmings.

Opposite Paris fashion ideas were widely circulated through fashion plates in magazines. This *toilette de dîner* of 1901, from *Queen* magazine, has French *art nouveau* trimmings and the *décolletage* acceptable for evening wear.

Copyright
HD
LONDON

Opposite These morning suits of 1911, with their cut-away fronts, were worn by businessmen. The more adventurous would have worn a modern suit with a Homburg hat, but they all changed into full evening dress for dinner.

Left Paul Poiret's theatre coat of 1912, in glossy silk charmeuse trimmed with black velvet and silver lace, has absorbed the principles of the dress reform movement in its unstructured simplicity.

The Needlewoman

A Magazine of Exclusive Fashions in Dress and in the Home

CONTENTS: Free Paper Pattern of this charming Fringed Evening Frock. Article on Fringes and How to Make them, by Laura E. Start. Directions for making and embroidering charming Evening Shawls, Bags and Dance Frocks. How to make Silk Wigs. Paris Fashions. *Monthly, Price 4d.*

At the Sign of Excellence

COATS CLARK

THREADS EMBROIDERIES COTTONS

Left Paris ideas filtered down to home dressmakers through magazines such as *The Needlewoman*. This issue of December 1926 told readers how to make their own fashionable, fringed dance frocks and shawls (probably in rayon) with Coats/Clark yarns.

Above Original designs for printed cottons showing a distant Cubist influence, by W. Fielden Royle (about 1928–38). His designs were sold to mass production manufacturers such as Tootals for everything from overalls to summer dresses.

IN THE COLOURS OF THE TRICOLOUR

JEAN PATOU

Very easy to wear and becoming is this écru knitted cotton suit with a knitted scarf in three bright colours and a hat in Panama.

Jean Patou strikes a bright, new note in his checked red and white crêpe marocain suit with navy blue belt, scarf and navy and white hat in fine cachemire or georgette. He makes the wide shoulder line with understanding of a woman's dislike of exaggeration. His waistline is set just where it should be, and there are long, simple sleeves to the jacket with the new fullness at the top.

In the colours of the tricolour once again Patou has designed this charming little ensemble in wool and cotton. The dress is in woollen crêpe, the coat in knitted cotton, the hat, scarf and glove tops in the three colours. These can be in woven material or hand knitted.

FREE Pattern *of this* **FROCK** *you can* **MAKE** *in* **3 HOURS**

Film Fashionland

6ᴰ
SEPT.
1934

● **FASHION**
Choice of Screen Styles with unique Pattern Service
Star Frocks for Sale
Louis Brooks on . . .
What the Stars will Wear
Enid Stamp Taylor's Cap and Bag Set

● **BEAUTY**
Toby Wing's Own Secrets
Skip for Body-Line
Improve Your Hands
Personal Service

● **FICTION**
Night after Bond Street
Bronze Angel
Chance is a Fine Thing

FREE Pattern *of this* **FROCK** WITH AND WITHOUT SLEEVES
As worn by **JOAN MARSH** RADIO PICTURES STAR

Left These fine wool and cotton summer clothes by Jean Patou, of August 1933, were both economical to produce and yet have the chic simplicity of 'between-the-wars' couture.

Above In the thirties, the magazine *Film Fashionland* offered free patterns of a 'film star' dress designed for and endorsed by a Hollywood star each month.

Left This Utility prototype design made in rayon crepe was designed to save on yardage and labour, with its scantily gathered, knee-length skirt and all-in-one-piece collar and centre front. It was widely copied by the ready-to-wear industry.

Right Christian Dior designed these sumptuous ball dresses in 1949, two years after the launch of his New Look. In silk tulle embroidered with sequins, they celebrate the resurgence of the craft of Parisian couture.

Left By the mid-1950s the fashion industry was producing excellent quality 'middle-class couture'. This *Vogue* advertisement of April 1956 shows a Marcel Fenez linen suit, selling at 20 guineas, which still retains the New Look cut.

Right In the sixties and early seventies Freemans, the long-established mail-order company, employed the Glaswegian pop star Lulu to draw in young consumers. In the 1971 catalogue she wears Courrèges-inspired boots and both mini and maxi skirts. Lulu continues to model for the company today.

...ashing double-breasted midi raincoat with big important ...and-up collar, all-round belt and two welt pockets. Fully Washable. *Material:* Diolen and cotton. *Colour:* stone.
...01   SIZES
10 12 14 16
...l lengths   42 42 42 42 in.
£12·95   (£12/19/–)   **Midi-Raincoat**

...ppy brimmed tie-dye effect hat. *Material:* wool felt. *Colour:* ...rple and lilac.
...2   £2·75   (£2/15/–)   **Hat**

...per summer boot, laced right up, with clever ribbon ...ping, full round toe, foam-backed lining and 2 in. shaped ...heel. *Materials:* canvas upper, resin sole. *Colour:* cream.
...04   SIZES
3 3½ 4 4½ 5 5½ 6 6½ 7 7½ 8
£5·95   (£5/19/–)   **Boot**

John Galliano is one of the most innovative of the 1980s generation of British designers. This 1989 outfit, a short jacket with soft lapels, shirt and asymmetrical skirt, has the draped fluid cut which is his trademark.

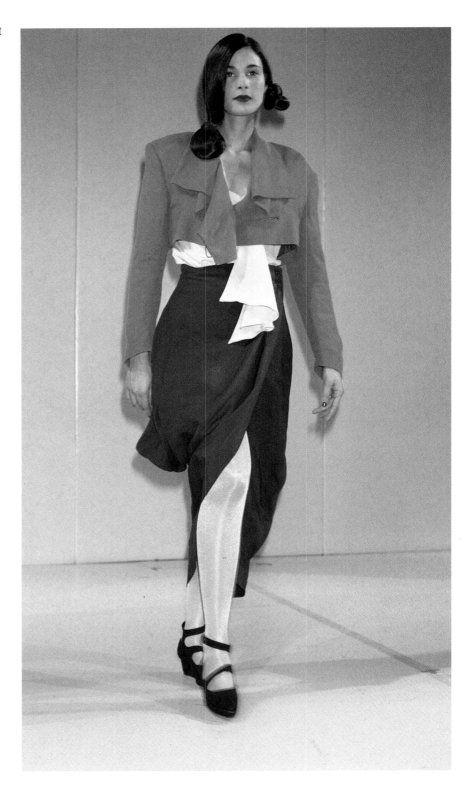

international editor of *Vogue*, felt compelled to preface the article Lee Miller wrote for American *Vogue* with what has become the standard justification. The extravagance had been patriotic: 'saving material and labour meant help to the Germans . . . it was patriotic to waste instead of to save. . . . If three metres of material were specified for a dress, the French found fifteen for a skirt alone.'[45]

Later it was said that the clothes were intended to be 'flaunted' at the Germans, to 'taunt' them, and they were deliberately exaggerated in order to make the dowdy German women (christened *souris gris* – grey mice) look as ridiculous as possible. The idea that the designers tried to save the French fashion industry by making clothes they themselves considered hideous is a little hard to swallow, but after the Liberation everyone hastened to dismiss the fashions of the occupation as an aberration. The wide shoulders, heavy wedge shoes, made of materials such as plastic, fibre-glass, wood and fur, and the towering hats and hairstyles, seemed strange to eyes unaccustomed to them. Yet the full skirts, tiny waists and general extravagance became key features of postwar fashion.

To understand why the New Look was so successful we need to see it in the context in which it first appeared. The '*corolle* line' as it was first christened, was France's secret weapon to wrest world leadership of the fashion industry back from Seventh Avenue, New York. Credit for its invention has gone to Christian Dior, who had worked for Lucien Lelong throughout the Occupation. Shortly after it ended the textile magnate Marcel Boussac set Dior up on his own. The gamble paid off.

Yet it was less that Dior really invented a completely new line than that he developed the themes which had been evolving since 1938, and which had been continued by French couture under the Nazis. As Hardy Amies wrote of the Occupation fashions: 'it was a silhouette that dealt in curves rather than straight lines. To make it graceful it had to turn into the New Look.'[46]

The New Look, however, did not appear until 1947. The immediate reaction of Parisian couture after the liberation had been to return to simple lines in order to counteract the American and British accusations of collaboration and to regain moral ground. It was also hoped to attract American buyers back to Paris. 'But,' said *Picture Post*:

the American buyers were not interested. Why pay extravagant prices and heavy customs duties for models similar to those already being made back in New York? Meantime, the American designers, delighted with their own success, liked to think of themselves as entirely independent of Paris. While before the war, there were few who did not cross the Atlantic each year, there are many today who have not been since 1939. Some indeed still refuse to have French fashion magazines in their showrooms.[47]

Dior's New Look of February 1947, with its wildly extravagant use of fabric and curvaceous lines, caused an international sensation. Not even the disapproval of the British Government could stop the demand for it.

Dior changed all this with his very first, February 1947 collection. By September 1947 *Picture Post* (despite the comments cited above) was also reporting ecstatically:

Dior's daycoats are ankle length – no more 'spiv' shoulders, but a tightly belted waist and full skirts over padded hips. Piguet's clothes have a lovely echo of Edwardian elegance. Even the fur which he uses lavishly for lining coats and suits is the period black sealskin. . . . Prices are fabulously high. . . . Many of the embroidered and fur-trimmed models are selling for as much as £250 [£3750].

These romantic, frivolous clothes have such a seductive appeal that your eye is 'in' remarkably quickly. Their utter femininity recalls the splendour and elegance of the Avenue du Bois [de Boulogne] before the 1914 war. Only in Paris could these clothes have been made: only in Paris could such a daring experiment have been undertaken.

Janey Ironside, later to be head of fashion at the Royal College of Art, said that the New Look was like 'a new chance in life, a new love affair'.[48] Here at last was some way of representing the fact that the war *was* over, that a longing for beauty and luxury was not a crime.

The New Look came to Britain when the country was in the grip of austerity and crisis. In the summer of 1945 the British for the first time elected a Labour government with a large majority, which gave Clement Attlee, who became Prime Minister, and his Cabinet, a mandate to create a new kind of Britain. So immediately after the war expectations were high. But Britain was almost bankrupt. Then came a devastating blow when the United States abruptly withdrew financial support, and a new loan had to be negotiated on unfavourable terms.

In addition, it came as a severe psychological shock to many that Britain was beginning the retreat from its Empire with the granting of independence to India and Pakistan. To put it bluntly, Britain was now clearly no longer top nation, and soon began to feel it was being squeezed between the United States and the Soviet Union. Although the Cold War did not really get under way until 1948, the wartime enthusiasm for the Soviet Union rapidly cooled; and this was linked with the sustained media attack on the 'socialism' that the Labour government was said to be attempting to impose. As if this were not all bad enough, the Labour government had the additional bad luck of fearful winters, particularly that of 1946–7, when fuel shortages and snowdrifts almost brought the country to a standstill. Rationing actually got worse, and for a time even bread was rationed, which it had never been during the war.

The ensuing mood of gloom and disillusionment no doubt partly came from exaggerated expectations of what could be achieved in two short years, and it was probably inevitable that the Labour Government would disappoint many of its supporters. On the other side there was the fear and anger of the Conservative party and of the sections of the middle class who identified with its views. 'Is the middle class doomed?' asked *Picture*

Post in 1949; and tales of crippling death duties and punitive taxes fuelled the paranoia of those who felt it was their duty and their destiny to rule.

On 19 April 1947, *Picture Post* summed it up:

In war, men and women will postpone considerations of personal good, to be gained when war is won – because each knows there are many who give up far more than he [sic] does. The soldier is the standard. In peace, that appeal to sacrifice does not work. 'If only the war would end,' we used to say. And then one day it was over. There was a great surge of happiness. For a day, the world was young again. We felt in our bones that things would never be so bad again. What has gone wrong?

The following month a letter from a twenty-seven-year-old housewife expressed exactly the same mood of hopes betrayed and sacrifices unrewarded. She complained that although she had been married for seven years, she had only been living properly with her husband for the past seven months, and had had to bring up their three children single-handed: 'I only thought of the time when the war would be over and *he* would be home. And now, what? We live in somebody else's house, and everything is rotten.'

For it was the housewife who bore the brunt of fuel shortages, food shortages and, perhaps worst of all, the housing shortage. Labour party idealists saw the Beveridge Plan for social security coupled with the new family allowances (now child benefit) as 'a new deal for housewives'. Women's domestic labour was recognised as hard work, and the idea was to help women do this work; but it was still *women's* work. Many government nurseries were closed down, and the belief that mothers should remain at home with their small children was very powerful.

After the war, food shortages worsened and there were still long queues – as here in Brixton in 1947.

Although there was no conspiracy to return women to the home, neither was there any challenge to the traditional view that a woman's place *was* in the home.[49] At the same time the government was begging married women to continue in paid employment for a few more years, especially in the manufacturing sectors that were producing for export to the United States, in order to close the 'dollar gap' and repay our debt to the Americans. There were also acute shortages of nurses and teachers. Yet there were also fears about the low birthrate, and hopes for larger families. Women, therefore, were receiving very contradictory messages from the government.

The Labour Government tried to maintain the ethic of wartime sacrifice into peacetime, and of communal effort as opposed to private gain or profiteering exploitation. But now people wanted something different. As one respondent to a survey about family allowances put it: 'I want some fun out of life – I'm not interested in raising the birthrate.'[50] What women wanted above all was some glamour. As Anne Scott James was later to express it:

All the squalor and discomfort and roughness that had seemed fitting for so long began to feel old fashioned. . . . I wanted to throw the dried egg out of the window, burn my shabby curtains and wear a Paris hat again. The Amazons, the women in trousers, the good comrades, had had their glorious day. But it was over. Gracious living beckoned once again.[51]

In a play about the services a character voiced the view that 'After khaki you want sky blue and frills',[52] while Alison Settle in the *Observer* found young women 'hungry for romantic dressing' and noticed 'a depression of spirits such as was unknown during even the blackest days of the war'. Even worse, she reported that 'many returned servicemen say they find British women tired, unglamorous, shabbily dressed'.[53] And the hunger for romantic dressing crystallised around the New Look.

In part, the dazzling impression the New Look made on British reporters was due precisely to its almost unbelievable contrast with wartime and postwar austerity. 'Austerity' was the keyword of the later forties; the New Look kicked austerity in the teeth. *Picture Post* raved about the:

Arabian Nights splendour of rich, regal velvets, brocades like shimmering moonlight, glittering gold and silver and pearl-encrusted embroidery, rustling taffetas covered with cobwebbed black lace, and the most lavish and extravagant use of fur.

Muriel Pemberton, then fashion illustrator for the *News Chronicle*, remembered the rustle and swirl of the huge, floating silk taffeta skirt at the House of Dior, which brushed against the faces of the closely-packed audience as the models swayed through the scent-drenched salon.

This was only one side of the British reaction. To some, the New Look caused absolute consternation. *Picture Post*, indeed, spoke with two

148

voices on the phenomenon and in almost the same breath as it responded to the sheer sensuous beauty of the rich materials and lavish silhouettes it protested:

Paris forgets this is 1947. The styles are launched upon a world which has not the material to copy them – and whose women have neither the money to buy, the leisure to enjoy, nor in some designs even the strength to support these masses of elaborate material. . . .

But whether you see in it a sensational bid to recapture the American market, or a cynical disregard for the world-wide shortage of textiles, there can be no question about the entire unsuitability of these new fashions, for our present life and times. In this country they are simply an economic impossibility. Think of doing housework, or sitting at a typewriter all day, or working in a factory, tightly corseted, and encumbered and constricted with layers of hip-padding and petticoats. Our mothers freed us from these in their struggle for emancipation, and in our own active workaday lives, there can be no possible place for them.[54]

The Labour Government was horrified. The new fashion seemed to spell further economic disaster. Sir Stafford Cripps, then at the Board of Trade and shortly to become Chancellor of the Exchequer, asked the British Guild of Creative Designers to keep the short skirt popular in Britain, thus saving precious material for the export drive. Mr Henry Scott of the Guild duly denounced the new long length.[55]

Opposition to the New Look from women was on three grounds. There were those who, like Stafford Cripps himself, objected to it on economic and patriotic grounds. Bessie Braddock MP dismissed it as the 'ridiculous whim of idle people'. Prunella Stack, of the Women's League of Health and Beauty, objected to the ridiculous extravagance. The British Housewives' League, a rightwing, or at least anti-Labour party organisation, also joined in the protests.[56]

Secondly, there were women (and some men) for whom the New Look was anti-feminist. Its echoes of the *Belle Époque*, which Dior himself nostalgically invoked, were seen as not only inappropriate but actually threatening, symbolising not really so much women's return to the home, as the recreation of the feminine woman as an upper-class luxury object. Feminist critics of the New Look feared that it would inaugurate a new era of idleness and conspicuous consumption, an ideal that was irrelevant to the majority of working-class women. Mabel Ridealgh, another Labour MP, objected that:

Women today are taking a larger part in the happenings of the world and the New Look is too reminiscent of a caged bird's attitude. I hope our fashion dictators will realise the new *outlook* of women and will give the death blow to any attempt at curtailing women's freedom.[57]

Thirdly, there was a puritanical reaction. As Mabel Ridealgh again put it: 'Padding and artificial figure aids are extremely bad, because they make for over-sexiness.'[58]

149

Opposite (top) *Peggy Hope, the buyer for Richard Shops in 1948, insisting that the company's middle market range reflects the new length, though the final product is still several inches shorter than the original New Look.*

Opposite (bottom) *In 1948 Princess Margaret wore this long length New Look dress to Glyndebourne. Her use of the New Look length caused much comment in the press.*

A lively correspondence on the issue broke out in *The New Statesman and Nation*. The subject was first broached in a regular column 'Critic', who condemned women as sheeplike for following the 'uncomely' new fashion. The writer Molly Cochrane responded, defending longer skirts as both more convenient (i.e. warmer) and because 'the ballet has taught most of us the aesthetic advantages of a longer skirt'. The writer and journalist Jill Craigie (today wife of Michael Foot) took up the issue in defence of the government position, although admitting that she actually liked the longer skirt.[59] She also suggested that it might increase the birthrate 'in that it favours the pregnant figure' (this seems a very strange argument given the tight waists – but then the main controversy was simply about the skirt length). But she tended to see in the New Look something of an economic conspiracy:

Phrases in the newspapers such as, 'you will be smart this winter if you wear your dress calf length,' are appearing with depressing frequency. This also goes for photographs of the new fashions, one of the first of which appeared in, of all papers, *The Daily Herald* [a Labour Party paper]. The fact that Princess Elizabeth's trousseau will be calf length must be counted as one of the major victories for the vested interests of the fashion houses. That in itself almost gives the new style official status.

There is, however, one really encouraging sign. There is a rumour that the Rank Organisation will continue to dress its film stars in short skirts.[60]

Hardy Amies contributed to the debate in the same issue, mounting both an artistic and an economic argument in favour of the longer skirt:

The American fashion industry has played up the situation . . . because it ensured that the large stores, where slumps were greatly feared in the Spring, would maintain their turnovers since the very fashion-conscious American public would be likely to feel it necessary to change their wardrobes completely. . . .

New fashions, however, are seldom created for solely commercial reasons. It should be noted that designers in Paris, New York and London have all been making longer skirts simultaneously, because they felt them to be right. . . . Contrary to what is often thought, there is no getting together of designers before launching something new.

The Board of Trade would, of course, be unwise to meddle with fashion. . . . It is very difficult to design for export only – in a void, as it were. Furthermore, the Americans are sensitive on this point and repeatedly say they want to buy typically British clothes. This snob appeal would disappear rapidly if our public were to wear clothes considered by them to be dowdy.[61]

But Hardy Amies must have confirmed the worst fears of some women when he went on to argue that:

the whole movement is part of a plan to emphasise women's best characteristics – curved shoulders, high busts, small waists, full hips and a good carriage. Speaking very personally, I feel that this must lead to more satisfactory relations between men and women, and in general to what the Americans call a more 'gracious' way of living.

The new clothes are, in a sense, a kind of protest against the feverish ill-planned years of the '20s and '30s – the era of the Bright Young Thing.[62]

There was some organised opposition to the new skirt length in the United States, where 1300 women formed a 'little below the knee club' and the legislature of Georgia announced its intention to ban the longer skirt.[63]

Protest, however, was useless. The huge success of the New Look almost instantly re-established Paris as the dominating force in world fashion, and the Americans flocked back. *Vogue* showed the new line in October 1947 both in its editorial section and in advertisements. Harrod's 'Miss Junior' still had her broad padded shoulders, but, 'note the fullness beneath a nipped-in waist and the longer skirt line, to create the new silhouette which Paris decrees for the youthful figure'. (No prices or coupon requirements were given.)

British fashion magazines were full of such compromises, and the resulting mixture of styles – padded shoulders with odd and assorted attempts at lengthening hemlines – often gave inelegant results. Magazines recommended various techniques to achieve the New Look. You were invited to insert a plaid or check section above and below the waist of a plain dress, or to add deep velveteen or fur to the hem of a fitted coat, or contrasting tiers into a skirt. Very few of these hybrid clothes survive today.

In the autumn of 1947 Dior showed his collection in London, and the clothes were also shown secretly to the Royal Family. Princess Margaret in particular was won over to the new style:

On March 3rd [1948] she appeared publicly in a pink nutria coat with three velvet rings at the hem. On March 17th she appeared in the same coat, but it now had four rings at the hem, an alteration which did not escape notice.[64]

Ironically, then, it was here at last that 'Make Do and Mend' came into its own: in pursuance of a fashion the government deplored. For the 'rings' were the British woman's answer to the problem of the longer skirt – indeed some new New Look garments came to be made with this feature, so much a part of the New Look did it become.

In this chapter, men have been for the most part offstage 'on active service'. Men's clothes in mid-century were conservative and changes in style gradual. The 'demob' suit – the issue of civilian clothes given to all men in the armed forces upon their discharge (demobilisation) – was an early source of postwar grumbles . . . and jokes. In the late forties the bespoke tailors of Savile Row tried to steer men towards a more dandified style: a more tightly fitting overcoat with a velvet collar and narrower trousers. We shall discover the fate of this in the fifties.

Male artists and intellectuals had always dressed distinctively and casually. In the twenties and thirties their clothes had still been influenced by the movements for dress reform. After the Second World War the influence on this group was increasingly American. In *Books Do Furnish A Room*, about the London literary scene in the grip of the freezing 1947 winter, Anthony Powell described the doomed writer X. Trapnel attempting an artistic style:

He was dressed in a pale ochre-coloured tropical suit . . . on top of which he wore an overcoat, black and belted . . . this heavy garment, rather too short for Trapnel's height of well over six feet, was at the same time too full, in view of his spare, almost emaciated body. . . . The walking stick struck a completely different note. . . . For the rest he was hatless, wore a dark blue sports shirt frayed at the collar, an emerald green tie patterned with naked women, was shod in grey suede brothel creepers. . . .

The general effect, chiefly caused by the stick, was the eighteen nineties, the *decadence*: putting things at their least eclectic, a contemptuous rejection of currently popular male modes in grey flannel demob suits with pork-pie hats, bowler-crowned British warms, hooded duffles, or even those varied outfits . . . that suggested recent service in the *maquis* [the French resistance movement].[65]

This passage suggests the way in which men as well as women in Britain were forced by the shortages of the first few years after the war to dress as best they could, rather than as they would have wished. (It is of interest that at this time the absence of a hat was still worth comment.)

It is therefore not surprising that the coherence of the New Look swept all before it. But its significance was not so much the 'caged bird attitude'; it was rather that it ushered in a period when fashion was to be

152

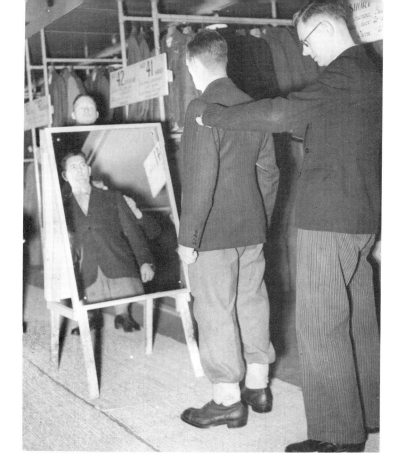

On demobilisation, every ex-servjceman was issued with a ready-made suit to start him off in civvy street.

more important – and more available – to everyone. The mass media spread the word; and mass production made the clothes available.

Margaret Trump, a junior saleswoman at Marshall and Snelgrove in the autumn of 1948, remembers the speed with which the haute couture New Look was translated into affordable, attractive fashion. This had already begun in the 1930s, but now the quality of reasonably priced copies, and the accuracy with which haute couture designs were reproduced, were greatly improved:

We advertised a model I really coveted: a neat shirtwaister style with a skirt of soft, unpressed pleats. It was printed . . . on a white ground, irregular wavy stripes of grey alternated with either yellow, pale green or a delicate shade of cobalt blue, and both colours were overprinted with an abstract design in black, which was accentuated by the small black spherical buttons and narrow belt.

The one I fancied was the blue/grey version, but at £12 9s 6d [£175], roughly five weeks' wages, I knew it was beyond my purse – an extravagance not to be thought of!

Then one weekend, window-shopping further up Oxford Street, I noticed in the window of C & A Modes a dress in the same style and the identical print, at barely a third the price – £3 17s 6d [£54.25]! The difference was in the fabric, a rather loosely woven, linen-look rayon; every other detail was the same. . . . I snapped up my cheap copy. I wore that dress all through the long heat-wave of summer 1949 . . . and when at last some of the seams began to fray (. . . that would never have happened to the Sea Island cotton original!) I cut off the bodice and made a summer skirt.[66]

This was truly the shape of things to come.

5

FASHION FOR ALL
1950-70

In retrospect, the 1950s has become the age of affluence, conservatism and women back to the home, of Cold War and anti-Communism. By contrast the 1960s are the years of liberation, of flower power and swinging London, or alternatively of the permissive slide towards indiscipline and lack of standards. In reality, there were strong lines of continuity between the two, particularly in the increasing consumerism of the domestic scene. Here, clothes played a central role, for these were the decades when fashion came to the fore. For the first time, fashion for all became a reality.

'The fifties' really began in October 1951, when the Conservative Party returned to power. The main cultural event of 1951, and Labour's last fanfare, was the Festival of Britain, originally planned during the closing years of the war. Serious preparations for the Festival had begun in 1947, following on from the 'Britain Can Make It' Exhibition, staged at the Victoria and Albert Museum in September 1946. Six thousand products made by 1300 firms were on display, and the crowds flocked to see them, although the experience must have been in some ways a frustrating one, since the displays were mostly of household goods made for export, as yet unavailable on the home market.[1]

The Festival, likewise, was intended to promote Britain's new scientific achievements and British design in textiles, furniture and ceramics, this time on a much larger scale. It should have celebrated the birth of a better and more equal Britain, as well as the democratic belief, which the Utility scheme had also expressed, that everyone should have access to goods made to a high standard of style and taste. But by 1951 the Labour Party's

Opposite The Festival of Britain in 1951 introduced advanced technology and design to a country starved of consumer goods.

155

'heroic reforming period' was well and truly over. The Festival became a contradictory event as it tried to express both the achievements of Labour in power and what the Beaverbrook Press was to proclaim – after Queen Elizabeth came to the throne in 1952 – as 'the new Elizabethan Age'. At one level it was a rather folksy attempt to summon up national pride at a time when Britain was becoming a 'second class' world power. Its emphasis on royalty and tradition reflected a society still in the grip of class distinctions. Yet it was forward-looking too, and showed a Britain on the threshold of becoming a different kind of society: a consumer society.

For many the Festival was successful in opening the eyes of the British public to a new world of style. As Arnold Wesker described it:

What do I remember? What everyone remembers: brave colours, exhilarating shapes, thrilling designs – the communication of courage. . . . Most vividly, though, I remember going into the decorating shop on the corner of Urstwick Road, E.8 . . . and asking why didn't they have the new wallpaper designs ? Wouldn't sell down here, they told me. . . . But I did buy a stunning three piece suite for my mother, and some rugs, on H.P. The rugs came from Heal's. Now *that* was courage – to go from Hackney to Heal's.[2]

The Festival had relatively little to say about fashion as such. Hardy Amies lamented that: 'there were no clothes; there was no fashion'[3]. It was an attempt, nonetheless, to create for the fifties a whole ambience in which style was the modern, the new, and in this, far from being the opposite of the sixties, it was very much their precursor. 'Festival style' came to be associated with 'Scandinavian' furniture and modernistic architecture. It inaugurated a fashion for printed textiles, formica, tiles and other domestic items which featured 'scientific' or 'modern' motifs, based for example on molecular structures (shades of the splitting of the atom). Some felt that 'South Bank style quickly deteriorated into a cliché for every coffee bar or renovated pub'[4], while others disliked its whimsical 'British eccentric' aspect – there was a period train designed by Emett the cartoonist – and some critics found aspects of the Festival, the Gardens at Battersea for example, fey and wistful. The importance with which design was regarded at the Festival, however, laid the foundations for 'that half-decade or so up to 1970 when British architecture and design had its greatest ever influence and prestige since the beginning of the twentieth century'[5].

The contrast is so often made between the cultural and social conformity of the fifties and the rebelliousness of the sixties that we tend to lose sight of the way in which these were two sides of the same coin; different phases in the development of consumerism. In any case, there was plenty of rebellion in the fifties, while the sixties was as much about individualism as about social change. For one thing the fifties saw the beginning of Rock and Roll with stars like Elvis Presley becoming a teenage cult.

What was different about the sixties was that the modern or 'contemporary' (a very Festival word) styles, as then developed, mocked and indeed destroyed the conventions of good taste and design so carefully built up after the war. The Festival aimed to educate taste; the sixties to subvert it.

While progressive Modernism was the fashion in architecture and interior design in 1951, fashion itself was still locked into the romanticism of the New Look and hedged about with convention and formality. Women were wearing stiff, sophisticated clothes, redolent of upper-class *hauteur*. There is a touch-me-not remoteness in many of the fashion images of the early fifties.

The fashionable age to be was somewhere between thirty and forty, and make-up was so heavy and formal that eighteen-year-olds looked positively middle-aged. There was still a prewar insistence on 'good grooming', ladylike deportment and tidy understated chic. Absolutely essential was a carefully thought-out appearance based on matching accessories and adherence to certain rules – for example, that hat, gloves, handbag, scarf and shoes should all match, and that black accessories should never be worn in the country.

Hemlines remained at below calf length until 1954 and rose only very slowly thereafter, and skirts were either very full or 'pencil slim' – both styles in which it could be difficult to feel comfortable. Most women still wore 'girdles', elastic roll-ons or all-in-one corsets; the least you could get away with was a suspender belt – and while today this garment appears as a provocative and essential component of glamour lingerie sets, in the fifties the dangling suspenders and arbitrary piece of material round the waist seemed the reverse of erotic. Brassieres were rigidly formed and worn beneath a full underslip. Stockings had seams which had to be kept straight (although the first, rather daring, seamless stockings appeared in 1953). The whole look was orderly, structured and 'feminine' in the most traditional sense.

The Age of Youth

It was widely believed that the postwar welfare and economic reforms had brought about a redistribution of wealth, but in the main such redistribution as did occur was within rather than between classes. In 1949 there were still two million unemployed, but during thirteen years in power, from 1951 to 1964, the Conservatives presided over a full

157

employment consumer boom. Britain was in decline relative to European rivals and to Japan, but productivity was rising faster than at any time during the twentieth century. During those thirteen years the cost of living rose by about 50 per cent and production and exports never kept pace with consumption; but wages rose on average by about twice as much as inflation. In 1951 there were 2 250 000 cars, and 1 000 000 TV sets; by 1964 the numbers were 8 000 000 and 13 000 000.[6]

Increased prosperity was relative, needless to say. Average weekly wages for men in 1951 were £8 8s 6d [£101]; in 1959 they had risen to £13 6s 6d [£118]. Many families were struggling to manage financially, and relied increasingly on hire purchase. There was a public refusal to acknowledge this. A few researchers tried to gain public attention for the continuance of poverty, but the poor were attacked as 'problem families', whose condition of life was due to their own inadequacies.

More money was spent on leisure. This was, even more than the 1930s, the era of massed (male) crowds at football matches, of mass courtship in dance halls, and, to a lesser extent than the 1930s, mass audiences in the cinema. More families were taking holidays and they began to go abroad. Even on a modest income, you could have aspirations, and rising aspirations were expressed perhaps more than anything else in the mass marketing of reasonably priced fashionable clothes.

The last debutantes were formally presented at court in 1958. Emma Tennant, who 'came out' in 1956, told *Vogue* that 'Everyone thinks the aristocracy is poor, but it is one big veil-pulling over the eyes. They are carrying on exactly as before. I don't see any difference between now, the 1950s, and the eighteenth century.'[7] It was the huge rise in the numbers of *nouveaux riches* debutantes that brought about the end of the ceremonies at Court. The most famous rich couple of the period, Sir Bernard and Lady Docker, were famous precisely for being *nouveaux riches*, their gold-plated Daimler, and Lady Docker's furs and diamonds, astonishing for their vulgarity as much as for their glamour. Despite the demise of the official presentations, the season continued in all other respects, with coming-out balls, cocktail parties, Henley and Ascot.

The popular view, however, was that this was now a society in which class no longer counted. Now it was age that defined the apparent social divide, a widening gulf across which the generations glowered at each other in amazed distaste. For one thing there just were more teenagers; from 6½ per cent of the population in 1956, they had risen to nearly 8 per cent in 1964, and settled at approximately 7 per cent in the late sixties and early seventies.[8] Their wages might be relatively low, but they had money to spend, not large sums, but a pound or so each week, when a 78 r.p.m. pop record cost 5s [£2.25] and a dress could be bought for £1 [£9].

'Young appears as the persuasive adjective for all fashions, hairstyles and ways of life,' commented *Vogue* in 1959, and the twin obsessions of young clothes and youth music were to dominate the atmosphere of the decade to come.

1956, rather than 1960, marked the change from the stuffiness of the late forties and early fifties to the more open and more hedonistic society we think of as 'the sixties'. The protest movements of the later fifties, particularly the Campaign for Nuclear Disarmament, created a new cultural climate in which the 'Angry Young Men'[9] gave voice to an iconoclastic yet idealistic mood of disgust with what they saw as a materialistic, class-ridden and backward-looking society.

In 1959 *Queen* magazine, which was to be the bible of smart young London in the sixties, published its 'Boom' number. This already sounded the note of hysteria which was to characterise the late sixties: 'FACING THE CRAZY SIXTIES: THE TENSE PRESENT'. 'Britain,' announced *Queen*, 'has launched into an age of unparalleled lavish living. . . . Nearly two thousand million pounds is pouring out of pockets and wallets and handbags and changing into air tickets and oysters, television sets and caviar, art treasures and vacuum cleaners, cigars and refrigerators.' At the same time *Queen* was radical; it ran articles on Red China, mounted attacks on 'the Establishment' and published Paul Foot's investigation into the controversial Hanratty case.[10]

The Profumo scandal distilled the relaxation in moral values and moral outrage at the hypocrisy of the British Establishment into one unforgettable moment, yet there was a curious innocence and optimism about the early sixties. A further change began to be evident by about 1967, for by then economic problems and unemployment were increasing, and a critique of the consumer society gained in force, again particularly among the young. This critique was to be expressed in styles of dress and 'lifestyles' generally (although this word only came into popular usage in the seventies).

In the fifties fashion models (mannequins as they were still called) became mass media stars, and associated with the aristocracy. Fiona Campbell Walter married Baron von Thyssen, one of the richest men in Europe; Jane McNeil married the Earl of Dalkeith (once one of Princess Margaret's escorts); and Bronwen Pugh married Lord Astor, at whose country estate, Cliveden, Christine Keeler was introduced to John Profumo. The best-known model of all was Barbara Goalen, 5 feet 8 inches (1.7 m) tall, who measured 33″, 21″, 33″ and had legs like a giraffe. She gazed superciliously down from a great height with raised eyebrows and sucked-in cheeks, her hands often clasped over the handle of a long rolled umbrella (essential accessory of the period).

Wallis fashion shops produced this American-style 'college girl' look, with the just-below-the-knee length, for the new teenage consumer. At 4 guineas, it was not as cheap as the advertisement, in **Woman's Day**, *30 January 1960, suggests.*

Smart 'n' tartan for only 4½ gns.! A very pretty bargain

Belles of Scotland

On the first London to Aldermaston march of Easter 1958, CND supporters wore duffle coats and donkey jackets which became symbols of non-conformity and protest.

The American version of these styles was the Beat look, found in the cafés and cellars of Greenwich Village in New York, and North Beach, San Francisco.

In the mid-fifties Audrey Hepburn, who originally came from Holland, and the French star Leslie Caron popularised a Left Bank *gamine* look as reinterpreted by Hollywood. Hepburn's huge 'doe eyes' became a new fashion in cosmetics; both she and Caron wore their hair cropped short, yet softly curling in a 'chrysanthemum' cut. Because they were Continental stars, they disrupted class-bound British stereotypes of beauty, as did Brigitte Bardot. When Bardot married Sacha Distel, her gingham and *broderie-anglaise* dress was copied everywhere. In 1959, Jean Seberg, who had appeared with cropped hair in Otto Preminger's film about Joan of Arc, starred in the first French 'New Wave' film, *Breathless*; her short hair became part of the new youthful sophistication.

Hepburn and Caron helped to create the vogue for casual fashions: flat ballerina pumps and black polo-necks. Leslie Caron actually was a ballet star (she had the lead role in *An American in Paris* opposite Gene Kelly); and there was a crossover here with Paris couture, for the New Look had also drawn on ballerina style with its full skirts and chignons. The rising

Paris designer Givenchy designed Audrey Hepburn's film wardrobes as well as the clothes she wore in private.

Barbara Hulanicki, whose Biba clothes were to become so influential in the late sixties, cites Audrey Hepburn as her youthful ideal:

Sabrina Fair [an Audrey Hepburn film] had made a huge impact on us all at college; everyone walked around in black sloppy sweaters, suede low-cut flatties and gold hoop earrings. . . . Audrey Hepburn and Givenchy were made for each other. His little black dress with shoestring straps in *Sabrina Fair* must have been imprinted on many teenagers' minds forever.[12]

The male version of the Left Bank look again incorporated the black polo-neck or baggy fisherman's sweater, the duffle coat, corduroy trousers, and, by the mid-fifties, jeans and often sandals. A jazz/folk music version of the dissent look was to wear a tweed jacket over a black or dark coloured woollen shirt with a red or white woolly tie. This was quite daring at a time when the general run of middle-class and working-class men wore conservative suits in dark colours and always white shirts and conventional ties. You could tell the difference because middle-class tailoring was of much better quality, and middle-class men usually wore waistcoats. When dressed casually, middle-class men wore cavalry twill trousers, suede chukka boots and a Paisley cravat in an open necked shirt; the concept of a whole separate set of casual wear as opposed to shabby clothes worn to work had not yet penetrated working-class lives to any great extent. Pearl Binder felt that male apparel was dreary in the extreme:

What is wrong with his daily life that causes him to shroud himself in his present mud-coloured garments? . . . Why is he in perpetual mourning? . . .

On the crowded streets of our great cities, in the bus, the train, the plane, the eye is saddened by the same dreary male uniform, shapeless and lacking in colour. Rich men, poor men, labourers, intellectuals, bankers, barrow boys, old men, young men, all today dress like robots. . . . Sartorial paralysis has set in.[13]

Amid the general conformity then, at a time when Continental was a code word for chic, youth fashions brought about a convergence between French and American style in creative combinations. Left Bank style was a largely middle-class approach to dress; the other major counter-cultural fashion of the period came, however, from working-class youths.

Teds and Mods

The Teddy boys (from 'Edwardians') of the early fifties appear to have started in south London, where they had links with an older tradition of working-class 'cloth-capped' delinquency, a prewar subculture. They, however, were the first subculture to be subjected to the investigation –

The sharp 'Mod' look, with its neat collar, narrow tie and trousers, was new when this photograph appeared in **Town** magazine in September 1962. The look originated among young wealthy East Enders.

Below *Roger Mayne's photograph of street life in 1956 shows a group of Teddy boys in North Kensington. Their slicked-back hair, drainpipe trousers, brothel-creeper shoes and long draped jackets aroused exaggerated hostility.*

and effectively the promotion – of the mass media. Thus, the clothes worn by a small majority of youths became a major mass media phenomenon and social scandal.

Their dress was an exaggeration, or a caricature, of the short-lived Savile Row style worn by guards officers and young men about town at the end of the 1940s. Hardy Amies was among those who had promoted it as a return to Edwardianism – the male equivalent of the New Look, perhaps. To the narrow trousers and velvet collar the Teddy boys added elements from the American West, transported across the Atlantic via rock and roll music and Western movies. The very narrow string tie, in particular, may have been derived from the villains in Westerns.[14]

The Teds first emerged into the public eye in 1953, when their theft of style from the upper classes was noted in the popular press. Within a year the wearing of the long, drape jacket with the velvet collar, the drainpipe trousers, the 'slim jim' tie and the crepe sole shoes, or 'beetle crushers' had become associated with delinquency, thuggery and 'cosh boys'. Magistrates told youths who appeared before them for some petty crime to go home and burn their Teddy boy apparel; and one father went so far as to hack his son's suit to pieces, claiming that 'since my son bought this thing a year ago his personality has changed'[15]. Soon, any youth who wore a Teddy boy suit became, by definition, a deviant, because, in the words of one 'family doctor', all Teddy boys were:

of unsound mind in the sense that they are all suffering from a form of psychosis. Apart from the birch or rope [!] depending on the gravity of their crimes, what they need is rehabilitation in a psychopathic [sic] institution. . . . Not only have these rampageous youngsters developed a degree of paranoia, with an inferiority complex, they are also *inferior* specimens apart from their disease.[16]

Lingering echoes of eugenics here!

The reaction to the Teds demonstrated, first, the enormous importance that the media and consequently the public – not to mention authority figures such as magistrates and doctors – attached to a *form of dress*; and secondly, just how narrowly were set the parameters of acceptable behaviour for the working-class teenager in the fifties. It seems that those in power simply could not endure the idea that working-class youths had the right to dress as they liked, especially in a way that imitated (or perhaps mocked) their betters, and that they spent large sums of money on the clothes. For Edwardian suits were not cheap. In October 1953, *Picture Post* reported that on wages of between £4 17s 6d and £12 per week [£52 and £130], Teds were spending as much as £100 [£1081] on one tailor-made outfit, and a drape suit would normally never cost less than between £17 and £20 [£184 and £216], while a pair of shoes cost £3 [£32]. Perhaps the whole episode expressed the general paranoia of the

165

generation gap. After all, teenagers were new. As the hero of Colin McInnes's *Absolute Beginners* said of his elder brother:

He's one of the generations that grew up before teenagers existed. . . . In poor Vernon's era . . . there just weren't any; can you believe it? . . . In those days, it seems, you were just an overgrown boy or an undergrown man, life didn't seem to cater for anything else in between.[17]

Ted dress remained firmly rooted in working-class areas, and, possibly because of this, did not infiltrate into or even influence mainstream menswear. In this it differed from the style of the Mods, which was most influential.

The Mods of the early sixties were said to have originated in the art schools in the late fifties, and to have had close links with the garment industry from the start.[18] Their style was 'cool', Italianate, with short hair and even make-up (for boys). They were relatively affluent; they rode Italian motor scooters, and some used amphetamines, known as pep pills or purple hearts. Mod girls wore advanced forms of contemporary fashions – beehive hairstyles and pointed Italian shoes, with shorter, full skirts and pale lipstick. This style was rapidly translated into High Street fashion via the influence of Mary Quant. Watered down Italianate male Mod styles were from the early sixties introduced in mass-produced versions in the High Street, retailed by chains such as Burtons. This company had seen a serious falling off in sales of semi-bespoke traditional tailored suits by 1953, and introduced younger styles with considerable success.[19]

By 1964 Mod culture, with the additional uniform of anorak and be-mirrored scooters, had developed a following of thousands. These rather subdued-looking youths, watched by the police, had just been involved in an 'incident' with Rockers at Clacton-on-Sea.

A new equality?

The mass media increased public awareness of youth subcultures, and played a central role in the development of general fashion consciousness as well. The 1950s was the heyday of the women's magazines. The readership of *Woman*, *Woman's Own* and *Woman's Realm* ran into millions, and they cost less than 6d [22p]. There were moderately priced glossies such as *Woman and Beauty* and *Vanity Fair*. Mary Grieve described the weeklies as the 'trade papers' of the housewife, and they did reflect some convergence of interests, if not of income, among women. Many working-class wives were better off than they would have been before the war, while for the first time many middle-class housewives were bereft of domestic help of any kind.

With the demise of the prewar 'little dressmaker', home dressmaking spread upwards through the middle class, assisted by improvements in paper patterns. These were now more accurate, and even couture patterns were widely available to the general public. For example, in April 1949 the *Brighton Evening Argus* reported 'a contract between *Vogue* pattern service and eight famous French couturiers – Balmain, Fath, Heim, Lanvin, Molyneux, Paquin and Schiaparelli'. Each pattern, which retailed at 10s [£6], carried the name of its designer. The designs themselves were chosen by buyers from *Vogue* patterns, who visited the couture collections each season. Evening classes in dressmaking meant that any woman with a little time and money could become sufficiently accomplished to make up at least an 'Easy to Make' pattern – the couture patterns were complex and required considerable skill.

In the early sixties new magazines – *Honey*, *Woman's Mirror* and, in 1965, the sophisticated *Nova* – catered to a younger and more diverse audience. Sales of the established weeklies began to decline, and it became clear that the market was fragmenting. No longer was there a homogeneous group: women, all of them interested only in fashion, cooking, children and interior decoration.

The image of the domesticated woman of the 1950s has contributed to the belief that women returned to the home after the Second World War. This never happened. Married women of all classes were going out to work in greater numbers than ever before. It was said that women could choose whether to stay at home or have a job, although the 'choice' was usually confined to part-time, low-paid work. There was a level of unease, however, and in some quarters a strongly held view that mothers *ought* to stay at home.

It was felt that 'the generation of Françoise Sagan and Brigitte Bardot' had lost interest in women's rights. Young women graduates may, how-

ever, have retreated into matrimony and motherhood because even a first class Oxbridge degree was useless without a typing course. Women simply could not 'hope to reach the top'. Yet the belief in a new equality within marriage persisted – and was symbolised in a mode of dress: 'they tend to some extent to dress alike – indeed their clothes, jeans, duffle-coats, sweaters, scarves, gloves, etc., appear to be readily and positively interchangeable.'[20]

In the sixties, unease intensified. The contraceptive pill, marketed in 1963, was credited with causing a revolution in sexual behaviour. This grossly overstates the extent of any 'revolution' that occurred, and the Pill was of less importance than other social changes. Young couples were marrying earlier, and large numbers of children were coming to be associated with the so-called 'problem families'. Contraception in general was slowly becoming more acceptable. The Church of England did not give positive support to contraception until 1958, and the Family Planning Association did not officially give advice to unmarried women until 1966. The Pill did not bring wholesale promiscuity in its wake, although female virginity became less of an issue. Yet a 1965 study found that only 12 per cent of the teenage girls in the sample had ever had sexual intercourse.[21]

The fashions of the sixties are often seen as directly reflecting the arrival of the Pill and the 'permissive society'. But, like so much else, sixties chic had its roots in the fifties, and among other things in the resurgence of Chanel.

High-sixties style: Quant, Twiggy, Ossie Clark

Chanel, in disgrace after the war, reopened her salon in 1953. One European reporter commented icily:

In spite of the instructions given to the critics, who were told to praise her, the public is aware that the first collection was shown to a silent audience. It is said [however] that . . . some important vendeuses have joined the firm.

But people were scarcely able to judge freely, on the day of the re-opening, the atmosphere was peculiar: the prewar decor, the mannequins with their very short hair, dressed in colours that evoked the past, in dresses made of fabric [jersey] which, since the day when Chanel first introduced it, has been absolutely transformed, and now, in the form in which she still uses, has a shoddy, lifeless appearance.[22]

But American buyers, it seems, did not care about Chanel's war-time activities, and by 1956 were purchasing her designs in large numbers. By 1960 Chanel's little suits had once more brought youthful simplicity back

into fashion. When she reopened she attacked the New Look as backward looking:

Elegance in clothes means being able to move freely, to do anything with ease . . . those heavy dresses that won't pack into aeroplane luggage, ridiculous. All those boned and corseted bodices – out with them. What's the good of going back to the rigidity of the corset? Now women go in for simpler lives.[23]

Mary Quant, backed by her husband, Alexander Plunkett Greene, opened their first boutique, Bazaar, in the Kings Road, Chelsea, in 1955. Although youthful fashions were still hard to find, department stores were opening special sections for the seventeen to twenty-five-year-olds, and chain stores – C & A, Neatawear, Etam and Dorothy Perkins – were beginning to cater for the young at a cheaper price range.

In 1963 Woollands of Knightsbridge opened a boutique within the store, which was modelled on Bazaar. This, the Twenty-One Shop, sold designs by all the new British designers and foreign ones, such as Marimekko of Finland and Emmanuelle Khan, who designed for the British firm Cojana as well.

The whole idea of the boutique was tremendously influential in the second half of the 1960s. Many a provincial town could boast its own boutique, often run by some graduates from the local art college. At their best, these boutiques provided unique, 'one off' designer clothing, often in cheap cottons, silks and synthetics – original styles at reasonable prices. The vast majority were economically non-viable, and most closed after two or three years' trading.

In 1961 a new French film star, Jeanne Moreau, appeared in *Jules et Jim*, and the 1920s clothes she wore, designed by Pierre Cardin, immediately looked like the latest Left Bank fashion. Gradually a whole new youthful way of looking and moving was developing. Soon models began to pose in the most unladylike way – with their legs wide apart, running, skipping, lying down, contorted in slovenly poses; and later in the sixties in exaggerated, decadent and even sinisterly anorexic ways.

Yet if, today, the fashions of the sixties seem to reduce women to vacuous Lolitas, at the time they did create a subjective feeling of liberation:

The fifties had been so sinful, so *old*. In my twenty-first birthday photograph my dark lips, vaselined lids, tightly waved hair, stiff black dress and pearl necklace age me poignantly; but by the time I reach thirty I'm dressed like a Kate Greenaway child in white stockings, flat shoes and high waisted dresses, with my cropped hair I look about twelve years old. There must have been a dislocation in travelling backwards so fast, so far.[24]

In this new world of the sixties, good taste became square. Forget the matching accessories – who now under the age of forty ever carried a handbag or wore gloves? Clothes did not even have to be well made any more. They were 'thrown together' to be worn for a few months. Colours

169

At Ascot in June 1968, Jayne Harris (left), show jumper and debutante, was turned away from the Royal Enclosure for wearing a trouser suit; she returned in a minidress. The following year, women in trousers were admitted.

were brighter and more daringly mixed. Miniskirts (popularly accepted from 1965) and trousers revealed the female leg more completely than clothes had ever done before.

Gradually the Kings Road began to change . . . full of new and unlikely people, all of the magical age in which they were adult but not old. . . . [The] women of Chelsea wore big floppy hats, skinny ribbed sweaters, key-hole dresses, wide hipster belts. . . . They had white lipsticked lips and thick black eyeliner, hair cut at alarming angles, op-art earrings and ankle-length white boots. They wore citron coloured trouser suits and skirts that seemed daily shorter. They rode on miniature motorbikes.[25]

The fashion models of the fifties would have been completely wrong for these clothes. In 1966 the editor of the *Daily Express* women's page was shown a photograph of Twiggy, her new short hairstyle cut by Leonard, the fashionable West End hairdresser. It was softer than Vidal Sassoon's geometric cuts, but even shorter and almost childish looking. On the strength of this, the *Daily Express* nominated Twiggy as 'the face of the year', and Twiggy (her real name was Lesley Hornby) from East London became the face not just of the year but arguably of the decade. She weighed 6½ stone (41 kg) and was sixteen years old. By this time fashion

was inescapably and totally geared to youth. Even the Queen had to raise her hemlines, though never more than a fraction above the kneecap.

The fashions of the early sixties with all their youthfulness and simplicity stayed within the parameters of 'normal' modern fashion as mapped out by Chanel and Patou in the 1920s; they were 'wearable' clothes for busy, sophisticated young women. But by 1967 the influence of the Underground – the hippie counter-culture – was being widely felt. Increasingly fashion moved towards excess. In 1967 skirts were so short that bottoms were almost visible, but soon they reached the floor and trousers were so wide they looked like skirts. Fashion in the last years of the sixties began to fracture so that cult hippie fashions, taken up by rock singers – Julie Driscoll and the Beatles, for example – represented for their wearers something quite apart and indeed hostile to haute couture, although the two might still influence each other.

Ethnic fashions could be worn in solidarity with the oppressed nations of the non-Western world – as students across the globe became politicised, particularly by the Vietnam War. Afghan coats embroidered on the outside and with the long wool worn as a lining; cheap Indian cotton printed full-length dresses with mirror embroidery; American Indian beaded headbands and fringed suede. As early as 1964 there had been a renewed interest within mainstream fashion for hand-knitted Fair Isle and crochet. By 1970, home-made clothes no longer seemed an inferior substitute for ready-made clothes; on the contrary there was a positive value attached to anything handmade, even if it were only a macramé belt or choker, as a reaction against the super shininess of PVC, the too-knife-like pleats of Terylene.

The vogue for garments you had made yourself extended to the rehabilitation of second-hand clothes. By the late sixties young women and men were scouring antique markets for frocks and suits from the twenties, thirties and forties. Shops such as Annacat in South Kensington specialised in the re-creation of starchy cotton Edwardian frilled blouses and shirts, which went so well with the velvet flares of the fashionable. Ossie Clark was designing droopy blouses and long frocks in muted crêpes and chiffons. Laura Ashley's 1968 bestseller was a widely-gathered, full-length Edwardian-style cotton print dress, complete with high collar and lace trimming. (A blue and white version may be seen in Brighton Museum.)

Fashionable men now dressed almost as flamboyantly as women. An important component in this trend was the intervention of haute couture into the male fashion market; from the mid sixties Pierre Cardin and other Paris designers were making ready-to-wear collections for them. Men had been wearing flowered ties since 1963 and these were followed

171

Wax models of the Beatles, in collarless Pierre Cardin suits, at Madame Tussauds, meet the real Beatles, wearing informal corduroy jackets and jeans, in 1964.

by flowery shirts (Liberty lawn again) with large collars. By 1968 thousands were copying pop stars, growing their hair, cultivating moustaches and beards, and wearing flamboyant jackets, trailing scarves, NHS 'granny' spectacles, 'grandad' cotton vests, high-heeled boots, kipper ties and hats with wide, floppy brims.

At the time, the much greater emphasis on male fashion was attributed to changing sexual attitudes and a relaxation in the moral climate. Martin Moss of Moss Brothers claimed that:

Men certainly became more interested in clothes after the war . . . but the really serious business started after the adjustment to the homosexual law. Before that, a man was afraid he might be thought a queer. Now the outlook is broader and has settled down, he can relax and be a peacock if he wishes.[26]

This comment refers to the 1967 reform which decriminalised sexual acts between consenting men over twenty-one in private. Whether men were really less frightened of being suspected of homosexuality, or whether the industry saw a potential market, men's clothing did become a little brighter and more adventurous. But although it was fashionable in the sixties to be a working-class lad made good, most of the new male style setters were upper class or pop stars. Pop stars had a working-class image to some extent, but the most famous – John Lennon and Mick Jagger, for

example – came from middle-class, college backgrounds. One of the first men to wear more colourful clothes was David Mlinaric, with his cinnamon suits worn with a yellow shirt and tie. It was he who reintroduced the frilled shirt, soon copied by the society and fashion photographer Patrick Lichfield, a cousin of the Queen. Lord Lichfield revealed to the *Observer* that he owned twenty-six suits, fifty shirts and fifty ties. Attempts to introduce completely new garments, such as the space age tunic top, met with little success, however, and even the polo-neck shirt, worn without a tie, had only a relatively brief vogue.[27]

Couture fights back

These then were the fashion styles, but how were they translated into mass market products? Although Paris was still the centre of the world fashion industry in the early postwar years, its mode of influence was changing. By 1955 couture prices had risen by 3000 per cent compared with their prewar level.[28] 'Only the woman over forty can afford today's prices,' Alison Settle told *Observer* readers in 1947, and she reported the New Look as a 'gamble on luxury modes'. In 1951 the *Daily Mail* was telling its readers that 'the rich customers now buy one dress where before they might have bought six'. This was part of a report headed 'Slump hits fashion houses'. In 1962 Jacques Heim told the *New York Times* that 'it was quite different in the old days. The wealthy woman came to Paris and would stay a month or two. Now they come by plane and almost want to leave before they have come.'[29] By the 1960s, the *New York Times* was reporting that there were only 3000 private customers for thirty-eight couture houses, for while the incomes of the rich did not change, their lives did, and they were no longer prepared to spend long hours in fittings and alterations.[30]

The Paris designers soon realised that they must find new ways of increasing their sales. By the 1950s they were adjusting to the fact that their wealth now came primarily from the sale of their designs to the mass market, rather than from individual private clients. This was achieved by the introduction of a number of new ways of selling designs and selling the haute couture names to the mass market. One way in which this was done was further to develop the system of licensing the reproduction of haute couture models which had begun to evolve in the 1930s as a defence against the illegal copying or pirating of designs. Pirating was still a problem in the fifties – at the height of his fame, Dior was said to be handling forty lawsuits a year on this issue alone – but the licensing system offered some protection and also proved a most fruitful source of revenue.

The wholesale buyers, who were now the most important haute couture clients, had to pay a substantial deposit to view the collections, which was set against any purchase they subsequently made. It was reported in the fifties that they also had to pay between 50 and 100 per cent more for models than a private client would pay. Instead of buying a finished model, the wholesalers could opt to purchase a toile – a canvas or linen copy of a model. With the toile they would also be given the necessary information about the amount of material needed for the garment, what buttons and other accessories and trimmings had been used, and where they might be purchased. Using these toiles, New York firms such as Macy's and Gimbels could reproduce thousands of copies of a $950 design for $80 a time. Alternatively, something much closer to the original could be reproduced, to be sold at a higher price as an 'Original Christian Dior [or whoever] Copy'.[31]

Couturiers also gave chosen wholesale manufacturers exclusive rights to copy their designs in a particular country, and began to design for wholesalers direct. In 1948 Jacques Fath visited the United States and negotiated a contract to design for the American wholesale manufacturer Joseph Halpert. Within two years, Fath's turnover had trebled. In 1954 he signed a contract to design a regular wholesale collection for wool merchant Jean Prouvost who made the clothes in Paris with American workers and Singer sewing machines. In 1950 Jean Desses signed a similar contract with I. M. Bagedonow. His designs, the 'Jean Desses American Collection', were retailed at around $100 each.[32] Couturiers began to organise their own wholesale subsidiaries overseas. Garments made in this way were sold with labels which clearly stated their origin.

Department stores such as Harvey Nichols and Woollands of Knightsbridge were making direct copies of Balmain and Lanvin couture models themselves in the 1950s. Harvey Nichols advertised:

Print coat dress; fitted, piped, back flaring – a wonderfully formal, unfussy way to dress for Ascot or a wedding. Copied in our own workrooms from the Balmain original; in various grey, navy or black prints – 39½ guineas [£430].

A further postwar development was in franchising or couture licensing. The licence is an agreement whereby the designer sells his name under contract to a manufacturer in return for royalties of between 3 and 10 per cent. It first became really widespread in the 1940s. Dior, for example, licensed his name to stocking firms in 1948, to glove manufacturers in 1952 and to the Rayne's shoe firm in 1955.[33] The practice had first begun when Chanel began to market her perfume in the 1920s. After the Second World War the mass sale of perfumes and perfume related goods began to expand rapidly.

Paris haute couture also developed its own ready-to-wear industry after the war. Alison Settle reported in 1949 that they were 'opening shops inside their grand premises where simplified versions of their models are sold at half price'. From the mid-fifties *prêt-à-porter* (the French term for ready-to-wear) was developing apace. Top model houses, and houses specialising in ready-to-wear, were having seasonal collective showings of their work specifically for trade buyers and the fashion press; marketing and advertising had become much more organised. In April 1956 British *Vogue* commented on this growing trend:

There is a quiet revolution going on in the French fashion industry. The traditional, unquestioned supremacy of the couturier and the little dressmaker has been brilliantly challenged by a growing, thriving ready to wear industry; top names, Lempereur (wonderful young clothes), Webe (excellent suits and coats), Pierre Billet and Alayne (delicious cotton dresses) and Givenchy-Université (Givenchy himself does the designs).

During the sixties, street style influenced Paris couture. This Yves St Laurent version of the hippy-Indian style was photographed by David Bailey for Vogue, *September 1969.*

Nevertheless, in France in 1956 it was reported that three out of five women still had their clothes made by a little dressmaker, or made their own clothes, while in the 1960s a copy of a Biba design, price 2 guineas [£14] in London, cost over £9 [£59] in a Paris chain store.[34]

By the late fifties, then, Paris haute couture was still developing as a modern industry. Its design leaders, on the other hand, were, by the late fifties and early sixties, appearing to lose touch with the new, youthful emphasis in clothes, and hence its sense of direction. After the sudden death of Christian Dior in 1957, the whole future of his fashion house and its huge commercial empire was threatened. Yves St Laurent was hastily promoted as his successor. His first 'trapeze' collection – following the waistless, looser-fitting A-line, H-line, Y-line and the sack line introduced in 1957 – was, fortunately for the company, rapturously received by the press. Their reports, bordering on hysteria, claimed that Yves St Laurent had 'saved' France – that is, the French fashion industry. In the autumn of 1960, however, St Laurent introduced a beatnik element into his collection. *Vogue* reported dubiously that 'the Beat look is the news at Dior . . . pale zombie faces; leather suits and coats; knitted caps and turtleneck collars, black endlessly'. This went down so badly that St Laurent, coincidentally absent doing his national service, was summarily sacked, to be replaced by Marc Bohan. A nervous breakdown followed, but St Laurent soon successfully reopened under his own name. He turned out to be fully in tune with the future, and has since had a much more sustained success than his former rival. The horror with which his initial foray into youth-inspired fashions was greeted demonstrates, however, the widening gap between the designers who had been established before or immediately after the Second World War, and a new generation.

From 1956, or even earlier, youth and youth movements were influencing fashion. There was simmering revolt even among the upper-class debs and the middle-class 'sub debs' confronted with formal, middle-aged styles:

Beatrice's coat was brown silk, a full-skirted coat dress, and mine was a revolting blue brocade with a huge shawl collar and an even more repulsive black velvet bow on the bosom. It was designed for a matron, not a fourteen-year-old.[11]

There were two sources for youth fashions: the mass market, and counter-cultural fashion. In mainstream fashion, there was a countervailing casual trend which came from Italy and the United States. The Italian look was the further development of 'separates', a continuation, really, of Chanel's sweater dressing and the sportswear Patou had adapted for daily life. Pleated skirts, twinsets, thick sweaters and even narrow, three-quarter-length trousers were beginning to appear as a casual form of dress. Young women could buy these at off the peg prices; the most innovative were made by Emilio Pucci, who used silk and silk jersey in vibrant shades of mango, heliotrope, and 'daring' colour schemes – pink and orange, or turquoise and chocolate. American teenage fashions for girls popularised cotton shirtwaisters worn with white ankle socks.

Counter-cultural fashions were not, as rational dress had been, *anti* fashion – that is, wanting to eradicate fashion. They were *alternative* fashions, assembled to express a critique of society, or to claim a group's, or an individual's, right to speak in its own – sometimes raucous – voice.

One kind of protest came from the educated young, in grammar and public schools and in art colleges and universities. Some of these joined social protest movements, particularly CND after 1958; most were probably involved in artistic and intellectual protest. The influence of folk music, for example the political music of Peggy Seeger and Ewan McColl, was important; and the trad. jazz bands of Humphrey Lyttelton and Chris Barber brought the music of 1920s New Orleans to a new generation hungry for an alternative to the sugary crooning of Donald Peers or David Whitfield. By 1956 Tommy Steele's first hit 'I never felt more like singing the Blues' was to be heard in every coffee bar.

What emerged from this radical culture was an 'arty' alternative to high fashion for the students of the mid to late fifties. Young women wore thick black, or sometimes dark green or maroon stockings, and full dirndl skirts that derived both from the Dorelia John fashions of prewar Chelsea and from the postwar cult of ballet. They wore items of male clothing: check shirts, oiled wool fishermen's jerseys from Norway (or men's jerseys from Marks and Spencer), and duffle coats from Millets or other army surplus stores. They wore tight 'drainpipe' trousers made of black velvet or Black Watch tartan, and were beginning to wear jeans.

Opposite Susan Small, a middle-market ready-to-wear company, hired the famous model Barbara Goalen to take their image up-market. Their New-Look gold and black rayon cocktail dress was shown at London's Fashion Fortnight in June 1952.

161

As 'Young Idea' editor at *Vogue*, Clare Rendlesham championed a number of new British talents. In 1964 she moved to *Queen*. There, on a black bordered page, she ran an 'obituary' of Balenciaga and Givenchy: 'The mood was fiftyish. The colours were drab. The evening clothes were dreary.' Fortunately a new Paris designer appeared to take the place of the fallen angels: Courrèges, and *Queen* was also the first to publicise his amazing 1964 space age collection with its miniskirts, trouser suits, short, square cut jackets that stood away from the body, square lines and flat-heeled white ankle boots with squared-off peep toes and ankle bows.

In 1962 Paris had thirty-two haute couture houses, employing 6000 staff, with 12 000 private customers, buying clothes retailing at from £250 to £1000 [£2062 to £8250].[35] They catered less and less for private clients, and by the late sixties their style ideas were being developed and promoted primarily to support or advertise their licences and franchises internationally.

From Utility to Biba: British style in the fifties and sixties

British design and British ready-to-wear clothing made great advances in the twenty-five years following the Second World War. The coupon system of clothes rationing ended for a wide range of garments on 1 February 1949; fewer and fewer Utility garments were advertised, and in 1952 this scheme was replaced by the Douglas Scheme. *Vogue* welcomed this change with the words: 'Once again it is a buyer's market. . . . Your discriminating shopping can keep quality up and prices down.' (*Vogue*, June 1952.)

Unlike Utility, the Douglas Scheme was purely voluntary. Whereas under the previous scheme the cheaper clothes were tax free, under the new one the tax threshold was lowered, so that even low price clothes were taxed, which obviously made clothes more expensive for the less well off. In addition, quality controls were abolished, and the Utility price and profit margin rules were ended. The Conservatives also abolished the Style Development Council, which Harold Wilson had pushed through when at the Board of Trade, and which had tried, for example, to rationalise women's sizing in clothing.

The 1950s therefore saw a move away from the project of central government planning for the clothing industry. Instead, on the wages front there was once more an uncoordinated scramble for wage increases by individual negotiations; the unionisation of the industry continued to be difficult and patchy, partly because of the large proportion of married women workers and the high turnover. Home work began to spread once

Opposite *Hippies at a pop festival in the late sixties.*

177

more, and increased further under the impact of the small-run boutique clothes in the late sixties and seventies.[36]

Britain's upper classes continued to buy their clothes from Paris, but increasingly looked to British haute couture as well. By the mid-fifties, largely as a result of the wide demand for Society dresses for the Coronation season of 1953, the future of London haute couture looked promising. London witnessed the rise of a new and talented generation of designers: Ronald Paterson, John Cavanagh and Michael Sherrard, and John Boyd and Otto Lucas in the millinery field, while the prewar houses such as Hartnell, Lachasse, Charles Creed and Hardy Amies continued with success. In 1956 it was recorded that a debutante's dress allowance for the Season might be as much as £500 [£4800], and her wardrobe would include a presentation ball dress to cost between £60 and £70 [£576 and £670], six cocktail dresses costing between £10 and £35 [£95 and £336], and four cotton dresses at the same price.[37]

Yet, with the exception of Amies who did manage to diversify, by the 1960s all these couturiers were struggling, with fewer and fewer clients, most of an older generation. So serious did the financial problems become that many closed their houses. Unlike the top Paris houses, they lacked the financial backing and the opportunities to expand into licensing and ready-to-wear. Against the thirty-four Paris houses, London in 1962 had only eleven, with 1500 staff and 2000 private clients. Hartnell's was still the largest house, with eight workrooms and 300 employees, while Amies had a staff of 135. The prices of their clothes ranged from £20 to £200 [£165 to £1650].[38]

There was common ground between the British haute couture houses and the top end of the ready-to-wear trade – firms such as Jaeger, Frederick Starke, Windsmoor and Deréta, whose most fashionable clothes were nearly as expensive as the couturiers' ready-to-wear lines. The ready-to-wear section of the industry was by this time much more co-ordinated. In 1950 Leslie Carr Jones, who built up Susan Small, had realised how much stronger British fashion would be were it to be properly organised. He was instrumental in the formation of the London Model House Group. Five years later it was replaced by the Fashion House Group of London, which united twenty-eight top-quality firms. The first London Fashion Week was held in 1958, for less than fifty wholesale buyers, but from then on London Fashion Weeks showed regularly in Paris, and by 1966 75 per cent of British ready-to-wear products were being exported.[39]

Manufacturing methods improved. Here, Marks and Spencer were in the vanguard, but many firms were now using American methods, in cutting and sizing, for example. Leslie Carr Jones described how at Susan Small:

Opposite *These New Look cocktail dresses of 1952 by Norman Hartnell were suited to the social formality of the period. The British couture industry was enjoying a period of success at this time, which lasted until the mid-sixties.*

We . . . evolved our own comprehensive sizing, precision pattern making, precision cutting in bulk with an electric knife and our own ideas of side and seam turnings. The dressmaker machinists became mechanics: they had a list of turnings and only had to follow the notches. In the old days it was so much hit and miss. Every garment was cut singly by a cutter and a girl fitted it up on a stand. If the girl was careful the dress fitted. If she was careless it didn't. It was very laborious.[40]

In the 1950s and 1960s British mass retailers such as Marks and Spencer and Wallis Shops relied primarily on Paris for their designs. Wallis, for example, was responsible for reintroducing the classic Chanel suit to British women, and from the late fifties bought so many Chanel toiles that the Paris firm offered the firm concessionary prices. Copies of a Chanel original costing £350 [£3100] at this period sold at around £40 [£360] in Wallis Shops. In the sixties Marks and Spencer would buy Paris models which were not adapted directly but acted to 'inspire' their design workrooms.[41] They also employed the British couturier Michael as a consultant designer. In his couture house clothes retailed at from 50 guineas [£450], whereas Marks and Spencer dresses in the fifties sold at around 1 guinea [£9].[42]

By the fifties, British ready-to-wear was able to offer its customers a wide choice. In 1954 for example, the dress shop chain Chanelle (near the top end of the ready-to-wear market) advertised a Dior copy, a fine woollen day dress with a pleated skirt, for 19½ guineas [£210]. At about the same time the *Brighton and Hove Herald* carried an advertisement for the up-market Cresta sale in which evening dresses were offered at between 11 and 21 guineas [£120 to £230] and tweed suits for from 6 to 9 guineas [£66 to £99]. A decade later the styles were much less staid, but prices had not risen very much. *Vogue* advertised one Susan Small outfit at 16½ guineas [£131]; 'heatwave colours and head to toe match' – in reds and pinks with flashes of green on grey. The set consisted of jersey sweater, stockings and turban in printed synthetic fabric, with miniskirt in red twill. *True Romances* magazine, although catering for a much less well off readership, was still able to offer 'designer' clothes, for example a Courtelle sweater by Charles Creed (another London haute couture designer) 'with snappy chequerboard front in black, white and yellow squares' for 3 guineas [£25].

There was so much variety in price, quality and design by the 1960s that in January 1965 the Consumers Association conducted its own investigation into the 'value' of four similar-looking black cocktail dresses. The couture version was made of expensive silk and wool fabric and sold at £66 13s 6d [£500]. The top level ready-to-wear/wholesale version cost £17 6s 6d [£130]. There was a Rembrandt design in the middle price range at 6 guineas [£47] and finally a chain store dress at £1 19s 11d [£15]. As part of the investigation all dresses were worn and cleaned; the

Rembrandt model emerged as 'best value for money', with the couture model as a rather poor second.[43]

The sparkle and 'snappiness' of the sixties designs was partly due to a resurgence of British dress design, which made a crucial contribution to the image and style of the period. Janey Ironside at the Royal College of Art could take much of the credit for this, as she had been nurturing a group of designers, among them Marion Foale and Sally Tuffin, John Bates and Jean Muir. And of course there was Mary Quant (who had trained at Goldsmiths' College), who brought the 'way out' ideas of the Chelsea Set to mainstream fashion. These designers did not operate at the mass market level. Indeed, by the 1980s, Jean Muir had gone right up-market and become a distinguished designer label, producing garments which cost upwards of £300.

The Royal College of Art designers were innovators. Their fashions were sold at relatively exclusive boutiques, such as Top Gear in the Kings Road. One 1965 Foale and Tuffin suit, made in fine brown and white herringbone tweed, had a long tunic coat with a velvet collar and a short hipster skirt. By the late sixties, their suits and long smocks were being sold at prices in the £30 to £40 price range [£200–£264]. Foale and Tuffin also pioneered the use of two different printed materials in one dress, which was to become almost a cliché of early seventies design. They used quality materials such as Liberty lawn to create high-waisted summer dresses and long smock dresses which were similar to those later mass-produced by Laura Ashley, but more elaborate and with more daring and more subtle colour combinations.

Mary Quant fashions too were relatively expensive, beautifully made from good materials. Even her cheaper, mass-produced Ginger Group clothes were available in only 180 British outlets. Mary Quant popularised the pinafore dress, that most useful garment of the early sixties, designing variations on the St Trinian's school tunic – some enterprising young women bought actual school tunics with box pleats from school outfitters, transforming them into a chic ensemble.

The cover of the very first issue of the *Sunday Times Colour Magazine*, itself a major innovation, in 1962, featured the top model of the early sixties, Jean Shrimpton, in a grey sleeveless Quant dress. Its high waist was emphasised by three bands of seven rows of piping studded at intervals with buttons covered in the same material. The blurb stated that the dress 'typifies the feminine look, away from the figure-denying line'. The dress cost 18½ guineas [£128], and Mary Quant was said to be 'the darling of the London young – now being accepted throughout the country'. She hijacked the beatnik fashions of the late fifties, the dark stockings, the flat shoes, the polo-necks, and transformed them into the

181

In the 1960s youthful fashions, designed by new young British designers and sold in boutiques, ousted classic British couture. The front cover of the first **Sunday Times Colour Magazine** *shows Jean Shrimpton, wearing a Mary Quant dress, photographed by David Bailey – all new stars of the period.*

latest fashion for the girl in the street. Fashion journalists were quick to seize on her ideas, and on those of the Royal College of Art designers, although not everyone liked her designs. They came as a shock to the older generation, and one *vendeuse* in the late sixties declared: 'I think the harshness and coarseness of her clothes bring out nasty reactions in men!'[44]

In 1963 Barbara Hulanicki, with her husband John Fitz Simon, started a mail order business. Their sleeveless pink and white gingham shift with a key-hole cut-out at the back of the neck and matching headscarf sold for £1.25 [£9]. Orders poured in, and it was this success that enabled them to open their first boutique, Biba, off Kensington High Street.

Biba and Mary Quant are usually lumped together as indistinguishable components of the sixties fashion impulse. Stylistically they were, but Biba's clothes were much cheaper. For example, in 1968 its mail order catalogue advertised an 'oyster coloured frock, gently flaring, wide droopy collar: Price £2 12s 6d [£17.50]'. The blurb added hopefully: 'We have taken great care that the larger sizes keep the correct proportions, so that they appear just as narrow and skinny looking as on smaller people.'[45] In any case the largest size was 14. Cheapness notwithstanding, Biba's very high fashion clothes were worn by pop personalities such as Kathy McGowan who fronted the TV music show *Ready Steady Go*, but although the Biba look became phenomenally popular, it too was never a mass-market operation. Biba was a London shop (although there was briefly a branch in Brighton), and however many young women from the provinces came to visit this shrine of style, it was because the clothes and the whole aesthetic of the shops were copied that they were influential, not because the clothes themselves were ever mass-produced.

Biba caught the mood of the late sixties, which was moving towards an aesthetic different from the space age brightness of Courrèges, or the Mondrian primary colours – black, white, acid yellow, red and blue – of Yves St Laurent in 1966. Already there had been a trend in interior design for Art Nouveau and Art Deco; Hulanicki decorated her shops in sombre colours and furnished them in period bentwood and ostrich feathers in Victorian vases. Soon, instead of little shift dresses, she was creating sleazy Jean Harlow satin evening wear (or perhaps it was for the boudoir – you could never be quite sure). She popularised 'off' colours reminiscent of the 1930s, or even of aesthetic dress in the 1890s. T-shirts, canvas and suede boots, and rubberised canvas riding macs were long-term bestsellers in these slightly weird colours – flesh, brickdust, aubergine. Meanwhile a whole cosmetic range brought back a forgotten era of the silent movies, when lipsticks were maroon and eyeshadow sepia.

Barbara Hulanicki, who began a mail order business, and then opened a boutique, continued to market her thirties look by post. This outfit in moss crêpe cost £9 12s 2d, an affordable price for many teenagers in the early seventies.

Cheap fashion: mail order and second-hand

At the lower end of the market mail order too improved and expanded, with more companies, more rivalry and more choice. Oxendales, Grattons, John Myers, Empire Stores and others advertised in the mass circulation women's magazines, and they continued to offer hire purchase, which was probably in fact their main attraction. They produced a staple fare of basic daywear. For example, the Oxendale Centenary Mail Order Catalogue (autumn/winter 1959) advertised the following:

Inexpensive, warm suit in hard-wearing, Rannoch imitation Harris tweed, classic, single-breasted, fitted jacket with flapped pockets: £5 19s 11d [£54].

For that vivid personality – enormous poppies in vibrant glowing colour printed on rayon satin of exceptionally rich quality – draped bustline, full, gathered skirt over stiffened attached petticoat: 95s [£45].

The catalogue showed no full-length dresses at all – the costliest clothes were pure wool suits and coats, and smart day dresses. The words 'inexpensive', 'imitation' and 'blended wool' give the quality away, and mail order was never considered smart or high fashion. In the 1950s it marketed to an entirely working-class clientele and an older age group, mostly living in the north of England and Scotland. In the 1960s Freemans employed the Scottish pop star Lulu to promote their new teenage lines with the aim of widening their clientele.

Many shopped through the Co-op, and, if their styles were not Paris, at least the quality was good and the dividend useful. In 1959 the *Brighton and Hove Herald* featured the local Co-op winter sale offers of 'Ladies coats reduced to £5' [£45] and one as low as £1 [£9]. Their dresses were reduced to 10s 6d [£4.50]. Mrs Patricia Miles, who worked as a sales assistant at Woolworth in Bournemouth, found £5 [£45] in 1959 to be 'very expensive' for a cotton Horrocks dress – and she considered herself 'not badly off'. She was married in a white wedding dress which cost her £8 [£72].[46]

The garb of poverty still existed. Roger Mayne's photographs of Southam Street, North Kensington, taken from 1956 to 1961, illustrate the 'forgotten poor' of the 1950s. Boys wear shrunken or baggy flannel shorts, young women are dressed in wartime glamour bands (for factory work) and 1940s style coats, and older women shuffle in slippers and overalls. Some of them are wearing long skirts reminiscent of 1948 rather than 1958, but there is also a picture of two young women on their way out for the evening, one in a tight skirt, the other in a full-skirted dress; these are contemporary fashions, fully in tune with the period. Roger

Mayne photographed the local Teds, and the new arrivals from the West Indies. These young men are clearly dressed to look smart in snap brimmed hats.[47]

The 1951 Rowntree Poverty Survey described the lives of families living on less than £6 a week [£72 today]. They found that a married woman of thirty-eight spent £14 2s 4d [£170] a year on clothes for herself. Her most costly investment was her overcoat (one every three years at 6 guineas [£75]). She bought one dress in three years at 2 guineas [£25].[48]

Many families coped by buying clothing on hire purchase. A man's suit might be paid off at as much as 10s [£6] a week. (The national hire purchase debt in 1951 was already £208 million.) Jumble sales and second-hand clothing were still a useful source of clothes for many families. The

In the fifties, fashion was still beyond the reach of the very poor. The older women in Roger Mayne's photograph of 1956 of Southam Street, North Kensington, wear forties-style clothes, although the young people look more up to date.

185

mother cited by Rowntree bought herself a second-hand raincoat and skirt every year for about 12s 6d [£7.50] and a second-hand jumper at 3s 6d [£1.80].

New fabrics, new markets

Along with the widening provision of fashionable clothes came a 'democratisation' of fabrics. It was no longer the case that a garment had to be made in silk or wool to be highly fashionable and exclusive. Clever marketing by the British Cotton Board in the mid-fifties enabled cotton to lose its 'tub frock' image, especially with the young. Crisp and starchy, it was ideal for the dresses of the post New Look period, with their tight fitted shirtwaist tops and very full gathered or pleated skirts, often belled out with broderie anglaise petticoats. The British Cotton Board promoted the fabric as easy-care, fashionable and crease resistant and it was used at every level of the fashion industry – even for informal couture evening dresses. The price range was wide: at the cheapest level, Eagle Mills of Huddersfield were selling a mail order full skirted cotton shirtwaist dress for 12s 11d [£5.85]. In 1958 *Vanity Fair* carried an advertisement for Victor Josselyn's printed, full-skirted cotton designs retailing at 6 guineas [£56]. Despite intense efforts the British cotton industry, which had been in decline since the First World War, could not compete with the cheaper prices and better finishes of the cottons from the United States in particular, and also India.

There was strong competition as well from man-made fibres, about which there was enormous optimism in the early postwar period. A whole new generation of synthetics based on coal or oil products had been developed. Rayon, which had never been entirely successful on its own, could be blended with these, while nylons, tricels and acrylics promised wonderful new qualities of durability, easy care, delicacy and fashion styling. Nylon, first marketed in the 1940s, was hugely successful, since it could be made into ultra-sheer stockings, which lasted better and were soon much cheaper than silk ones, and into fine transparent lingerie and drip-dry shirts. Polyester, the first fully synthetic yarn made from a petrol base, was also developed in the 1940s, and by 1955, as Terylene, was being used to make permanently pleated skirts, chiffon dresses and a wide range of nightwear, as well as bed linen and furnishing fabrics. Acrylic yarn, a type of plastic made from oil, could be fashioned into hard-wearing sweaters, jersey fabrics and carpeting. Crimplene, Dacron, Acrilan, Courtelle, Orlon and Dralon were all variants on these fibres. They were made into fashion garments which were also, for the first time, long-lasting and economically priced. These had long been the goals of fashion producers at the mass level, and since synthetics seemed to provide the answer they were produced in huge quantities.

Apart from a few experiments couturiers largely ignored synthetics until the mid-sixties when a new range – PVC, Lycra, vinyls, foam-backed Crimplenes and various plastics – had an enormous, although brief, success at couture level. Ungaro's space-age teenage designs were deliberately made up in mostly synthetic fabrics. Paco Rabanne made dresses out of plastic discs linked with metal. The vogue for these passed quickly, but perhaps what made them different from the other synthetics was that they were not trying to imitate natural fibres; they were made

Taking over everywhere the new, fresh look in clothes. Tailored suit, lined, in checked jacquard jersey by JERSEYCRAFT, is in Courtelle—completely washable. In checks of lemon, pale green, olive, cherry, light blue, royal, navy, beige, all with white, sizes 10-18. It's at all good stores, price **15 gns.** By *Koupy Boutique*

Wear clear blue-and-white for a go-ahead day "

SO **PRACTICAL**—WHEN
IT'S COMPLETELY WASHABLE

ON THE UP-AND-UP —a new kind of clothes! Example: the executive-style houndstooth check, feminine version, in double-knit jacquard jersey. Business asset: now it's in Courtelle—firm, comfortable, and really, truly *washable!*

Anyone with fashion-acumen knows that Courtelle is a safe investment. Courtelle makes the clothes you wash at home

(no shrinking) and simply drip-dry (no sagging or stretching). When time's precious, Courtelle takes care of itself.

Take a look in the shops — Courtelle clothes are there to give a new, pretty look to your busy life.

COURTELLE *

Regd. Trade Mark for the acrylic fibre made by Courtaulds Limited, 16 St. Martin's-le-Grand, London, E.C.1

Courtauld's promoted their new synthetic fabric Courtelle in Vogue *in March 1960 as washable, durable, yet smart for the business woman. This suit by Koupy Boutique retailed at 15 guineas.*

187

into garments which precisely exploited the artificial qualities of the materials.

By the mid-sixties many believed that there was a marked decline in the quality of the making up of clothes – for instance, machine-stitched hems even on expensive skirts, jackets without linings, and so on. 'Today, clothes can be thrown together, sold quickly and thrown away,' commented Leslie Carr Jones.[49] In the era of nearly full employment in the 1960s no one would any longer admit to needing 'durable' or 'economical' clothes. For the youth market at least, clothes were made to be worn for a few months only.

From the early seventies it was becoming obvious that synthetic fibres lacked the virtues of the wool and silk they imitated. Acrylics were simply not as warm as wool and garments stretched or pilled (roughened) when washed, while most had a hard, unsympathetic 'feel'. Nylon dresses, shirts and underwear acted like steamers in hot weather, since they were impermeable and retained the heat and sweat of the body. In addition the changing aesthetic – the turn towards retro-chic, naturalism and ecological concerns – caused synthetics to fall out of fashion, and they were left to linger on in their unappreciated durability in jumble sales and Oxfam shops.

Although the miniskirts and Courrèges boots, the kipper ties and long hair, the granny spectacles and full-sleeved shirts, almost *are* the Sixties of the collective memory, naturally enough most women and men never went in for the extremes of outrage dressing. Women were not allowed to wear trousers into the Royal Enclosure at Ascot until 1969, a year after men had first been admitted in lounge suits (which very few of them wore). The majority of women could not wear trousers to work at all. In 1970 most professional women were still wearing the 'uncluttered' 1960 uniform of dress and jacket with a smooth, neat hairstyle, although by this time the fashionable were beginning to wear their hair loose, wild and curly. Schoolgirls made unsuccessful attempts to wear trousers to school in cold weather. One young woman was refused entrance to an exclusive London restaurant because she was wearing a trouser suit; having removed the trousers she was allowed in wearing the tunic top only, which passed muster as a minidress. Semi-nudity was more acceptable than bifurcated garb. Men were still expected to wear ties in smart restaurants or clubs, notwithstanding the vogue for Nehru jackets and polo-neck cotton shirts.

In any case, the stereotype of the miniskirted dolly bird began to seem not very liberating after all, as fashions turned from the space age to the inner world of hallucinogens and exoticism. The fashions of the later sixties represented less a sense of liberation than a sense of crisis, confusion and questioning. By that time inflation and unemployment were rising in Britain. On the world stage not only John Kennedy and Martin Luther King but also Bobby Kennedy had been assassinated. Near revolution in France (as it seemed at the time); the Black Panthers in the American ghettoes; the Soviet intervention in Czechoslovakia; above all the Vietnam War – all these bore out the *Queen* forecast of 1959: 'The tense present – the crazy sixties', in ways more serious than that magazine had no doubt intended. Fashion necessarily reflected these tensions, so many of which deeply involved the young. The obvious conflict over style leadership in the world of fashion: between couture and ready-to-wear, between Paris and London, and between the generations, merely joined the many symptoms that pointed not just to an overheated British economy, but to a crisis in democracy, even to an overheating world.

6

$\mathcal{S}$TYLE FOR ALL 1970-90

There have been enormous social changes during the past twenty years. Some writers have argued that they amount to an upheaval on a par with the Industrial Revolution and that we are living in 'post-industrial' or 'post-modern' times. While this appears overstated, a narrower use of the term 'Postmodernism' may capture the disorienting aspect of contemporary society. The term seems first to have been used in art and architecture as – to put it very crudely – a label for pastiche and the haphazard appropriation and mingling of various historical and exotic styles and motifs. Opinion is divided as to whether this is merely nostalgic and indiscriminate or whether it embodies new and less élitist, because more accessible, popular forms.[1]

The postmodern label would certainly fit the way fashion seemed to be going in the seventies. Then, many saw the diversity of haute couture as the 'end of fashion', claiming that there were no longer any rules, that women could wear what they liked, or alternatively that fashion had lost its way and that Paris was in decline. Yet ironically, just at the moment when fashion was pronounced dead, fashions started to appear from all sides, a superfluity of styles: fashions, not fashion.[2] With hindsight, it seems at least possible that this compulsive pluralism of fashion styles was part of the general postmodern aesthetic movement.

The social, political and economic problems that had emerged during the late 1960s intensified during the 1970s and 1980s. The popular image of the 'affluent' 'consensus' society had left out so much. These overused words had been terms for a society in which higher living standards brought social peace. The 'consensus' was a peaceful society, free of

Opposite *By the 1970s cheap youth fashions were being sold in every High Street. This smock and trousers by Geoff Banks, for Miss Selfridge in 1972, is modelled by Josy Numa who worked for Courrèges, the Paris designer. Black models were never used before the 1960s and not until December 1987 did a black model appear on the cover of British* Vogue.

social strife. Living standards were indeed rising throughout the postwar period. On average, low wage earners were better off in real terms at the end of the fifties than at the beginning, and much better off than their parents. Unfortunately, the gap between the low paid and the rich, or the high salaried professional remained. In the seventies and eighties this gap widened, particularly after 1985. Now, affluence no longer brings consensus; on the contrary.

In the 1970s, there was increasing discontent and social polarisation; and some sections of the community were radicalised as an awareness of the continuing inequalities grew. Economic crisis, trades union militancy and the reappearance of protest movements outside existing political structures changed the British social landscape. Old established divisions of class and gender seemed to be breaking up in a society that was moving in different directions simultaneously.

By 1971 there were one million unemployed, and after 1979 the figure climbed above three million. This was accompanied by structural changes in the British economy (and other Western economies as well as the United States) such that new patterns of employment have emerged. In some sectors the gap is widening between a highly skilled and highly paid élite of workers (including some, although a minority, of professional and managerial women), and a mass of unskilled, low paid, non-unionised and often part-time workers, many of them women. Many of these women in turn are migrant workers and/or from black and ethnic minority groups. All this has created a subjective sense of working-class fragmentation and to some extent a loss of working-class identity. At the same time the middle sections of society are growing larger, and new subdivisions have appeared. Estate agents' salespersons, hairdressers, social workers and security personnel are but a few who occupy an amorphous and diverse lower middle class.

Meanwhile, other group identities have emerged more strongly. The women's movement of the 1970s and 1980s pushed the issue of discrimination against women to the fore, and one of the early sources of indignation was the way in which the mass media and the culture generally depicted women. Fashion, and its relationship to a cult of feminine beauty and slenderness, was one target here. More and more women have been entering employment during the last twenty years, although certainly not on equal terms with men, and, worried about the shortage of labour envisaged as a result of the ageing population, the present government has recently stated its wish to support this trend.

Lesbians and gay men were more visible in these decades. Despite continuing prejudice, they made an important contribution to style and the cultural scene.

A third factor which has complicated old class and gender divisions is race. Afro-Caribbean, Asian, African and many other groups and communities have protested in many different ways against a society to which they make an essential contribution, but in which they are often exploited, stereotyped and abused.

The ecological and peace movements have focused on concerns about the environment, nuclear weapons and nuclear energy, pollution, the extinction of many species and even the death of the planet. As the 1980s moved to their close these issues were just beginning seriously to worry established political parties and influence their thinking.

Back to the classics

Despite the 'confusion' of fashion in the seventies, with its riot of alternative garb, couture fashion continued to produce 'classic' styles. In mainstream fashion the search was for 'elegance' and 'wearability'. Partly this was a reaction against the excess of the years 1967–73; partly it was a response to the oil crisis of 1973 (when world oil prices were abruptly raised by OPEC). After that, even rich women wished to spend less on clothes, or if they spent a lot, wanted the clothes to last. Besides, other aspects of consumption were becoming more important; in France, 8.4 per cent of national income was spent on clothing in 1970, but this had fallen to 7 per cent by 1980; by contrast, the amount spent on leisure, sports and holidays had risen. This was consistent with an increasing vogue for sportswear of all kinds as a kind of functional fashion. Similar trends were apparent in Britain and in the United States.

Also, because more women were going out to work, they wanted wearable clothes that were not going to date rapidly. So hemlines settled around the knee; extravagantly flared trousers gradually ceded to *'la ligne cigarette'*, and classic skirts, blouses, sweaters, coats and suits could be worn for years on end without becoming seriously dated.[3]

In fact, it was not just that fashion split in two. Style differences, some obvious, others noticeable only to the initiated, marked off the fragmenting or subdividing classes. 'Fashion for all' in the 1940s and 1950s meant that the New Look began with Dior and 'filtered down' to all levels, diffused everywhere by mass manufacture. 'Style for all' suggests a subtle difference, or a more complex reception of fashion. It is no longer a simple linear process of one fashion following another and gradually being diffused. Different groups adopt different fashions and make them their own.

193

Fragmented style

Whether part of the spirit of the Postmodernist age or not, pastiche and retro-chic were among the most important trends of the early to mid-seventies. This 'nostalgia mode' – the revamping of fashions from a slightly earlier period – was already noticeable in the 1960s. The 1967 film *Bonnie and Clyde* popularised thirties fashion; *Viva Maria*, which starred Jeanne Moreau and Brigitte Bardot in 1965, and *Far from the Madding Crowd* (Julie Christie and Terence Stamp), 1968, drew on Edwardian fashions and frills.[4] The success of Biba, based to a large extent on retro-chic, spanned the period from the mid-sixties to the mid-seventies, and Biba style was on the cusp between 'fashion' and 'style', marking the transition from one to the other.

Some have admired retro-chic for its 'irony', and even as an ideal feminist fashion – it dispensed with extravagance but was full of camp chic.[5] Retro-chic reappeared as a pastiche of the 1970s in the spring 1989 Paris collections, when Martine Sitbon, Jean Paul Gaultier and Christian Lacroix all showed this 'pastiche of a pastiche'. (Martine Sitbon was on a French-exchange, learning English in Brighton, in the mid-seventies, and acknowledges that her current clothes are a fantasy memory of that time.) Writing of this 'seventies revival', Sarah Mower of *Vogue*, far from seeing it as subtle or ironic, dismissed it as 'stylistic bankruptcy'.[6]

In the 1970s, it was the 1940s that were coming back into fashion, from Yves St Laurent versions to second-hand 'frocks'. One exponent of forties style was Lee Bender, whose dress shop chain Bus Stop rivalled Biba in catering to the young and trendy. Like Biba she, too, had a shop in Kensington Church Street. Her style – puffed sleeves, sweetheart neck-lines, jazzy colours and materials that bordered on sleaze (deliberately shiny rayon or nylon for example) – had an affinity with the mid-seventies glam-rock of David Bowie's Ziggy Stardust. Platform sole shoes, worn by both men and women, became clumpier and clumpier and were constructed in variegated primary colours.

The haphazard mixing of different styles of retro and ethnic fashions, which often overlapped one another, made possible the making of many different 'statements'. Hippie fashions for lace, long skirts and a lavish assortment of old silk scarves, beads and hats, antique prints and shrunken Fair Isle sweaters had seemed to represent the creation not only of a lost past but also of some more 'natural', Cotswoldy communal life. This had an unconscious resonance with the aesthetic dress of the 1890s. Leather, glam-rock (copied from David Bowie and Gary Glitter), red lipstick, platform soles and second-hand fur coats evoked an entirely different world, a reminiscence of *film noir* rather than aesthetic dress, of decadence rather than authenticity.

Yet what they shared was 'retro' or pastiche itself. The clothes created a myth, or many myths, about the 'past' – or sometimes about a mythic 'America' – and hopefully imbued the wearer with the glamour of nostalgia. At the same time, the skill with which a diverse assortment of bits and pieces from different periods and cultures was put together was highly individualistic and even élitist; it might be a 'poor' look if you wore second-hand clothes, but it showed you had time to spend if not money, in searching out the unique garment, and taste in choosing the one little frock that was 'right for you'.

The appeal of retro dressing was that a trawl through the Portobello Road or the North Laine shops in Brighton might yield the reward of a genuine Burberry, a real silk slip or blouse, a genuine Harris tweed jacket, even an original 'middle-class couture' suit. Therefore, the code of 'classic good taste' was never abandoned, indeed it could reappear quite

The pop group Culture Club, particularly its famous lead singer Boy George, created a 'gender bending' style of dress. He used ethnic motifs (Jamaican dreadlocks and Hasidic Jewish hat) and flaunted make-up. Girl fans copied his style, which influenced mainstream fashion in the mid-1980s.

openly in male modes, which made young men resemble Edward, Prince of Wales, in the 1920s, Leslie Howard, the true Brit Hollywood filmstar of the thirties, or a whole covey of rising TV and cinema stars playing upper-middle-class men of the between-the-wars period. Perhaps the apotheosis of this look came with the television adaptation of Evelyn Waugh's novel *Brideshead Revisited* in 1981.

The avant-garde had already grown tired of hippie naturalism by the mid-seventies, and in 1976 Punk first caught the attention of the public. This counter-cultural movement which caused alarm drew on themes similar to Surrealism and was really a classic case of avant-garde shock tactics. An assault on all received notions of taste, it is significant in being almost the only one of the postwar youth/culture/music movements fully to have integrated women. The style alluded to sado-masochism, porn sleaze and tawdry glamour and inscribed itself by means of shaven or partially shaven heads and a sort of anti-make-up (reddened eyes, black lips, make-up painted in streaks across the face or in a pattern) on the surface of the body. Punks created an alienated space between self and appearance by means of these attacks on their own bodies; this was truly fit wear for the urban dispossessed, constructed out of the refuse of the material world: rusty razor blades, tin cans, safety pins, dustbin bags[7] and even used tampons.

The Punk style seems to have started in the autumn of 1974. Then, Malcolm McLaren, who had formed and was promoting the Punk rock band the Sex Pistols, renamed the Kings Road shop he owned with Vivienne Westwood. It had started life as Let It Rock in 1971 and had become Too Fast to Live, Too Young to Die the following year. Now it was simply called Sex (and would become Seditionaries in 1977). There Westwood designed bondage trousers and clothes based on leather, corsetry, rubber and 'kinky gear'. The dedicated ugliness, noise and anger of the Punk bands, including the women's band Siouxsie and the Banshees, quickly became notorious and the power to shock reached a cultural climax in 1977 with Derek Jarman's Punk film *Jubilee*.

In the mid-seventies this seemed far removed from haute couture. Paris was, however, influenced by alternative fashion and devised a layered look which drew on a wide variety of ethnic styles. Yves St Laurent, for example, designed a Russian collection, but this was not incompatible with 'classic' long coats and boots and full skirts. New Italian, American and Japanese haute couture and ready-to-wear designers were challenging the stylistic dominance of Paris, and British designers began to come back strongly in the early 1980s. In Italy, in the early eighties, Giorgio Armani and Cerruti led the way in producing a version of what became known as 'power dressing', with Marlene Dietrich trousers and straight

Opposite In the late 1970s the unfamiliarity and aggression of Punk clothes aroused deep hostility. A decade later Matt Belgrano, here travelling on the London Tube, has become a media star. In his multi-coloured Mohican haircut and clothes, he features in advertisements and chat shows.

Since the 1950s British colleges of art and design have produced two generations of young creative designers. This leather skirt by Bill Gibb was one of his earliest designs from his degree collection at St Martin's School of Art, London, in June 1972.

cut jackets for women and men. Versace produced flamboyant fashions in which fur, leather and gold featured prominently. In the mid-eighties a new Italian designer, Romeo Gigli, began to produce softer, more fluid clothes, and by 1990 fashion style generally was moving towards a new, more sinuous version of classicism, with wider trousers, richer, softer colours and the use of softly draping materials such as crêpe: a renewal of 1930s elegance without the pastiche feel of the seventies versions.

The influence of American designers such as Norma Kamili with her use of grey sweatshirt fabric and Calvin Klein and Ralph Lauren's classic simplicity brought American style to an international level. Power dressing, also from the USA, took a more flamboyant turn in the mid-eighties under the influence of the TV soap operas *Dallas* and *Dynasty*. Millions around the world watched these fantasies of American wealthy lifestyles, and many of the fashions were adopted in modified form for the High Street. Padded shoulders and big jackets appeared again, together with shiny materials, matching hats, tight skirts, high heels, hair carefully tinted and layered to flow copiously but stay off the face, and peach blusher and lip gloss created a look that was artificial yet banal. This was – and is – a successful High Street style when translated into leather jackets (black or coloured) and tight, short denim skirts or, sometimes, jeans, and sweaters ornamented with sequins or satin appliqué embroidery.

A more lavish and formal version has been adopted as a public style of dress by the slowly increasing numbers of women in the professions and the media, for example, women politicians. At the very top, members of the Royal Family, and especially Princess Diana, have worn couture versions. Power dressing is associated with the use of bright, often harsh colours – royal blue, magenta, jade green. For public figures these are functional, since they enable the wearer to stand out from the crowd.

A related style was the American 'dress for success' look, an ultra-cautious, conservative approach for women making an assault on the boardroom (or, more likely, the lower ranks of line management). Writing in the *Observer* in 1984, a rather embittered City woman banker, who felt she had to use a pseudonym, complained that the joining together of the two words 'woman' and 'banking' appeared to be a contradiction in terms, and 'the young woman with Christian Dior glasses and a Jaeger suit' appeared unable to convince colleagues that she was as capable as her male counterparts.[8] The 'dress for success' model appears to mean treading an impossibly thin line between masculinity and femininity. To look mannish would put men off; but it would also put them off if you flaunted your feminine sexuality. The outcome is a kind of suppressed, sexless, air hostess look; a neutral-coloured or black coat and skirt that may be mass produced from manmade fibres, or beautifully cut in real wool at the couture level; careful shoes and dark stockings; careful peach make-up and tidy hair. In 1988, a *Guardian* correspondent described how a dreary 'Euro-uniform' was taking over the business centre districts of capital cities throughout the EEC – women and men dressed in dark, sober, executive suits, with leather briefcases and sleek hair.[9] To help women achieve the required look, 'style counsellors' have multiplied. They offer (usually expensive) advice on style 'etiquette' and colour matching.

The new generation of professional women and female financiers has never attempted to radicalise their collective uniform by wearing trousers. Today, trousers have completely lost their power to shock, in the sense that no one any longer thinks them indecent or sexually provocative; but the taboo on trousers is still used to police women in most professions, a significant symbol of the fact that women have yet to be accepted on equal terms in any of the higher echelons of employment, especially management, business and banking.

199

The conservatism of professional dress would seem to be a far cry from Punk yet, perhaps surprisingly, a number of Punk motifs have been incorporated into mainstream fashion. Critics compared Punk in its initial manifestation to Surrealist art of the 1920s and 1930s, which had aimed to shock with its use of obscene imagery and irrational juxtapositions. Yet Surrealism, originally so anarchic and anti-Establishment, eventually contributed many motifs to advertising, and Punk, too, has proved surprisingly adaptable as well as enduring. By the mid-eighties, the Punks had been assimilated to British eccentricity, as much a tourist attraction in the Kings Road as the changing of the guard at Buckingham Palace, and Punk style had modified the mainstream.

Bright red lipstick and black eye make-up, boldly dyed or streaked hair, and 'ugly' short hair cuts – shaved necks and spiked crowns stiffened with gel – replaced the naturalism of free floating hennaed curls; four earrings in one ear became a style cliché; black leather, short skirts and black tights became a metropolitan work uniform for young women in the late 1980s. Many young men also took the hairstyles and the tough image. This stylistic shift was partly due to the influence of the Parisian haute couture designer Jean Paul Gaultier, who always claimed that his inspiration came from the Kings Road.

The impact of Japanese haute couture is difficult to gauge, although it received enormous publicity in the early 1980s. At their most uncompromising the Japanese couturiers used a cut and structure wholly alien to that of Western dress. It concealed rather than emphasised the shape of the body, and was not even constructed with conventional armholes and fastenings. In the spring of 1983, the Comme des Garçons collection by Rei Kawakubo, dubbed in rather bad taste the 'Post Hiroshima look', created a sensation:

Down the catwalk, marching to a rhythmic beat like a race of warrior women, came models wearing ink-black coat dresses, cut big, square, away from the body with no line, form, or recognizable silhouette.

 The fabric is full of surface interest; velvet mixed with hand-cut cord, cotton woven with wool, with funnels of fabric falling into a cowl neck or tied round the body at random. . . . From the soles of her rice-paddy slippers or square-toed rubber shoes to the top of her black rag-tied head (lower lip painted a bruised blue), this is a creature from a race apart.[10]

More rudely, these unfamiliar garments were described as: 'a whole cornucopia of shapeless, arbitrary Zen styles, executed in impeccably Zen shades of earth, granite, foam and dung, and in fabrics which would appear to have been somewhat carelessly stored in cesspits since the early Edo period. . . .'[11]

The extreme versions of the Japanese style do seem to have proved untranslatable into High Street fashions, but, along with Punk, they rein-

The ragged 'post-Hiroshima' collection by the Japanese designer Rei Kawakubo for Comme des Garçons, of spring 1983, was mocked as radical and feminist, but was nevertheless influential.

forced the vogue for black, and contributed to the generally bulky and shapeless look of some mid-eighties styles, especially the long, square jackets with voluminous skirts, flat heels, and knitwear which looked as if it was inside out with the seams showing. The challenging influence of Japanese haute couture certainly contributed to the urban sobriety of fashion in the mid-eighties.

The Japanese did not have it all their own way at the Paris 1983 collections. Ranged against them were the rival Paris designers Thierry Mugler and Azzedine Alaia who showed tight-fitting, sexy clothes. The *Times'* fashion correspondent concluded: 'I am intellectually with the Japanese in their search for clothing that owes nothing to out-worn concepts of femininity. But both Claude Montana and Chloe can have my body to dress.'[12] In retrospect the Japanese style of the early 1980s seems to have been the logical conclusion of an alternative society 'recession dressing' look and an expression of the 'aesthetic of poverty', harking back to the 1970s rather than prefiguring – as it seemed at the time – the shape of things to come.

Mass advertising campaigns competing for the lucrative jeans market have drawn on youthful British nostalgia for the dress and music of 1950s America. Lee Jeans used a 1950s car to promote the 'Red Star' Rough Ride jeans in 1988.

Just as there was continuity between the fifties and the sixties, despite the surface contrasts, so, in fashion at least, there is much to link the seventies with the eighties, although superficially it is easy to contrast counter-cultural and ethnic fashion in the 1970s with 'designer madness' and the return to more conventional forms of display in the 1980s. One aspect of this continuity is the steady popularity of jeans.

In the fifties, James Dean in *Rebel Without a Cause* became the epitome of the alienated adolescent and made jeans the symbol of teenage rebellion. Marlon Brando in *The Wild One* did the same thing for the black leather jacket, an even more threatening garment. In the sixties, blue jeans were again the symbol of youth and the spirit of 1968. In the early seventies jeans were one of a number of kinds of work clothes – boiler suits, dungarees, cord trousers and donkey jackets – that became virtuous because of their association with manual toil. Later on they were given a new lease of life for the opposite reason, by becoming designer jeans: the same denim, the same shape, but with a label – Gloria Vanderbilt, say – sewn on the back pocket or waistband.

"ROUGH RIDE"
The new commercial from Lee

If these jeans seemed too new, too fake, you could buy 'stonewashed' or 'distressed' jeans, or genuine second-hand ones from the United States, actually torn by the previous owner. Cheap jeans were available from Hong Kong, later from Taiwan and other countries producing basic clothing at the bottom end of the market. The 'genuine' second-hand article could cost almost as much as designer jeans – £40 in the summer of 1988. By this time there was also a specifically British craze for equally genuine, but new, original 501 (fly button) jeans, in either blue or black denim, and a look that reproduced the original 1950s American teenager with uncanny accuracy, popularised by Levi's memorable advertising campaign. Both jeans and the leather jacket – the original signifier of the teenage outlaw – could live on as classic rather than as rebellion garments. The secret of their enduring popularity may be partly that they form an element of several divergent and indeed contrasting modes of dress.

Jeans still form an essential item in a number of sub-cultural styles which have continued to flourish in so far as they reflect the stubborn vibrancy of some groups in the face of changed, troubled and more repressive times. Punk-derived styles have continued to be fashionable in gay male and lesbian circles, while there has been raging controversy among lesbians about extreme bondage styles and – at the other extreme – ultra-feminine dressing.

Gay culture represents a minority, but it has always had an important influence on mainstream culture. In the early eighties gay style was an integral part of the nightclubbing scene. The new clubs were the stage for 'the blurring of sexual divisions in an orgy of costume'. This became known as blitz culture. (Blitz was the name of the club where it all started.) The style was known as New Romantic – to be followed by a rapid kaleidoscope of style, particularly for extravagantly dressed 'peacock' men. Gay or straight, they played with transvestism: a feminine masquerade for men. This was gender bending.[13] (The style of the romantics eventually influenced some of the clothes designed for Princess Diana in the early eighties, especially the large organdie collars and droopy bows.)

Black style has also always been important, going back to the birth of jazz at the turn of the century and right through the forties, the period of zoot suits and be-bop. Before skinheads or Mods were heard of, 'the young Stevie Wonder, on the cover of his *Little Stevie* album, 1962, sported the clothes that were to become the mainstays of skins' and Mods' wardrobes. These were shiny Sta-prest short trousers, Fred Perry top and dark sunglasses.'[14] In the 1970s, nightclub culture was the setting for the development of new styles by the rising generation of black Britons, who

203

invented the 'casuals' style taken up by white teenagers in the early eighties, when label clothes, cashmere sweaters and Burberrys were the vogue among the young. In the mid-eighties there were Armani-based black styles and, more recently, a return to sportswear label styles.[15]

These were largely male styles. Black women began to be more visible in the presentation of mainstream fashion in the eighties. *Vogue* featured a Black model on its cover for the first time in December 1987, but a Black woman has yet to appear on the cover of magazines such as *Woman* and *Woman's Own.*

Some young professional-class Asian women have also developed their own styles, moving away from the traditional sari towards a style, for evenings at least, based on the 'loose tunic (*kameez*) and baggy Indo-Pakistani trousers (*shalwar*) of the north'. These fashions were shown in late 1988 at a dinner given by the Asian City Club, 25 per cent of whose members are women, who would in most cases wear Western clothes to work.[16] A new magazine, *Libas*, now caters specifically to this market.

All these groups are relatively small, but their existence, and their demand for their own styles, testifies to changes in British society that are part of the fragmentation or subdivision mentioned at the beginning of this chapter. At the same time, new British designers have emerged from the Black community: Bruce Oldfield and Joe Casely-Hayford, for example. Oldfield dresses Princess Diana and Joan Collins; Casely-Hayford dresses big stars such as Annie Lennox, Michael Jackson and Sade, and also sells his designs in outlets such as Joseph, Harrods and Harvey Nichols in London.

One of the most important features of eighties style has been the success of style magazines such as *The Face*, *i-D*, and *Blitz*. These magazines both took up street styles and publicised new avant-garde designers. For the first time, a male as much as a female audience was addressed. Designers and manufacturers have increased their interest in men's fashion in the 1980s, and a growing interest in male fashion and even face and body products has been reflected in the emergence of new style magazines directed at them. In 1988 Nick Logan, publisher of *The Face*, launched *Arena*, to be followed by an American men's magazine, *QD*. The newly glamorous, male style setter of the eighties became as familiar in magazines and advertisements as his female counterpart, with his hair, short at the back, long at the front, sleekly gelled, his looks mean and tough, yet simultaneously blankly narcissistic. This new man is the empty object of anyone's desire, his sexuality ambiguous. It is unclear whether his beauty is destined for men or for women.

Juliet Ash has dated the new direction in menswear to 1984, and suggests that it happened because of two factors:

204

Vivienne Westwood's 1981 'pirate look', with a slim short skirt, was one of several fashion trends which she originated. Another was the mini-crin skirt of 1987, which later influenced Christian Lacroix.

First, in the design world gay male designers at last had the confidence to design flamboyantly for their own sex . . . and young women designers were similarly gaining the confidence to design clothes for men, whether through an acknowledgement of the challenge that designing menswear presented or through sheer lust.[17]

The 'New Man' who was talked up by the media – a non-macho, caring person who could express his feelings – was a myth. 'What was more interesting than the New Man as fashion victim and consumer in 1984–5 was . . . the simultaneous advent of menswear designed by women designers, particularly in Britain.' Jean Muir's designs for men appeared in *Vogue* in July 1986, and at the London fashion shows in the autumn of that year Wendy Dagworthy, Ally Capellino, Katherine Hamnett, Elaine Challoner and Amanda Quarry all showed menswear.[18]

Rebellion impossible

The word 'lifestyle' and the fashions with which it is associated have undergone a significant change in the 1980s. In the early 1970s 'lifestyle' went with 'politics' and denoted an alternative way of life which could include squatting, the search for spiritual self-improvement and radical activism. Alternative dress was part of this lifestyle, and particularly the appropriation of second-hand clothes.

Today 'lifestyles' is a marketing term, a cliché of the designer catalogues. Even the uniform of jeans and leather jacket has lost – according to one commentator at least – the last remnants of deviance:

> The leather biker jacket, far from signalling danger, has become a well-behaved modern classic. . . . Leather has become respectable whilst pretending to be wild; double-think style for a generation that has forgotten how to be angry.
>
> Biker style is the end of the line for what was once called street fashion – youth style confronting establishment dressing with clothes that would deliberately disturb the status quo. This is partly due to apathy . . . and partly . . . to a reluctance to shock. . . . But mostly it is the result of the commercialisation of style which has made rebellion impossible. . . . No one may wear an outlaw style without its being written up, stolen and sanitised for the high street. . . .
>
> Traditional images of revolt have been used to sell establishment products.[19]

The photographs that illustrated this *cri de coeur* were of 'outlaw' fashions selling at from £90 to £900: not exactly within the price range of the urban underclass.

Meanwhile, second-hand clothes are no longer an expression of choice, but an unwelcome necessity. For, as poverty and unemployment have increased, so have second-hand shops. No longer, though, is it such fun to search the rails for a genuine 1940s suit. Antique markets still have their little boutiques, but now the tweed suits and silk blouses change hands at anything from £20 to £80. Meanwhile the Oxfam and Age Concern shops with their indeterminate, indestructibly shabby coats and

Since the late 1960s second-hand shops have once again become an important source of clothes: on the one hand for the radical or more avant-garde young in search of originality and nostalgia, on the other for growing numbers of unemployed and really poor, including older women and men.

Crimplene dresses offer cheap clothes to pensioners, the unemployed and students. Second-hand clothes in the late 1980s, therefore, tend to convey a very different meaning from the wistful chic and ironic tawdriness that the hippies lent them twenty years ago. One Glasgow mother, her husband among the long-term unemployed, described, just before Christmas 1988, how she spends the family Giro of £61.19 a week:

Most of your money goes on food. But my kids hardly ever have fruit. They have vegetables but it's out of tins. Same with meat, not fresh, always tins, the only shop around here is the van and he's awful expensive. I do go up the market where you get cheap bashed-in tins of stew. . . .

The other thing is clothes. When I get the Child Benefit each month [£87] I go and buy the clothes for the children but it's all cheap stuff and it never lasts. I bought them shoes, not cheap, £7.99 a pair, but if I could have paid £15 they would last much longer. For my clothes I go to the second-hand shop. Even there it's quite expensive. It cost me £7 for two dresses and a cardigan. Otherwise I wait for the jumble sales for my pants, bras, jumpers.[20]

Couture in the eighties

By the end of the 1980s Paris haute couture had changed almost beyond recognition from what it had been in the 1930s. The designers were no longer dressmakers for an exclusive private clientèle. There are now only abut 3000 women in the world who can afford haute couture originals (only six of these are British) at prices which start at £1000 and reach £30 000 for a full-scale evening dress. An exclusive hand-beaded garment can cost as much as £60 000. Even Ivana Trump, wife of the billionaire who built the Trump Tower complex in Manhattan, has announced that in future she will buy American couture. The Paris design establishment has become one of the major world industries, but there are clearly tensions between its international marketing role and its status as the world centre of fashion design.

The departure of Romeo Gigli from Milan to Paris in the spring of 1989 (Versace has also left for Paris, and so has Valentino from Rome) would seem to underline the dominance of Paris in the marketing of couture and *prêt-à-porter*, yet the changing economics of the whole fashion industry place conflicting pressures on the haute couture houses. The trend towards franchising, licensing and ready-to-wear which became so evident in the 1950s and 1960s intensified markedly from the early 1980s, and now forms the basis of the industry.

This means that the fashion designers themselves have to fulfil divergent functions. They must continue to produce variations on the 'wearable', 'classic' designs, which can be copied in many different price ranges for ready-to-wear, but they must also create sensational prototype new lines which will generate publicity and thus feed the glamour image

207

upon which the sale of their scents and other 'accessory' products is based.

Haute couture is still a showcase for the miraculous dressmaking skills, fabulous fabrics and elaborate modern technology that go to the making of design originals today, but the relevance of the designs themselves is not always clear.[21] Many of the garments shown on the catwalks are intentionally exaggerated to win front-page publicity and to suggest trends rather than to be copied exactly. Since there is no longer the discipline of having to produce directly for individual private customers, there must be an increased risk that these designs will prove to be out of touch with what is acceptable to the public. On the other hand, the continual production of wearable classics risks being dismissed as 'boring' (which is how some fashion journalists described the spring 1989 Milan collections).

In other words, there is a curious paradox at the heart of the contemporary fashion industry. As its empire expands further and further, the fashion design on which it is ultimately based is in danger of becoming ever more divorced from the millions of women who wear the designer label, middle-market or bucket-shop versions of garments of which the label itself is more significant than the actual design.

Christian Lacroix is a case in point. In 1986 he launched his couture collection, with backing from the Dior financiers. He made headlines with his short, puffball skirts, rose prints and *décolleté* necklines, leading to journalistic predictions of a 'New New Look' and the return of women to the home. Despite the general hype, some fashion journalists reacted with dismay. As it turned out, 'acres of off-the-shoulder, short, frilly frou-frou things stolidly stayed on the rails for three seasons running; to their great consternation, retailers found they could hardly *give* them away'.[22] In late 1988 Lacroix issued a newsletter, which admitted to 'problems' in selling his first ready-to-wear collection, although he blamed the difficulties on the puritanism of the Americans.[23] Presumably his backers are now hoping that the next ready-to-wear designer collection will be more successful, and counting on a successful perfume launch to recoup their massive investment.

Today, haute couture could not possibly survive on private customers – and the houses employ more staff than the sum total of private buyers. Especially in France, they are increasingly run by specialised finance operations, and this has meant that designers themselves are no longer in direct financial control. For example, Madame Grès, a doyenne of French haute couture since the 1930s, was last year the victim of a take-over deal, as a result of which twenty out of her thirty-one employees were not paid for many months.[24]

One of the most successful of the fashion empires, Dior, earns only 3 per cent of total income from haute couture. The house of Balenciaga signed thirty-four new licensing agreements in 1988, from women's ready-to-wear to hosiery. Sales from their licensing division rose from 36 000 000 francs to 72 000 000 francs (£3 600 000–£7 200 000) in 1987, and were said to be likely to double again in 1988.[25]

The selling power of international couturier names is so lucrative that counterfeiters risk imprisonment to cash in. The *Observer* reported on 3 March 1985 the trial of three men jailed for producing counterfeit Chanel No 5. They had been able to do this because 'Chanel's UK subsidiary,

THERE ARE WOMEN
WHO KNOW HOW
TO BE LATE.

watches/lighters/pens/jewellery

YVESSAINTLAURENT
Collection

In the style-conscious 1980s, famous designer names have been used increasingly to launch million-dollar licensed products on to the market. This has brought designer labels to the mass market. Yves St Laurent advertises the complete power-dressers' kit, aimed at women as well as men.

209

Chanel Ltd, sells Chanel No 5 only through 1200 selected outlets, [such as] Harrods.' Non-approved retailers wishing to sell the exclusive products have to find other ways of obtaining them. It would appear that Chanel limit their outlets in order to retain the exclusiveness of their product and also because their profits are already so huge:

Chanel Ltd imports its supplies, ready packaged, from its French parent. Figures given in court . . . revealed that at the time of the arrests, the real Chanel No 5, in 14 ml bottles, was bought by Chanel Ltd for between £4.00 and £4.50 a bottle.

They then sold this to retailers at £14.71 per bottle. The recommended retail price was £27.50. . . .

During the trial, defence lawyers suggested that the bulk cost of Chanel No 5 to the French manufacturing company could be as low as 50p.

It is instructive to compare the financial success of the big French haute couture empires with the situation in which British design has again found itself at the close of the 1980s. London design saw a renaissance developing through the decade, with new names such as John Galliano, Jasper Conran, Bruce Oldfield, Rifat Ozbek, Arabella Pollen, Vivienne Westwood, Betty Jackson and Bodymap enjoying rapid success. In this they were assisted by the fortuitous but fortunate emergence of Princess Diana as a fashion leader. The Princess deliberately associated herself with the promotion of British fashion and has been a great asset to the industry. Her clothes, particularly the hats, collars and accessories, have been copied at every level.

There are serious problems, however, for the majority of the many talented designers who still emerge from the British art and design schools. Although big firms such as Next and Marks and Spencer take on young talent, it has become almost a cliché to point out that many British designers have been forced to go abroad in order to gain the jobs and recognition they deserve. Many Italian companies, well aware of the shortcomings of their own art schools, either buy British textile designs and re-sell them to Britain, or else employ British designers, for example Keith Varty at Byblos and Elizabeth Griffiths at Missoni, both of whom trained at St Martin's School of Art.

Two problems were already emerging in the early 1980s. There was a 'political controversy' as to whether fashion departments in art schools should be turning out artists or industrial designers. It seemed as if there was a 'class' or snob divide in Britain between the designers and cutters and other technicians. Jean Muir stated her belief in the importance of a thorough grounding in practical skills and knowledge of the industry:

'I don't want to be negative. . . . Of course I want to see instinctive, marvellous, creative designers. But, at best, you are going to find one of those a year. The rest aren't even taught properly the way the sys-

Opposite (right) The Royal Family has always influenced British fashion. Since her marriage Princess Diana has been the most important Royal fashion star. She chooses British design fashions to help promote the British fashion industry. The blue silk evening dress she wears here is by the Chelsea Design Company, November 1987.

Opposite (left) This strapless (polyester crêpe) evening dress, sold through Freemans' mail order catalogue in 1987–8 at £39.95, reproduces the Princess Di style in evening wear for the popular market.

tem works, let alone how to do good pattern making and cutting. I don't expect them to be able to cut like Balenciaga – or even to be as good as me. But I think that far too much emphasis is put on the sketch.'

Jean Muir set out her views in a trenchant paper to the Royal Society of Arts in November 1981. She said that the separation of design and manufacturing in Britain meant that any embryo designer should be taught to undertake both roles. 'Why should we complain or boast that many of our good young designers go abroad?' she asks. 'Surely that should point to the fact that we are not training them for the situation as it exists in this country.'[26]

In response to this, and to like criticisms from British manufacturers, it appeared that many courses had become more industry conscious. Jeff Banks, on the other hand, took a rather different view:

'It would be a great shame to limit the creative expansion of the colleges . . . creative stimulation is what arts education is about. We need to have people in designing, retailing and marketing who have an understanding of what style, design and taste can achieve. Nowadays there are machines to cut patterns and computers to grade them. It is industry that has failed to appreciate what creative designers can do.'

He takes six to ten graduates a year into his company, *but then puts them through his own training scheme.* At the end of his course he says that students (who receive a diploma) 'will have a thorough grounding in fashion and retailing. They can all make a contribution . . . it's the fault of industry if it cannot appreciate how to use design talent and abilities within a corporate organisation.'[27]

At the same period, *Vogue* was blaming the government and British industry for not realising what a valuable asset British design talent and the British fashion industry were. This continues to be the underlying problem: just as British haute couture in the late fifties was unable to follow Paris into the franchising and licensing, so the underfinancing and consequent lack of international status continues today. It is hardly surprising if young British designers descend to what one fashion correspondent described as 'slovenly presentation' and 'egotistic posturing' or that British couture is regarded as 'eccentric', when business and finance appear to regard it as in some way aberrant and not worth support.[28] This is extraordinarily short-sighted, for British clothing exports amount to £1.2 billion, of which, in 1986, £163 million went to the United States, and the industry employs nearly half a million persons, roughly 9 per cent of the whole manufacturing force.[29]

By contrast, Italian and French ready-to-wear has blossomed. Giorgio Armani and Jean Paul Gaultier produce ready-to-wear or 'diffusion' lines costing in the range of £200 to £700 for a suit or dress. Giorgio Armani's turnover has reached almost £200 million a year. At least one British designer, Katherine Hamnett, has managed to break into this big league. Originally famous for her protest T-shirts, Hamnett was signed in 1989 by the Italian company CGA, and her clothes will now be sold internationally as well as in 350 mixed designer stores in Britain.[30]

Related to the intensive marketing of design clothes is the trend towards publication of *free* glossy magazines, supported entirely by advertising, in which fashion plays a key role. One of the earliest was *Portrait*, launched in 1981. It is distributed only to 100 000 high-value properties in London. Today, there are 500 such magazines, compared to 70 when *Portrait* first appeared. They are very profitable, and market an exclusive lifestyle as much through their advertising as through their editorial copy.[31]

The retail revolution

It is impossible to discuss designer clothes in isolation from the retailing methods that have transformed shopping, not only in Britain, but all over the Western world, and indeed in the majority of urban centres of the entire globe. The decline of the department store has accelerated. Many, of course, survive successfully. On Kensington High Street in London, where there were four department stores in the 1950s, one now remains. In the early seventies, Biba took over another, Derry and Toms. There she created a whole Biba universe, retaining complete the Art Deco interiors, carpets and fittings. Young women flocked to hang out in its cavernous ground floor, with the sepia walls, window seats, dim lighting and throbbing music, but a boutique couldn't be reproduced on this giant scale. The venture failed in 1975 and the limit point of both retro-chic and department store shopping had been reached. Sadly, but in the spirit of the coming decade, the store interior was gutted, to be replaced by the banal beige carpets and neon lighting of yet another M & S and BHS. In 1987 the Next flagship store opened almost opposite, but despite its café and interiors section, this is not a department store on the old model, where the leisured woman could spend a whole morning, meet friends for coffee or for lunch and have dress fittings in private cubicles; it is somewhere between a small shop and a large chain store.

The top department stores, Harvey Nichols, Harrods and Fortnum and Mason in London, for example, have followed the American pattern – found at its most glamorous in Bloomingdale's, New York – and gone for shops within shops, where clothes are arranged according to designer labels. More significant is the general changing pattern of High Street retailing, with a massive development of boutique chains. Next is the most obvious example, but Principles and Laura Ashley and, in London, Hobbs and Warehouse (financed by Sears), are other examples.

These, for the most part middle-market operations, have aimed to capitalise on the success of expensive boutiques selling designer originals or ready-to-wear. Consequently they have promoted their clothes as

*Some designers associate themselves with particular subcultures. Sarah Whitworth, of **Deadlier Than The Male**, sells her corseted Victorian-inspired evening wear from Hyper-Hyper, which houses many designers in High Street, Kensington. Her clothes are admired alike by elegant party-goers and followers of the 'Goth' street style.*

'designer label' clothes in their own right, though at lower prices. The pioneer of the designer boutique was probably Joan Burstein's South Molton Street shop, Browns. Joan Burstein's parents had owned the Neatawear chain, which had been very successful at selling low-priced High Street underwear and young women's fashions in the years after the war, but which faltered disastrously in the sixties. Joan Burstein herself had worked at Feathers, one of the Kensington High Street boutiques that blossomed in the wake of Biba, Bus Stop and the hippie trail.

In 1970 she opened Browns with a display of haute couture ready-to-wear from Daniel Hechter, Emmanuelle Khan and Cacherel, and soon followed with Sonia Rykiel, Missoni, Comme des Garçons and, today, Romeo Gigli. She brought Milan and Tokyo to the smart women of London, and the result has been that many of these designer names now have their own shop fronts. Emporio Armani, opened in 1989, is the latest of these. The Joseph and Whistles shops have followed her in catering to relatively rich youngish buyers who want genuinely exclusive clothes.

Although most of these are metropolitan enterprises, boutiques have blossomed in towns and cities in other parts of the country. The *Observer* described one called Pollyanna in Barnsley, Yorkshire, seemingly an unlikely place for the sale of Jean Muir and Romeo Gigli, but Rita Britton, the owner, and a Barnsley woman herself, says that ordinary local women buy her clothes. One, a sixty-year-old occupational health nursing officer, spends about £400 a year on Jean Muir classics. Another, at twenty-five years old the manageress of a middle-market clothing shop in the town, spends about £100 a month at Pollyanna, keeping it a secret from her ex-miner boyfriend. A forty-four-year-old antiques collector, photographed wearing a Jean Muir black leather jacket, price £1150, and matching skirt at £450, would not reveal how much she spent: 'Let's just say I spend a lot of money.'[32]

The Joseph shops went in for high tech interiors, but the more general pattern has been to follow the retro-period feel that Biba pioneered in the sixties, and furnish small shops with polished wooden shelves and a veneer of 'old fashionedness'. This trend is not confined to the marketing of clothes, but is a general part of the 'heritage industry'. The interior styles of both domestic furnishing and of retail chains such as Crabtree and Evelyn, which sell toiletries and some foods (jam and pickles), have all been marketing a fantasy of the 'traditional', related to tourism. Central areas of some of Britain's oldest cities − York is a good example − have become pedestrian precinct shopping malls lined with these small shops, which promote an image of individuality, whereas in reality they are outlets for huge conglomerates. This 'traditional' style has also cashed in on the ecology consciousness of the eighties. The toiletries of

Crabtree and Evelyn and Body Shop, and the flowery cottons of Laura Ashley provide a commercialised version of the lost, cottagy, rural past.

The clothing industry, like many others, has seen the development of monopolisation, and by 1987 ten companies controlled 50 per cent of the British clothing trade. Burtons, whose chief executive is Sir Ralph Halpern, owns Debenhams, Top Shop, Top Man, Principles, Principles for Men, Evans, Dorothy Perkins and Harvey Nichols: 1417 outlets and 9 per cent of the British retail market.[33] Conran-Storehouse plc owns BHS, Mothercare, Richard Shops, Habitat and Heals. Laura Ashley sales rose by 29 per cent in 1986, to reach £77.4 million.[34]

George Davies's Next chain has been the most publicised of successes such as these. With 687 outlets, their profits in 1987–8 reached £92.4 million.[35] Davies launched the Next chain of women's fashions shops from the shell of the menswear chain Hepworths. Next has always stated

The Next chain, founded by George Davies in 1984, was the first to develop a new trend in High Street marketing: chains of small shops selling a 'total look' (clothes, accessories and jewellery) or even a complete lifestyle (interior decoration and furniture). These two outfits are from the Next mail order catalogue for spring/ summer 1989.

that the aim is to market a 'look' and to save the busy woman or man shopper – now seen as a professional or business person in a hurry – from having to toil from one store to the next in the search for shoes to match the bag that goes with the suit.

Next was able to exploit shoppers' disillusionment with the department store. In 1983 the *Observer* reported on a recent survey of shopping preferences undertaken by Source Information Marketing, which suggested that shoppers were finding the department store 'anonymous', and were demanding the 'old-fashioned' services of intimate surroundings and personal attention.[36] Paradoxically, those were precisely the services that the department stores had once prided themselves on offering; and in fact boutique chains have not returned to the old-fashioned hard sell with the shopper's choice intensively monitored in the changing room by a saleswoman. What Next did was to bring together a fantasy of old-time shopping and 'aspirational buying' – the desire of newly affluent members of the twenty-five to thirty-five age group to wear an approximation of designer clothes.

The point about Next is that the outlets are not independent but, as with Marks and Spencer, are a link in the chain of the total enterprise. Like Benetton, the whole operation is closely controlled with monitoring of design, computerised stock-taking systems and warehouse control.

It was Marks and Spencer that pioneered the factory-to-shop system (at the beginning of the century) in order to bring quality and reasonable prices to the High Street. Marks and Spencer still maintains tight quality control on the firms that supply its cloth and its finished garments, and may demand that production runs be switched at a moment's notice if a line is not selling fast enough. Benefits to firms who supply Marks and Spencer are that they are paid promptly and helped to develop new products and with advice on sources of raw materials. There is also the subsidiary business of selling the M & S rejects of which there is a fair supply because of the very exacting St Michael standards (although the rejects may not carry the M & S St Michael label).

There have also proved to be disadvantages to the dependent relationship, which became evident in 1979. This was the year 'when Marks and Spencer cut its prices by the equivalent of £17 million – and demanded that suppliers shoulder half the burden'. It was a response to one of the first acts of the new Conservative administration headed by Mrs Thatcher: to raise VAT. As a result, some suppliers suffered, and the experience 'brought home to M & S how close its control over the suppliers had become, and how dependent some of them had grown. Since then, St Michael has encouraged the manufacturers to stand alone a little more.'[37]

216

The problems resurfaced in the mid-eighties. One commentator suggested that the 'feudal control' exerted by Marks and Spencer over suppliers was not to the general benefit of the industry as a whole:

The decline in the United Kingdom textile industry during the 1970s may have been made worse by its dependence on St Michael, since this dependence prevented some British companies from diversifying sufficiently to cope with the flood of Far Eastern imports.[38]

Marks and Spencer was embarking on an enormous programme of modernisation and expansion, and had to squeeze the profits of its suppliers, especially on the clothing side. In the summer of 1988, 780 redundancies and the closure of a knitwear factory were announced by Corah, which relied for two-thirds of its business on Marks and Spencer.

The relationship with the suppliers was not the only problem. In 1987 St Michael:

took too many of its fashion items too far up market. This led to flat clothing sales in the six months to September [1987] and a drop in market share estimated at a striking one per cent by Verdict Research, the leading retail consultancy. That is equivalent to the loss of business worth around £50 million.[39]

This was part of the attempt to compete with the new designer consciousness of the 1980s. In the consensus years of the fifties and sixties Marks and Spencer managed to satisfy a wide range of purchasers. In the increasingly divisive society of the 1980s this has become more difficult. Glossy ads for Marks and Spencer appeared for the first time in the up-market fashion press in 1987. Yet at the end of the day neither they nor Next can ever be 'designer labels', and Marks and Spencer at least are to some extent trapped by their image as providers of good quality and a modicum of choice at relatively affordable prices.

This is only one example of another paradox of the fashion market. Aware of new subdivisions in what remains a class society, market researchers responded by 'market niching', that is by trying to classify these subdivisions in purchasing terms, thus providing for new wants and at the same time enabling suppliers to avoid some of the risks of trying to accommodate customers whose characteristics are unknown.

Fashion stylists and fashion forecasters, whose advice is increasingly sought, have become the new professionals of the industry – their role to predict coming trends. Consultants study trends from a wide field – from the business itself, social and economic factors, street fashion and developments in film, art exhibitions, design and the media. Colours, for example, are anticipated two years in advance by the international dye companies such as ICI in Britain and Montefibre in Italy. Fashion fabrics are organised into a number of age- and style-based themes each year and shown at international textile fairs such as Premier Vision in Paris and Interstoft in Frankfurt, eighteen months ahead of their appearance

in the shops. At the international ready-to-wear collections in Paris, Milan, New York and London, the colours and fabrics come together with seasonal styling to produce the clothes seen in the High Street six months later. The paradox is that this has led not to more choice but to greater conformity and sameness as the results of the predictions are mass marketed and retailed all over the world.

One solution for Marks and Spencer has been diversification away from clothing. Some of its local stores have been turned into up-market food emporia, and they are also expanding into the financial services sector. Theirs is already (1988) the biggest charge card company in Britain, with 2.2 million credit card holders, and St Michael unit trusts and insurance policies were launched in the autumn of 1988.

M & S is not alone in having introduced 'In-house credit' as there are now also charge cards for Next, Habitat, and other multiples such as Boots. This is an important part of the consumer boom, which in turn is part of a generally increased emphasis on shopping as a major leisure-time activity. In an eerie way shopping – consumption – is replacing manufacture in many parts of Britain. To give just one example: a northern clothing tycoon has bought up the old textile factory at Saltaire, a model industrial town built by the nineteenth-century tycoon, Sir Titus Salt, and is to turn it into a shopping mall. As the department store concept, where everything was under one roof, has waned, diversification emerges in new forms and the whole world becomes a shop. Even cultural institutions such as the Beaubourg in Paris, and the Victoria and Albert Museum and the Barbican in London become 'leisure environments' in which shopping plays an essential part, both for the entertainment of visitors and the profits of the institution.

'Drifting down' – the credit squeeze

Despite the efforts of the fashion forecasters, new problems emerged in the late 1980s. One victim of a widely experienced downturn in sales was George Davies of Next: he and Next parted company in December 1988. Next profits had been 'drifting down like autumn leaves'. Stockbrokers who had been forecasting profits of £150 million for 1988–90 had to revise these downwards to £70 million. Growth began to slip backwards in the prosperous south.[40]

An important factor in the problems faced by Next was that its mail order catalogue *Next Directory* did not achieve the success that had been predicted for it. It was launched in January 1988 and was the outcome of the 1986 merger with the mail order company Grattan. The *Guardian* reported that £24.1 million had been invested in the business, and about 120 000 copies of the £3 hardback directory (with matt black designer

Opposite In the face of competition from the new High Street chain stores, long established companies such as Marks and Spencer have had to up-market their image – here advertising a 100 per cent synthetic jacket at £49.95 and a 'Couture rose' skirt in viscose at £19.99 in 1989.

219

cover) had soon been requested. George Davies predicted sales of between £20 and £25 million in the first six months, after which the company would go into profit. He also expected that returns of stock at 15 per cent would be much lower than the mail order average of 50 per cent. His aim was to reach the up-market 'class AB' purchasers normally thought not to shop by mail order. Unfortunately sales did not come up to expectations. This was attributed to the postal strike that took place in the spring.[41]

Jeff Banks' Warehouse had been running its Bymail catalogue for several years, and in July 1988 the giant GUS/Kay mail order company launched its new catalogue which for the first time included designer clothes by Jasper Conran, Benny Ong, Roland Klein, Mary Quant and Burberry. This initiative was the result of their market research, which showed their customers anxious to buy top of the range designer label garments. Freemans have followed with a whole range of catalogues, including, in March 1989, 'Editions – the complete life style survival kit'. This is aimed at younger customers and sells cheaper ranges; one, of 'natural' dresses, jumpers and skirts in 55 per cent linen and 45 per cent viscose is priced at from £44 for a suit to £12 for a jersey. Home shopping absorbed 13 per cent of total sales of women's and children's clothing in the 1980s.[42]

As the 1990s approach, old problems have returned to afflict the retail clothing business. There are two important reasons why retail in general, and clothing in particular, have been hit. One is demographic change: the ageing population. 'The thirty upwards age group is sharply increasing, while, by the end of the century, there will be a million fewer sixteen to twenty-four year olds in the UK alone.'[43] The youthful styles of Lacroix and others and the wilder excesses of haute couture may simply not appeal to older women, and indeed the whole fashion industry, geared primarily to youth since the sixties, appears to be shifting its emphasis.

The 'empty nesters' – well off couples whose children have left the nest and are no longer a financial burden – may find themselves with extra disposable income, but they will not necessarily spend it on more clothes. Meanwhile the design conscious salary earners in their twenties and early thirties will have changed gear to become parents and mortgage holders, and there will be fewer of them in the next generation. High interest rates leading to high mortgage payments were part of an anti-inflationary strategy at the end of the 1980s, and the consequent downturn in spending began to appear.

One response by the retailers was to promote easy credit. In the run up to Christmas 1988 many stores were offering up to 20 per cent off total purchases to new credit card holders, although the Retail Credit Group, whose members are the big retail firms, was adamant that the panic about 'plastic money' was unnecessary. They stated that although the amount of spending on credit cards rose by 30 per cent between March and December 1988, 'the level of actual borrowing (the debt carried forward each month) remained more or less the same'. Between 40 and 50 per cent of credit card shoppers pay off the full amount of their debt every month, thus incurring no interest charges at all.

David Legg, chief executive of Burton Group Financial Services, says: 'People are actually borrowing relatively less now and it's a myth that retailers are doing fantastic business at the moment.' That explains why there are so many pre-Christmas sales.[44]

The downturn in trade has led retailers to make ever more frantic efforts to attract custom. In the winter of 1988–9 many shops had special evenings for card holders. In some cases discounts were offered; another attraction was some form of entertainment, thus further breaking down the distinction between shopping and other forms of amusement.

The *Guardian* reported a Marks and Spencer event, where there were free refreshments and three bands, Eddie Clayton on the ground floor, a steel band on the first floor next to lingerie, and the Fortuna String Quartet from Hampstead Garden Suburb in the Penny Bazaar. The correspondent described the scrum for the free wine and mince pies, but customers also bought in large quantities. Meanwhile, nearby, cardholders at Liberty, dressed in black cashmere or furs, were emerging from *their* credit card evening, carrying little party bags containing a packet of pot pourri.[45]

Despite these intense efforts, sales in early 1989 were low. Christmas sales hung on until February. Top Shop even advertised cuts in its new incoming ranges.

Technology and the workforce

On the manufacturing side technological innovation has continued. Laser power, electronic air and water jet looms and a vast array of computerised equipment have increased speed, flexibility and, it is said, mass creative possibilities, although we have already noted that computerised stock taking, for example, can also lead to greater conformity. Among machines shown at the 1988 IMB Trade Fair in Cologne, newly developed equipment included the 'EBS electronic button stitcher', for 'hand sewn front buttons' and – for jeans and outerwear manufacture – 'the Automatic Stitch-counting Overlock Unit', which used photocell edge-sensing technology. The Bullmer's CNC 2000 fully automatic cutting system 'carries out grading and lay making, to achieve optimal cutting efficiency'.[46] Japan has very nearly reached the stage of developing totally computerised garment production, in which no human hand is needed.

Textile designs for print, knit and weave can now be generated by computer aided design equipment. With some, the design can be typed in one end and a knitted garment or woven length comes out at the other. In September 1988 *Knitting International* published a mathematical algorithm developed by the Shenkar College of Textile Technology and Fashion, in Israel, which can create computer-generated designs for textiles. Those responsible declared that this would 'shorten [fashion] cycle times and achieve faster delivery'.

Yet technological innovation continues to co-exist not only with the stylistic conformity which it may actually intensify, but also with the most archaic methods and sweatshop conditions both in factories and in the home. This particularly affects women worldwide. What some economists refer to as the globalisation of the economy has internationalised the fashion industry. One tactic is to send cut out garment pieces from (say) West Germany to Sri Lanka, the Philippines or Pakistan; ultra-cheap local labour is used for the making up of garments which are then shipped back to the country of origin for finishing. Girls as young as eleven or twelve may be exploited, earning a few pence for sewing each garment, and this process, furthermore, retains all the technological expertise in the West. Another effect of computerisation has been the reassignment of labour processes. In some cases the whole sequence of production has been broken down. The unskilled and repetitive functions may be subcontracted out, in which case the firm may lose its central factory altogether and become 'an agglomeration of "detached workshops"'. Another feature is for a division of the workforce between a skilled élite and a reserve of temporary workers taken on and laid off according to requirements – not that there is anything very novel about that.[47]

In the 1970s the textile factories of 'Polyester Road' in South Korea were said to be recreating the very worst conditions of the original Industrial Revolution in pre-Victorian Britain. In many of the 'world market factories' of south-east Asia the situation is even worse than in the Victorian period. At least in the nineteenth-century West there was the possibility for unionisation and improvements in pay and conditions; whereas today in the Far East the new industrial conditions have often been supported by undemocratic governments who have attempted to emasculate trades unions and erode civil liberties.

At the same time, the balance between East and West has changed to some extent. In Hong Kong, one of the earliest sites of cheap clothing manufacture, a new generation of firms producing quality fashions has

appeared (and a similar evolution is predicted for South Korea). Yet simultaneously a feature of the global economy is the emergence of 'the Third World in the First World'. For example, in some factories wages are now higher in Hong Kong than in Scotland. In Britain, a weakening of the unions and high unemployment rates have led to an increase of casualised, often part-time work and home working for a predominantly female workforce, many of whom are immigrants or black. Similar economic patterns are seen in Silicon Valley and in the Texas border areas in the United States, where the most exploitable form of labour is that of 'undocumented' workers (i.e. without work permits) leaving Mexico and other Latin American states to obtain work at any price. Clothing manufacture is at the very heart of these operations.[48]

Yet these unpromising new conditions have produced considerable militancy in some cases. The vice-president of the Bangladesh Garment

Exploited, low paid, non-unionised labour is still a major feature of the British (and world) garment industry. Since the nineteenth century successive generations of women and immigrants – at first Jews from Central Europe, later workers from former British colonies – have been the clothing industry's homeworkers. This is a Bangladeshi/Bengali machinist in Tower Hamlets, London.

223

Workers' Federation has pointed out that in spite of the exploitative work and conditions, the very fact of earning a wage at all 'has given 150 000 young Muslim women the chance to be economically independent temporarily, and thereby to defy the taboos of an orthodox society'. The possibility of work has created a catalyst 'for a bigger struggle for women's independence'.[49] There have been similar reports of militancy in South Korea and other parts of south-east Asia – and for that matter Scotland.

In a curious way, the product itself – fashion – is the emissary, or visible effect of this new stage in the exploitation of the southern hemisphere by the northern hemisphere. Western fashion is becoming global fashion, at every level. The poor of the Third World wear the same Taiwanese T-shirts as the inhabitants of British 'sink estates'; even the People's Republic of China is engaging in Western-style haute couture, in spite of the fact that Western fashion was previously considered to be a form of 'cultural pollution'. Gorbachev's Soviet Union is stepping up its attempts to develop its couture and fashion industry along Western lines. In the Arab states, the consumption of fashion by the wealthy even affected Paris haute couture, and resulted in the development of evening models in particular that were more sumptuous than ever. At the same time, in Fundamentalist states such as Iran, Western women's fashion is perceived as it was formerly in China, as part and parcel of Western degeneracy.

Finally, ecology consciousness has continued and increased throughout the 1980s. One initial effect of this was the preference for natural fibres. Among other things, this led to the rehabilitation of linen. In the early postwar years it was considered unsuitable for even the higher levels of the mass market because it crumpled so easily, but today that very quality is proof that it is a natural fibre, and its return to popularity has been hastened by the many period and 'Empire' movies (*A Passage to India*, for example), because it has become associated with retro-chic. There was, therefore, a shift in the hierarchical status of fabrics in recent years, and newly developed synthetics have also been completely upgraded in the 1980s. The latest technology has been used to create new synthetic variants such as stretch Lycra, Spanzelle and fine jersey rayons, and polyesters that look exactly like silk but don't crease. All kinds of rayon and cotton mixtures are now emerging from Japan into European couture. Jean Muir uses the rayon jersey for her designer models. These latest fabrics drape beautifully, feel soft and have got rid of the shine that was so unappealing. They are a far cry from the tough, crimped rayon of the 1930s and the Crimplene of the 1960s. They are also as expensive as natural fibres. The British synthetics industry, which has been less innovative, is finding the challenge from Japan hard to compete with. In

In the last five years technology and design improvements have made possible new up-market rayons and synthetics, used by influential designers such as Jean Muir who created this red matt jersey rayon jump suit, priced at £550, for her spring 1989 collection.

spite of this trend, 1989 saw closures and layoffs at the Manchester Courtauld factory, due, the company said, to the weakening demand for synthetics.

The continuing campaign against fur, which has been particularly successful in Britain, leading to a significant drop in sales, has further increased demand for innovative synthetics. Although some campaigners argue that fake furs are as bad as the real thing, because they still give the impression that there is beauty in human beings wearing fur, exciting new fur fabrics have been produced and they too can be expensive and exclusive, not shunned by haute couture.

Conclusion

How far then have we come in 140 years of fashion and garment making? These years essentially cover the whole period of Paris haute couture, from the dominance of Charles Frederick Worth to the current evolution of the Parisian, American, Japanese and Italian couturiers of 1990. Glamour and exclusivity are as potent commodities as ever.

The export of clothing manufacture from the home to the factory is not complete; but the vast majority now buy mass-produced clothing, rather than relying on themselves or a local dressmaker to sew something to their own specifications. Despite the continuous economic growth and technological development of Western society in the twentieth century, the frightful conditions of garment factories, sweatshops and outworkers have not disappeared; in fact they have reappeared with a vengeance in the seventies and eighties.

The position of women has changed out of all recognition since the 1860s and yet in a curious way changed hardly at all. Both in Western capitalist countries and worldwide, women, whether married or not, form a vital component of the workforce. Yet they remain responsible for the bulk of household work and child care. In the fifties and sixties this used to be referred to as 'women's two roles', and was said to be the effect of 'choice' rather than the double exploitation of badly-paid part-time work outside the home and unpaid, unshared domestic work in the home. The women's movement has created a greater awareness of the problem, although so far no solution has emerged. Meanwhile, the 'two roles' pattern has been exported all over the world. It is, says one feminist sociologist, 'the result of a model of "progress" that places increasing economic responsibilities on women without redefining their role as the mainstay of family life in the home'. What this means in non-Western countries is that 'by transposing this model onto the very different cultural patterns of the Third World, together with the conditions that pro-

225

duced it, we have helped to create extreme distortions in women's lives in the rest of the globe'.[50]

In the West, economic changes have not affected all women uniformly, but on the contrary have widened the division between the wealthy and the poor. The position of many working-class women has worsened relatively and possibly absolutely since the 1960s with the decline of the manufacturing sector. In 1968, for example, women sewing machinists earned 98 per cent of the average wage for full-time women workers; now they earn only 76 per cent.[51] Meanwhile, 'the economy has been better at creating jobs for well-educated women than jobs for women at the bottom end of society. The largest increase in participation in the workforce has been among . . . better off [women]. In 1968, women married to managers and professional men were only four-fifths as likely to work as the wives of men in manual jobs. Now . . . they are more likely to have a job.'[52]

It is this relatively privileged group that has been associated with the designer fashions and imitations of designer style that were so much to

Fans follow the style of their preferred bands. These young Brosettes, dressed like their heroes, show off their 'official Bros' souvenirs and clothes after the Bros concert at Wembley in December 1988.

the fore in the 1980s. Fashion is still primarily a feminine domain, although gender difference has been reworked in the same period and men increasingly included into the appreciation of style.

By contrast, there have been, throughout the whole period we have explored, women and men who rejected fashion, but who nevertheless used distinctive forms of dress to signal their social and aesthetic beliefs. Equally, throughout the period second-hand clothes have featured, although in fluctuating degrees, as a source of both fashion and decency.

One of the clichés of the era of mass-produced fashion since the 1920s has been the belief that modern clothing wipes out class difference. Today we can clearly see that, on the contrary, mass-produced fashion makes possible the enunciation of social distinctions more minutely than before. These distinctions are not confined to class, but relate to generational, ethnic, regional and subcultural groups. Dress codes signal perhaps more subtly than ever an individual's exact location in the hierarchy of work and status. The contrast is no longer between silk and rags, although differences in the quality of clothes is still very marked, but rather between, say, 'Sloane Ranger' style and 'polytechnic dressing' (lecturers in 1968 jeans and hairy jumpers – also known as Liberal Party style), between teenage 'casuals' in bomber jackets and expensive sports shoes by Reebok and Converse, and art students in matt black and Doc Marten boots. Some of these 'uniforms' are deliberate, some virtually unconscious.

What has also not changed is Western uneasiness about consumerism itself. We seem unable to escape our curious ambivalence towards it; fashion, novelty and display grow and intensify, even under the threat of ecological disaster, yet equally persistent – albeit as a minority view – is the puritan tradition which would do away with fashion altogether. The exploitative and unequal conditions in which garments are often produced and the inaccurate but potent association of fashion with feminine frailty, should not lead us, however, in the name of women's rights or decent work conditions, to blame adornment itself.

Fashion is neither a conspiracy to seduce us into 'unnecessary' expenditure, nor is it a realm of unfettered choice and untainted pleasure. In contemporary Western society it is sometimes associated with glamour and ideal beauty as well as extravagance and self-indulgence. Yet a more equal social system would not necessarily lead to the abolition of fashion, although this is what the dress reformers believed. It is also what anti-socialists have argued; they have insisted that an egalitarian society must inevitably bring with it a grey uniformity. The mere fact that dress and adornment figure so largely in the critique both of socialism and of capitalism suggests that whatever the social system, we will in the foreseeable future continue to articulate our niche in the world, and our aspirations, our most intimate feelings and our crudest social claims in the way we dress and look.

John Flett, reflecting the current fashionable interest in natural body-revealing lines, designed this organic tube, here worn with a 'samurai' jock strap, in spring 1989.

Notes

Chapter 1

1 *Vogue* (1989), April.

2 SAUNDERS, Edith (1954), *The Age of Worth*, London: Longmans, p. 75, quoting FEUILLET, Madame Octave, *'Quelques Années de Ma Vie'*, 1865.

3 KONIG, René (1973), *The Restless Image*, London: Allen & Unwin.

4 For example, VEBLEN, Thorstein (1957), *The Theory of the Leisure Classes*, London: Allen & Unwin. (Originally published in 1899.) Veblen continues to be used widely in fashion literature, to an extent that his place within contemporary sociology would not seem to justify. More interesting sociologists, notably Georg Simmel, figure hardly at all. Other examples of writers who stress the irrationality of fashion are: BARTHES, Roland (1967), *Système de la Mode*, Paris: Editions du Seuil; BAUDRILLARD, Jean (1981), *For a Critique of the Political Economy of the Sight St Louis*, Mo: Telos Press; and FLUGEL, J. C. (1980), *The Psychology of Clothes*, London: Hogarth Press.

5 NEWTON, Stella Mary (1974), *Health Art and Reason: Dress Reformers of the Nineteenth Century*, London: John Murray, p. 2.

6 For an extended exploration of these arguments see WILSON, Elizabeth (1985), *Adorned in Dreams: Fashion and Modernity*, London: Virago.

7 LAMPARD, Eric (1973), 'The Urbanising World', in DYOS, H. H. and WOLFF, Michael (1973), *The Victorian City: Images and Realities*, Vol. 1, London: Routledge & Kegan Paul.

8 MARX, Karl, and ENGELS, Frederick (1970), *Manifesto of the Communist Party*, in *Selected Works*, London: Lawrence & Wishart, p. 31. (Originally published in 1848.)

9 HUNT, E. H. (1981), *British Labour History 1815–1914*, London: Weidenfeld & Nicolson, p. 100.

10 Ibid., p. 100.

11 SCHMIECHON, James H. (1984), *Sweated Industries and Sweated Labour*, London: Croom Helm, p. 11.

12 THOMPSON, E. P., and YEO, Eileen (1984), *The Unknown Mayhew: Selections from the Morning Chronicle, 1849–50*, Harmondsworth: Penguin, p. 406.

13 Ibid., p. 407.

14 BURN, W. L. (1964), *The Age of Equipoise*, London: Allen & Unwin, p. 97, quoting STAPLETON, Dr J. W. (1860), *The Great Crime of 1860*.

15 GARTNER, Lewis P. (1960), *The Jewish Immigrant in England 1870–1914*, London: Allen & Unwin, p. 81, quoting Arthur Baumann M.P. in the *National Review* XII. no. 69, November 1988.

16 HUNT, E. H., op. cit., p. 21.

17 HIGGS, Edward (1986), 'Domestic Service and Household Production' in JOHN, Angela, ed. (1986), *Unequal Opportunities: Women's Employment in England, 1800–1918*, Oxford: Basil Blackwell.

18 FLUGEL, J. C., op. cit., coined this phrase. See also LAVER, James (1969a), *A Concise History of Costume*, London: Thames & Hudson; and LAVER, James (1969b), *Modesty in Dress: An Inquiry into the Fundamentals of Fashion*, London: Heinemann.

19 SALA, George Augustus (1859), *Twice around the Clock*, London: Houlston & Wright, p. 83.

20 BURN, W. L., op. cit., p. 26.

21 WAUGH, Nora (1968), *The Cut of Women's Clothes*, London: Faber & Faber, p. 218, quoting Mme CARETTE, *My Mistress, the Empress Eugénie*, undated.

22 CHAPON, François (1984), *Mystère et Splendeur de Jacques Doucet 1853–1929*, Paris: Clattes, p. 56.

23 VANIER, Henriette (1960), *La Mode et Ses Métiers*, Paris: Colin, p. 194, quoting *Le Figaro*, 22 March 1866. Original prices were 3200–7000 francs and 10 000 francs.

24 SAUNDERS, Edith, op. cit., p. 118, quoting the *Illustrated London News* (1864).

25 DAVIDOFF, Leonora, and HALL, Catherine (1987), *Family Fortunes*, London: Hutchinson.

26 RUSKIN, John (1960), *Sesame and Lilies*, London: Allen & Unwin, pp. 144–5. (Originally published in 1865.)

27 For example, in 1876 the adopted daughter of John Simon, a pioneering physi-

cian and public health campaigner, and his wife Jane, née O'Meara, was divorced by her husband for adultery. She later married the co-respondent Thomas Bolton, a prosperous businessman and subsequently Liberal MP for North-east Derbyshire. See LAMBERT, Royston (1963), *Sir John Simon (1816–1904) and English Social Administration*, London: McGibbon & Kee.

28 See, for example, GAY, Peter (1984), *The Bourgeois Experience: Victoria to Freud*, Vol. I, *The Education of the Senses*, Oxford: Oxford University Press; GAY, Peter (1986), Vol. II, *The Tender Passion*, Oxford: Oxford University Press; CHITTY, Susan (1974), *The Beast and the Monk: A Life of Charles Kingsley*, London: Hodder & Stoughton; and MENDES, Susan, and RENDALL, Jane, eds. (1989), *Sexuality and Subordination: Interdisciplinary Studies of Gender in the Nineteenth Century*, London: Routledge. Mendes and Rendall stress how little we still know about the sexual lives of Victorian women, while Peter Gay and Susan Chitty investigate the passionate and active sexuality of at least some Victorian middle-class women as well as men.

29 NICHOLSON, Shirley (1988), *A Victorian Household: Based on the Diaries of Marion Sambourne*, London: Barrie & Jenkins, p. 84. Marion Sambourne was paying Madame Bosquet £38 [today £1352] for a dress in the 1880s.

30 See DAVIDOFF, Leonora (1983), *The Best Circles*, London: Croom Helm.

31 TAYLOR, Lou (1983), *Mourning Dress: A Costume and Social History*, London: George Allen & Unwin, pp. 140, 194, 303.

32 MORLEY, John (1971), *Death, Heaven and the Victorians*, London: Studio Vista, p. 23.

33 HOLCOMBE, Lee (1973), *Victorian Ladies at Work: Middle-Class Working Women in England and Wales, 1880–1914*, Newton Abbot: David & Charles.

34 ROSEN, Andrew (1974), *Rise Up Women: the Militant Campaign of the WSPU 1903–1914*, London: Routledge & Kegan Paul, Chapter 1. STRACHEY, Ray (1928), *The Cause*, London: Bell.

35 See GREENSLADE, Cindy (1987). 'Progress versus Fashion: An Investigation into the Relationship between Dress Reform and the Women's Movement in Great Britain and America, 1860–1900', Brighton Polytechnic: unpublished BA (Hons) thesis, p. 32, for a discussion of the problems of wearing Reform Dress.

36 NEWTON, Stella Mary, op. cit., pp. 127–8, quoting WARD, Mrs Humphry, *Robert Elsmere*, 3 vols., London, vol. 1 (1901).

37 ORMOND, Leonée (1968). 'Female Costume in the Aesthetic Movement' in *Costume*, no. 2, p. 38, quoting FRANCILLON, R. E., *Mid Victorian Memories* (1913), p. 212.

38 PINCHBECK, Ivy (1930), *Women Workers and the Industrial Revolution, 1750–1850*, Oxford: Oxford University Press.

39 GINSBURG, Madeleine (1972). 'The Tailoring and Dressmaking Trade 1700–1850' in *Costume*, no. 6, pp. 64–71.

40 Ibid., p. 66.

41 Ibid., p. 68.

42 DODD, George (1843), *Days at the Factories: or the Manufacturing Industries of Great Britain Described; Series 1. London*: Charles Knight & Co., p. 154.

43 THOMPSON, E. P., and YEO, Eileen, op. cit., pp. 200–1.

44 LEVITT, Sarah (1986), *Victorians Unbuttoned: Registered Designs for Clothing, their Makers and Wearers, 1839–1900*, London: Allen & Unwin. See also LEVITT, Sarah (1988), 'Clothing Production and the Sewing Machine', *The Textile Society*, vol. 9, Spring, pp. 2–13.

45 BEAZLEY, Alison (1973), 'The Heavy and Light Clothing Industries 1850–1920' in *Costume*, no. 7, p. 56.

46 Ibid., and LEVITT, Sarah (1988), op. cit., p. 12.

47 LEVITT, Sarah (1988), op. cit., p. 12.

48 ADBURGHAM, Alison (1981), *Shops and Shopping*, London: Allen & Unwin, p. 123.

49 Ibid., pp. 117–18.

50 Ibid., pp. 283–7.

51 MILLER, Michael (1981), *The Bon Marché: Bourgeois Culture and the Department Store, 1869–1920*, London: Allen & Unwin.

52   BEAZLEY, Alison, op. cit., who refers to BRISCOE, Lynden (1971), *The Textile and Clothing Industries of the UK*, Manchester: Manchester University Press.
53   ADBURGHAM, Alison, op. cit., pp. 134–5, quoting prices from Debenham and Freebody's *New Fashion Book* of October 1870.
54   LEVITT, Sarah (1988), op. cit.
55   MAYHEW, Henry (1984), *Mayhew's London*, ed. Peter QUENNELL, London: Bracken Books, p. 210. (Originally published in 1861.)
56   This section has drawn extensively on GINSBURG, Madeleine (1980), 'Rags to Riches: the Secondhand Clothes Trade 1700–1978' in *Costume*, 14, pp. 121–35.
57   Ibid., p. 127.
58   Confirmed by Dr BYNUM, Archivist at the Wellcome Research Institute of the History of Medicine, London.
59   BELL, Quentin (1947, 1968), *Of Human Finery*, London: Hogarth Press.

Chapter 2

1   GORDON, Lady Duff (Lucile) (1932), *Discretions and Indiscretions*, London: Jarrolds, p. 80.
2   THYNNE, Daphne, Marchioness of Bath (1951), *Before the Sunset Fades*, Warminster, Wiltshire: The Longleat Estate Co.
3   See ELLMANN, Richard (1987), *Oscar Wilde*, Harmondsworth: Penguin, for a discussion of the Aesthetic Movement in Britain. Walter Peter was an art critic writing in the 1870s and 1880s. His most famous work was *Marius the Epicurean*.
4   GROSS, John (1969), *The Rise and Fall of the Man of Letters: Aspects of English Literary Life since 1800*, London: Weidenfeld & Nicolson, quoting BENNETT, Arnold, writing under the pen-name of TOLSON, Jacob, on 'Books and Persons' in *The New Age*, between 1908 and 1911.
5   ZIMMECK, Metta (1986), 'Jobs for the Girls: The Expansion of Clerical Work for Women, 1850–1914', in JOHN, Angela, ed. (1986), *Unequal Opportunities: Women's Employment in England 1800–1918*, Oxford: Basil Blackwell, pp. 164–5.
6   ROAD, Alan (1987), 'Memoirs of a Secretary, or, as Miss Angell would put it. . . .', *Observer*, 25 January.
7   GISSING, George (1985), *The Odd Women*, London: Virago, p. 17. (Originally published in 1893.)
8   FRASER, W. Hamish (1981), *The Coming of the Mass Market*, London: Macmillan, p. 178.
9   PEMBER REEVES, Maud (1979), *Round about a Pound a Week*, London: Virago, p. 64. (Originally published in 1913.)
10   BELL, Lady (1985), *At the Works*, London: Virago, p. 69. (Originally published in 1907.)
11   Ibid., p. 52.
12   MOORE, George (1895), *Esther Waters*, London: Dent, p. 65. (Reprinted 1983.)
13   Ibid., p. 165.
14   Thorstein VEBLEN, whose work reflects some of these concerns, is an example of the way in which, when taken to extremes, the critique of dress became a wholesale condemnation of cultural life itself. Adolf LOOS, a Viennese designer and writer, wrote an influential article in 1908 which also condemned all forms of ornamentation: this article was an early manifesto, effectively, of the Modern Movement.
15   NEWTON, Stella Mary (1974), *Health, Art and Reason*, London: John Murray, pp. 116–17, quoting *The Rational Dress Society Gazette* of 1888.
16   Ibid., p. 183.
17   BALLIN, Ada (1885), *The Science of Dress in Theory and Practice*, London: Sampson and Low.
18   Quoted in WALKLEY, Christine (n.d.), unpublished lecture notes.
19   Ibid., quoting GIELGUD, Kate, *Autobiography – tennis dress design*. For the influence of girls' education, especially sport, on fashion and dress reform, see GREENSLADE, Cindy Jayne, op. cit. and FLETCHER, Sheila (1984), *Women's First: The Female Tradition in English Physical Education, 1880–1980*, London: Athlone Press.
20   Quoted in TINLING, Teddy (1983), *Sixty Years in Tennis*, London: Sidgwick & Jackson, p. 24.
21   This section draws extensively on MARDLE, Jill (1984), 'Cycling for Women in the 1890s', Brighton Polytechnic: unpublished BA (Hons) thesis.
22   MARDLE, Jill, op. cit., p. 11, quoting SWANWICK, Helena (1935), *I have been Young*, London: Victor Gollancz.
23   Ibid., pp. 13–14, quoting *The Lady Cyclist*, 1893, vol. 1, part 2, p. 86.
24   Ibid., pp. 6–8, quoting *The Lady Cyclist*, 1893, vol. 1, part 3, p. 121.

25   Ibid., p. 20, quoting *The Lady Cyclist*, 1893, vol. 1, part 1, p. 49.
26   HAYNES, Alan (1983), 'Murderous Millinery: the Struggle for the Plumage Act, 1921', in *History Today*, July, pp. 26–31.
27   ELLMANN, Richard, op. cit., p. 244, quoting BLACKMORE, Trevor (1911), *The Art of Herbert Schmalz*, pp. 43–4.
28   Ibid., pp. 243–4, quoting DE BREMONT, A. (1911), *Oscar Wilde and his mother*, p. 89.
29   Ibid., p. 44, quoting DE BREMONT, A., *Life among the Troubridges*, p. 169.
30   Ibid., p. 244, quoting *The Bat*, 30 March 1886.
31   MORRIS, William (1986), *News from Nowhere and Selected Writings and Designs*, Harmondsworth: Penguin, pp. 234–5. (*News from Nowhere* originally published in 1890.)
32   Ibid.
33   WALKER, Lynne (1987), 'Design, Class and Gender in Edwardian Britain', in *Fan* (Feminist Art News), vol. 2, no. 5, p. 14. See also CALLEN, Anthea (1977), *Angel in the Studio: the Women's Arts and Crafts Movement 1870–1914*, London: Astragal Books.
34   We are grateful for the information in this section which draws on HANDLEY, Susanna (1983), 'Aesthetic Dress 1910–1939', Brighton Polytechnic: unpublished BA (Hons) thesis. See also SWAIN, Margaret (1978), 'Mrs Newbery's Dress', in *Costume*, no. 12.
35   HANDLEY, Susanna, op. cit., p. 35 (footnote).
36   Ibid., p. 74 (footnote). The student was Louisa Starr, and the quotation is taken from an article she wrote for the *Strand* magazine in 1891.
37   PRITCHARD, Mrs Eric (1902), *The Cult of Chiffon*, London: Grant Richards, pp. 27–8.
38   HANDLEY, Susanna, op. cit., and LATHAM, Patricia (1974), 'House of Liberty', in *Costume*, no. 8, p. 61.
39   LLOYD, Clara Frances (1976), 'Liberty's Embroidery Workrooms' in *Costume*, no. 10, pp. 86–90.
40   Quoted in LATHAM, Patricia, op. cit., p. 61.
41   Ibid.
42   The Directory (*Directoire*) was the executive body of the Revolutionary government of France from 1795 to 1799.
43   STEELE, Valerie (1988), *Paris Fashion: A Cultural History*, Oxford: Oxford University Press, p. 219.
44   PROUST, Marcel (1981), *Remembrance of Things Past*, vol. III, *The Captive*, pp. 375–6, translated by C. K. Scott Moncrief and Terence Kilmartin. (Originally published in 1923 as *A la Recherche des Temps Perdus: La Prisonnière*.)
45   Ibid., vol. I, *Swann's Way*, p. 460. (Originally published in 1913 as *Du Côté de Chez Swann*.)
46   NEWTON, Stella Mary, op. cit., p. 163, quoting *The Woman Worker*, June 1908.
47   MORRIS, Jenny (1986), 'The Characteristics of Sweating: The Late Nineteenth-Century London and Leeds Tailoring Trade', in JOHN, Angela, ed., op. cit., p. 100.
48   Ibid.
49   This section draws extensively on WATSON, Linzi (1985), 'The Influence of Jewish Immigrants on the Women's Ready-to-wear Trade in Britain, 1880–1939', Brighton Polytechnic: unpublished BA (Hons) thesis, quoting POTTER, Beatrice.
50   WALKLEY, Christine, op. cit.
51   MORRIS, Jenny, op. cit., p. 116.
52   Ibid.
53   BLACK, Clementina (1983), *Married Women's Work: Being the Report of an Enquiry undertaken by the Women's Industrial Council*, London: Virago, p. 68. (Originally published in 1915.)
54   EWING, Elizabeth (1974), *History of Twentieth Century Fashion*, London: Batsford.
55   LLOYD, Clara Frances, op. cit., pp. 86–90.
56   BRITTAIN, Vera (1978), *Testament of Youth*, London: Virago, p. 34. (Originally published in 1933.)

Chapter 3

1   PRIESTLEY, J. B. (1987), *English Journey*, Harmondsworth: Penguin, pp. 375–6. (Originally published in 1934.)
2   SPRING RICE, Margery (1981), *Working Class Wives*, London: Virago, p. 144. (Originally published in 1939.)
3   SOKOLOFF, Bertha (1987), *Edith and Stepney*, London: Stepney Books, p. 45.

4   SPRING RICE, Margery, op. cit.
5   SAMUEL, Raphael (1983), 'Suburbs under Siege: The Middle Class between the Wars', *New Socialist*, no. 11, May/June, p. 28.
6   Ibid., p. 28
7   Ibid., p. 29.
8   Ibid., p. 28.
9   CHISHOLM, Anne (1979), *Nancy Cunard*, Harmondsworth: Penguin.
10   MACKINNON, Janice R., and MACKINNON, Stephen (1988), *Agnes Smedley: The Life and Times of an American Radical*, London: Virago.
11   GRAVES, Robert, and HODGE, Alan (1971), *The Long Weekend: the Living Story of the Twenties and Thirties*, Harmondsworth: Penguin, p. 34. (Originally published in 1941.)
12   Ibid., p. 271.
13   HOLTBY, Winifred (1978), *Women in a Changing Civilisation*, Chicago: Academy Press, pp. 118–19. (Originally published in 1935.)
14   Archives, Willenhall Lock Museum, Wilkinson and Roddell, Cherry Street, Birmingham. *New Year Show Catalogue*, January 1933.
15   BEATON, Cecil (1954), *The Glass of Fashion*, London: Weidenfeld & Nicolson.
16   GRAVES, Robert, and HODGE, Alan, op. cit., p. 269.
17   Ibid., p. 118.
18   Musée Historique des Tissus, Lyon (1975), *Les Folles Années du Soie – François Ducharne et son atelier de dessin d'après les souvenirs de Bernard Lorjou*, exhibition catalogue, p. 16.
19   CHARLES-ROUX, Edmonde (1976), *Chanel*, London: Jonathan Cape, pp. 229–30.
20   STEELE, Valerie (1988), op. cit.
21   WILSON, Robert (1926), *Paris on Parade*, Indianapolis: Bobbs Merrill, p. 82.
22   NYSTROM, Paul (1929), *The Economics of Fashion*, New York: Ronald Press, pp. 167–8.
23   SETTLE, Alison (1937), *Clothes Line*, London: Methuen, p. 8.
24   Royal Pavilion, Art Galleries and Museum of Brighton (1985), *Norman Hartnell*, exhibition catalogue, p. 34.
25   See EWING, Elizabeth (1974), op. cit., p. 129.
26   This section draws extensively on the work of HAYE, Amy de la (1986), 'The Role of Design within the Commercialisation of Women's Ready-to-Wear Clothing in Britain during the Interwar Years, with Specific Reference to the Cheapest Levels of Production', Royal College of Art: unpublished MA thesis, and *Fashion Source Book: A Visual Reference to the 20th Century*, London: Quarto (1988).
27   EWING, Elizabeth (1974), op. cit., p. 130.
28   HAYE, Amy de la (1986), op. cit., p. 94.
29   Ibid., p. 95.
30   ALLINGHAM, Margery (1986), *The Fashion in Shrouds*, London: J. M. Dent, pp. 35–6. (Originally published in 1938.)
31   HAYE, Amy de la (1986), op. cit., p. 136.
32   Ibid.
33   GRIEVE, Mary (1964), *Millions made my Story*, London: Victor Gollancz.
34   HAYE, Amy de la (1986), op. cit., p. 24.
35   MORTON, H. V. (1926), *The Spell of London*, London: Methuen, p. 92.
36   Ibid.
37   CHESTERTON, Mrs Cecil (1926), *In Darkest London*, London: Stanley Paul, p. 5.
38   CHESTERTON, Mrs Cecil (1928), *Women of the Underworld*, London: Stanley Paul, p. 31.
39   HOGAN, Kathy (1985), 'Courtaulds Rayon: Advertising and Publicity – 1920–1955', Brighton Polytechnic: unpublished BA (Hons) thesis, quoting COLEMAN, D. C. (1980), *Courtaulds: An Economic and Social History*, Oxford: Oxford University Press, vol. III, p. 314.
40   MORTON, H. V., op. cit., pp. 93–4.
41   HOGAN, Kathy (1986), 'Public Relations for Courtaulds Rayon 1920–1955', in the *Textile Society Newsletter*, vol. 5, p. 3.
42   CHARLES-ROUX, Edmonde, op. cit., p. 271.
43   LEESE, Elizabeth (1976), *Costume Design and the Movies*, Benbridge: BCW Publishing Ltd.
44   Quoted in HAYE, Amy de la (1986), op. cit., p. 101.
45   HOLLANDER, Anne (1978), *Seeing Through Clothes*, New York: Viking/Penguin, pp. 342–3.
46   Quoted in WHITE, Jerry (1986), *Campbell Bunk: The Worst Street in North London*, London: Routledge, p. 166.
47   HAYE, Amy de la (1986), op. cit., p. 80.
48   PRIESTLEY, J. B., op. cit., p. 125.
49   BURMAN, Barbara, and LEVENTON, Melissa (1987), 'The Men's Dress Reform Party, 1929–37' in *Costume*, no. 21.
50   STACK, Prunella (1988), *Zest for Life. Mary Bagot Stack and the League of Health and Beauty*, London: Peter Owen.

Chapter 4

1   BEAUVOIR, Simone de (1980), *The Prime of Life*, Harmondsworth: Penguin, p. 385. (Originally published as *La Force de l'Age* in 1960.)
2   MORGAN, Troy (1986), 'An Assessment of the Make Do and Mend Campaign during the Second World War', Brighton Polytechnic: unpublished BA thesis, p. 19. We have made extensive use of Troy Morgan's work in this chapter.
3   BALMAIN, Pierre (1964), *My Years and Seasons*, London: Cassell, p. 225.
4   TULLIS, John, nephew of Molyneux, in private correspondence with Polly Binder.
5   See MARLY, Diane de (1980), *The History of Haute Couture*, London: Batsford; FAIRLEY, Roma (1969), *A Bomb in the Collection: Fashion with the Lid Off*, Brighton: Clifton Books.
6   CALDER, Angus (1971), *The People's War: Britain 1939–45*, London: Panther, p. 261.
7   Ibid., p. 309.
8   Ibid.
9   RILEY, Denise (1983), *War in the Nursery*, London: Virago.
10   CALDER, Angus, op. cit.
11   EWING, Elizabeth (1974), op. cit., p. 148.
12   Personal communication from Cicely Turner.
13   FITZGIBBON, Theodora (1983), *With Love: An Autobiography 1938–1946*, London: Pan Books, p. 199.
14   MITFORD, Nancy (1974), *The Pursuit of Love* in *The Best Novels of Nancy Mitford*, London: Hamish Hamilton, p. 134. (*The Pursuit of Love* was originally published in 1945.)
15   *Vogue*, October 1941.
16   Alison Settle Archives, 'Notes on the 1943 London Collections', Brighton Polytechnic.
17   Personal communication from Nancy Weir.
18   CALDER, Angus, op. cit., p. 435, quoting HENREY, Mrs Robert, *The Siege of London* (1946), and GORDON, Jane, *Married to Charles* (1950).
19   MORGAN, Troy, op. cit., p. 42, quoting personal communication from Anne Parker.
20   See CALDER, Angus, op. cit.
21   WHITE, Doris (1980), *D for Doris, V for Victory*, Milton Keynes: Oakleaf Press, p. 63
22   CALDER, Angus, op. cit., p. 322.
23   MORGAN, Troy, op. cit., p. 42.
24   STEELE, Katy (1986), 'The Response to the Women's Utility Clothing Scheme during the War Years 1941–1945', Brighton Polytechnic: unpublished BA (Hons) thesis. We have been indebted to Katy Steele's work throughout this section.
25   COLEMAN, D. C. (1980), *Courtaulds – an Economic and Social History*, Cambridge: Cambridge University Press, vol. III, p. 56.
26   EWING, Elizabeth (1974), op. cit., pp. 145–6.
27   Ibid., p. 143.
28   HOLDEN STONE, James de (1946), 'The Designer and the Print Dress' in *Art and Industry*, vol. 40, April, p. 100.
29   NEWBY, Eric (1985), *Something Wholesale: My Life and Times in the Rag Trade*, London: Picador. (Originally published in 1962.)
30   EWING, Elizabeth (1974), op. cit., p. 148.
31   Alison Settle Archives, 'Notes on the 1943 London Collections', Brighton Polytechnic.
32   The London couturiers involved in the Utility prototype design scheme were Captain Molyneux (who was Chairman of the Designers' Committee), Charles Creed, Elspeth Champcommunal from the London House of Worth, Peter Russell, Victor Stiebel, Digby Morton, Lachasse and Hardy Amies. The Victoria and Albert Museum, London, was presented with a selection of the original prototype designs, which were all anonymously attributed. The Queen's dressmaker, Norman Hartnell, was not part of this committee, but he did design a standard Utility range for the London ready-to-wear

company Berketex. The Victoria and Albert Museum also has an example of one of these designs. Our thanks to Avril Hart of their Textiles Department for this information.

33   Lou Taylor Textile Collection, Brighton Polytechnic. From Courtaulds, Nottingham.
34   NEWSOM, John (1948), *The Education of Girls*, London: Faber & Faber, p. 103.
35   *Vogue*, October 1942.
36   STEELE, Katy, op. cit., quoting SCOTT-JAMES, Anne (1942), 'Deborah Kerr shows off the Utility Clothes' in *Picture Post*, March.
37   Ibid., pp. 59–68.
38   Ibid.
39   Ibid., quoting *The Times* (1943).
40   MORGAN, Troy, op. cit., p. 55.
41   Ibid., quoting personal communication from Sheila Hamilton.
42   PANTER-DOWNES, Mollie (1985), *One Fine Day*, London: Virago, pp. 75–8. (Originally published in 1946.)
43   Ibid., p. 89.
44   *Vogue*, August 1944.
45   Ibid.
46   AMIES, Hardy (1984), *Still Here – An Autobiography*, London: Weidenfeld & Nicolson, p. 47.
47   *Picture Post*, September 1947.
48   SISSONS, Michael, and FRENCH, Philip (eds.) (1986), *The Age of Austerity, 1945–51*, Oxford: Oxford University Press, p. 118. (Originally published in 1963.)
49   See WILSON, Elizabeth (1980), *Only Halfway to Paradise: Women in Postwar Britain, 1945–1968*, London: Tavistock.
50   SLATER, Elliott, and WOODSIDE, Moya (1951), *Patterns of Marriage*, London: Cassell.
51   SCOTT-JAMES, Anne (1952), *In the Mink*, London: Michael Joseph.
52   Quoted in WILSON (1980), op. cit.
53   Ibid., p. 84.
54   *Picture Post*, 17 September 1947.
55   PHILLIPS, Pearson, op. cit., p. 129.
56   Quoted in PHILLIPS, Pearson, op. cit., p. 130.
57   Ibid., p. 132.
58   Ibid., p. 131.
59   *New Statesman and Nation* (1947), 4 October, p. 270.
60   Ibid., p. 271.
61   Ibid.
62   Ibid.
63   LANG, Kurt, and LANG, Gladys (1961), 'Fashion: Identification and Differentiation in the Mass Society' in ROACH, Mary Ellen, and EICHER, Jane Bubolz (eds.) (1966), *Dress Adornment and the Social Order*, New York: Wiley.
64   PHILLIPS, Pearson, op. cit., p. 34.
65   POWELL, Anthony (1971), *Books Do Furnish A Room*, London: Fontana, pp. 114–15.
66   TRUMP, Margaret (1986), 'When I was at Marshall and Snelgrove' in *Costume*, no. 22, p. 92.

Chapter 5

1   ADDISON, Paul (1985), *Now the War is Over: A Social History of Britain 1945–51*, London: BBC and Jonathan Cape, p. 192.
2   BANHAM, Mary, and HILLIER, Bevis (1976), *A Tonic to the Nation: The Festival of Britain 1951*, London: Thames & Hudson, p. 187.
3   Ibid., p. 108.
4   BANHAM, Reyner (1976), 'The Style: "Flimsy . . . Effeminate"?' in ibid., p. 195, quoting BARRY, Sir Gerald, Director of the Festival.
5   Ibid., p. 197.
6   BOGDANOR, Vernon, and SKIDELSKY, Robert (1970), *The Age of Affluence 1951–1964*, London: Macmillan; and HARRIS, Jennifer, HYDE, Sarah, and SMITH, Greg (1986), *1966 and all that: Design and the Consumer in Britain, 1960–1969*, London: Trefoil Books.
7   Quoted in SWANNELL, Jane (1906), 'Debs or Plebs; the Disadvantages of being a Privileged Member of Society', in ASH, Juliet, and WRIGHT, Lee (eds.) (1986), *Components of Dress: Design, Manufacturing and Image Making in the Fashion Industry*, London: Comedia/Routledge, p. 78.
8   HARRIS, Jenny, HYDE, Sarah, and SMITH, Greg, op. cit., p. 19.
9   The 'Angry Young Men' were a group of writers given this collective label by the media. Their early novels, plays and criticism were said to constitute a moral and political attack on British society in the fifties. Colin Wilson, Kingsley Amis, John Osborne and John Wain were important figures and the label was sometimes extended to include the women novelists Iris Murdoch and Doris Lessing. In fact, the politics and preoccupations of these writers were widely divergent, as their subsequent development has shown.
10   See COLERIDGE, Nicholas, and QUINN, Stephen (eds.) (1988), *The Sixties in Queen*, London: Ebury Press.
11   HULANICKI, Barbara (1983), *From A to Biba*, London: Hutchinson, p. 43.
12   Ibid., pp. 54, 61.
13   BINDER, Pearl (1958), *The Peacock's Tail*, London: Harrap, pp. 11–12.
14   FRITH, Simon (1983), *Sound Effects: Youth, Leisure and the Politics of Rock and Roll*, London: Constable.
15   Quoted in ROCK, Paul, and COHEN, Stanley (1970), 'The Teddy Boy' in BOGDANOR, Vernon, and SKIDELSKY, Robert, op. cit., p. 305.
16   Ibid., p. 301.
17   MCINNES, Colin (1984), *Absolute Beginners*, London: Allison & Busby, p. 17. (Originally published in 1959.)
18   MELLY, George (1972), *Revolt into Style: the Pop Arts in Britain*, Harmondsworth: Penguin.
19   HILL, Peter (1987), 'Sharp Schmutter – Italian Suits – 1955–66', Brighton Polytechnic: unpublished BA (Hons) thesis, p. 23.
20   MILLER, Betty (1958), 'Amazons and After' in *The Twentieth Century*, August, p. 180.
21   SCHOFIELD, Michael (1965), *The Sexual Behaviour of Young People*, Harmondsworth: Penguin.
22   BERTIN, Celia (1956), *Paris à la Mode: A Voyage of Discovery*, London: Victor Gollancz, p. 177.
23   Quoted in WILSON, Elizabeth (1985), op. cit., p. 89.
24   WILSON, Elizabeth (1986), 'Memoirs of an Anti-Heroine' in *Hallucinations*, London: Radius, p. 6.
25   PRINGLE, Alison (1988), 'Chelsea Girl' in MAITLAND, Sara (ed.) (1988), *Very Heaven: Looking Back at the 1960s*, London: Virago, pp. 37–8.
26   FAIRLEY, Roma (1969), *A Bomb in the Collection: Fashion with the Lid Off*, London: Clifton Books, pp. 115–16.
27   MARLY, Diana de (1985), *Fashion for Men*, London: Batsford, p. 135.
28   WHITE, Nicola (1986), 'The Commercialisation of the Paris Couture Industry, 1947–55', Brighton Polytechnic: unpublished BA (Hons) thesis, p. 7, quoting *Les Femmes d'Aujourd'hui*, 3 April 1955. We are grateful to Nicky White's work throughout this section.
29   Ibid., p. 46, quoting 'French see Revolution in Couture' in the *New York Times*, 3 June 1962.
30   Ibid., p. 8, quoting the *New York Times*, 12 September 1965, p. 50.
31   WHITE, Nicola, op. cit., p. 15, quoting BERTIN, pp. 46 and 49.
32   WHITE, Nicola, op. cit., p. 44, quoting LATOUR, Anny, p. 257.
33   WHITE, Nicola, op. cit., p. 13, quoting *Promotion des Ventes Christian Dior* (1980), Paris: Edition Push, p. 5, and *Harper's Bazaar*, March 1952.
34   FAIRLEY, Roma, op. cit., p. 176.
35   GARLAND, Madge (1962), *Fashion*, Harmondsworth: Penguin, pp. 42–3.
36   EWING, Elizabeth (1974), op. cit., pp. 151–2.
37   PRINGLE, Margaret (19??), *Gilded Butterflies*, ?
38   GARLAND, Madge, op. cit., pp. 42–3.
39   FAIRLEY, Roma, op. cit., pp. 46–7.
40   Ibid., pp. 56–7.
41   WHITE, Nicola, op. cit., p. 42, quoting from a personal interview with J. Wallis, April 1986.
42   FAIRLEY, Roma, op. cit., p. 27.
43   HALLIDAY, Leonard (1966), *The Fashion Makers*, London: Zenith, p. 95.
44   FAIRLEY, Roma, op. cit., p. 48.
45   Ibid.
46   Personal communication from Mrs Patricia Miles, aunt of Ann Wise, Curator of Costume, Worthing Museum, 1988.
47   MAYNE, Roger (1986), *The Street Photographs of Roger Mayne*, catalogue of an

exhibition at the Victoria and Albert Museum.

48 ROWNTREE, S. (1951), *Poverty and the Welfare State*, p. 117, London: Longmans.
49 FAIRLEY, Roma, op. cit., p. 56.

Chapter 6

1 Events such as *perestroika* and *glasnost* in the USSR and the developments in the Socialist bloc generally, including the People's Republic of China, together with the rise of Islamic Fundamentalism, and a number of political and social changes in the West, have been taken as signs of a global upheaval that is not only economic and political but existential, calling all received notions into question, particularly, the assumptions of the European 'Enlightenment' of the eighteenth century in the West and 'actually existing Socialism' in the East. This upheaval, and its penetration into every aesthetic, intellectual and social area of life, is often referred to as Postmodernism. The debate about Postmodernism has been carried on at a largely academic level. However, for a brief overview, see NORMAN, Phillip (1988), 'Faking the Present' in the *Guardian*, 10 December. Some of the key texts on the debate are HEBDIGE, Dick (1988), *Hiding in the Light*, London: Routledge; JAMESON, Fredric (1984), 'Postmodernism, or the Cultural Logic of Late Capitalism', in *New Left Review*, no. 146, July–August; and JENCKS, Charles (1985), *Modern Movements in Architecture*, Harmondsworth: Penguin. Prince Charles's views on architecture reflect a relatively conservative inflection of Postmodernist positions on architecture. Likewise those of Rod Hackney. Different positions within Postmodernism do not, however, correspond neatly with the normal 'right' and 'left' of the political spectrum.
2 DELBOURG-DELPHIS, Marylene (1981), *Le Chic et le Look*, Paris: Hachette, p. 284.
3 Ibid., p. 234.
4 Thanks to Rafael Samuel for pointing out the significance of *Far from the Madding Crowd*.
5 FRASER, Kennedy (1985), *The Fashionable Mind: Reflections on Fashion 1970–1982*, Boston: David Godine.
6 MOWER, Sarah (1989), *Vogue*, March.
7 HEBDIGE, Dick (1979), *Subculture: The Meaning of Style*, London: Methuen.
8 DALLEN, Ruth (1984), 'Bankers and Skirts', in the *Observer*, 29 January.
9 WALKER, Martin (1988), 'A Pigsty without Frontiers', in the *Guardian*, 15 November.
10 MENKES, Suzy (1989), 'Feminist versus Sexist' in *The Times*, 22 March, p. 11.
11 CARTER, Angela (1989), 'The Recession Style', in *New Society*, 13 January, p. 65.
12 MENKES, Suzy, op. cit.
13 EVANS, Caroline, and THORNTON, Minna (1989), *Women and Fashion: A New Look*, London: Quartet Books, pp. 35–8.
14 JEAL, Nicola (1988), 'Black Style' in the *Observer*, 27 November, pp. 35–6.
15 Ibid.
16 KHAN, Naseem (1989), 'City Dazzlers Don't Say Sari' in the *Observer*, 8 January, p. 48.
17 ASH, Juliet (1989), 'Tarting up Men: Menswear and Gender Dynamics' in ATTFIELD, Judy, and KIRKHAM, Pat (eds.) (1989), *A View from the Interior: Feminism, Women and Design*, London: The Women's Press, p. 30.
18 Ibid.
19 DU CANN, Charlotte (1988), 'The Rebel Machine' in the *Independent*, 1 December, p. 19.
20 IRVINE, Carol (1988), 'The Real Voice of Poverty' in the *Guardian* 14 December.
21 MOWER, Sarah (1989a), 'Couture in Crisis', in the *Sunday Times*, 29 January, p. 3.
22 MOWER, Sarah (1989b), 'Fashion gets Real and Faces up to the Nineties', in *Vogue*, February, p. 94.
23 MOWER, Sarah (1989a), op. cit.
24 *International Textiles* (1988), no. 691, p. 10.
25 GIRAUD, Françoise (1987), *Dior*, London: Thames & Hudson, p. 296, and *International Textiles*, op. cit.
26 Quoted in MENKES, Suzy (1984), 'Yes, but is it an art or a craft?', *The Times*, 5 July, p. 8.
27 Ibid.
28 RUMBOLD, Judy (1988), 'The Midriff Crisis', in the *Guardian*, 10 October.
29 ROBSON-SCOTT, Marki (1987), in the *Observer*, 15 March.
30 HUME, Marion (1989), 'Hamnett Soars to Designer Stardom', in the *Sunday Times*, 5 March, p. 5.
31 FISHER, Paul (1989), 'Free, Fat and Flashy', in the *Guardian*.
32 JEAL, Nicola (1988), 'Paris Yorkshire', in the *Observer*, 11 December, p. 39.
33 JOHNSTON, Libby (1987), in the *Independent*, 13 July.
34 *London Evening Standard*, 30 September 1986.
35 *The Independent*, 2 December 1988.
36 BRAMPTON, Sally (1983), in the *Observer*, 6 November.
37 KAY, William (1983), 'How they Sold their Soul to St Michael', in *The Sunday Times*, 19 June. It is interesting here to note that S. R. Gent, a major clothing supplier to Marks and Spencer, paid for glossy advertisements for Marks and Spencer in *Vogue* in Autumn 1988 for the first time.
38 PESTON, Robert (1988), 'The Counter Revolution', in *The Spectator*, 23 July.
39 Ibid.
40 *The Independent*, 12 April 1989, p. 25.
41 *The Guardian*, 13 (1988) and the *Independent*, 12 April 1989, p. 25, which reported a loss of £15 million on Next's mail order *Directory* for the year to 31 January 1989.
42 *Clothing World* (1988), on US/KAY mail order catalogue, July.
43 MOWER, Sarah (1989b), op. cit.
44 Quoted by DRUMMOND, Maggie (1988), 'Clever Girl's Best Friend?' in *The Sunday Times*, 4 December, p. 8.
45 ELLISON, Jane (1988), 'When Marks and Sparks Fly', in *The Guardian*, 15 December.
46 *Clothing World*, July 1988.
47 MITTER, Swasti (1986), *Common Fate, Common Bond*, London: Blue Press, p. 122; and ELSOM, Diane, and PEARSON, Ruth (1981), 'Nimble Fingers make Cheap Workers: An Analysis of Women's Employment in Third World Export Manufacture', in *Feminist Review*, no. 7, Spring.
48 See DAVIS, Mike (1984), 'The Political Economy of Late Imperial America', in *New Left Review*, no. 143, January–February.
49 MITTER, Swasti, op. cit., p. 75.
50 SCOTT, Hilda (1984), *Working our Way to the Bottom: the Feminisation of Poverty*, London: Pandora, p. viii.
51 FRY, Vanessa, and MORRIS, Nick (1984), 'Richer for Poorer', in *The Guardian*, 18 January.
52 Ibid.; see also MARTIN, Jean, and ROBERTS, Ceridwen (1984), *Women and Employment: A Lifetime Perspective*, London: HMSO.

APPENDIX

Purchasing power of the pound, 1860–1989

From the Bank of England's Retail Price Index January 1989

Year	Value	Year	Value	Year	Value	Year	Value
1860	28.62	1895	37.75	1930	18.55	1965	7.67
1861	27.89	1896	38.08	1931	20.09	1966	7.35
1862	28.62	1897	36.80	1932	20.95	1967	7.09
1863	29.59	1898	36.49	1933	21.68	1968	6.91
1864	29.99	1899	36.80	1934	21.68	1969	6.51
1865	29.59	1900	35.60	1935	21.47	1970	6.20
1866	27.89	1901	35.31	1936	20.95	1971	5.72
1867	26.22	1902	34.75	1937	20.37	1972	5.28
1868	26.70	1903	34.48	1938	19.38	1973	4.90
1869	28.07	1904	34.21	1939	19.81	1974	4.38
1870	28.07	1905	34.48	1940	17.66	1975	3.68
1871	28.07	1906	36.49	1941	15.70	1976	2.96
1872	26.38	1907	33.43	1942	15.36	1977	2.54
1873	26.07	1908	32.68	1943	15.42	1978	2.31
1874	27.20	1909	32.68	1944	15.42	1979	2.11
1875	28.07	1910	32.44	1945	15.20	1980	1.79
1876	28.81	1911	31.96	1946	15.15	1981	1.58
1877	28.07	1912	30.84	1947	15.05	1982	1.41
1878	28.81	1913	30.84	1948	14.55	1983	1.34
1879	30.84	1914	31.06	1949	13.90	1984	1.28
1880	29.59	1915	27.37	1950	13.43	1985	1.22
1881	30.20	1916	22.80	1951	12.92	1986	1.15
1882	29.99	1917	18.63	1952	11.43	1987	1.11
1883	31.06	1918	16.40	1953	10.95	1988	1.07
1884	31.50	1919	13.99	1954	10.81	1989	1.00
1885	33.17	1920	13.64	1955	10.38		
1886	34.48	1921	11.62	1956	9.86		
1887	35.60	1922	15.98	1957	9.46		
1888	35.60	1923	17.24	1958	9.12		
1889	34.75	1924	17.38	1959	8.94		
1890	34.75	1925	17.11	1960	8.97		
1891	34.48	1926	17.59	1961	8.79		
1892	34.48	1927	17.59	1962	8.40		
1893	35.60	1928	18.32	1963	8.18		
1894	36.49	1929	18.40	1964	8.02		

$\mathcal{B}$IBLIOGRAPHY

ADBURGHAM, Alison (1981), *Shops and Shopping, 1800–1914*, London: Allen & Unwin

BARTHES, Roland (1985), *The Fashion System*, London: Jonathan Cape

BELL, Quentin (1968), *On Human Finery*, London: The Hogarth Press

CHARLES ROUX, Edmonde (1975), *Chanel*, London: Jonathan Cape

CUNNINGTON, Cecil Willett, and Phyllis (1951), *The History of Underclothes*, London: Michael Joseph

CUNNINGTON, Phyllis, and LUCAS, Catherine (1967), *Occupational costume in England from the Eleventh Century to 1914*, London: A. &. C. Black

ETHERINGTON SMITH, Meredith (1983), *Patou*, London: Hutchinson

EWING, Elizabeth (1974), *History of Twentieth Century Fashion*, London: Batsford

EWING, Elizabeth (1978), *Dress and Undress: A History of Women's Underwear*, London: Batsford

FAIRLEY, Roma (1969), *A Bomb in the Collection: Fashion with the Lid Off*, Brighton: Clifton Books

GINSBURG, Madeleine (1982), *Victorian Dress*, London: Batsford

HEBDIGE, Dick (1979), *Subculture: The Meaning of Style*, London: Routledge

HOLLANDER, Anne (1978), *Seeing Through Clothes*, New York: Viking/Penguin

KONIG, René (1973), *The Restless Image*, London: Allen & Unwin

LATOUR, Anny (1988), *Kings of Fashion*, London: Weidenfeld & Nicolson

LEESE, Elizabeth (1976), *Costume Design and the Movies*, Benbridge: BCW Publishing Ltd

LEVITT, Sarah (1986), *Victorians Unbuttoned*, London: Allen & Unwin

MILLER, Michael (1981), *The Bon Marché: Bourgeois Culture and the Department Store 1869–1920*, London: Allen & Unwin

NEWTON, Stella Mary (1974), *Health, Art and Reason: Dress Reformers of the Nineteenth Century*, London: John Murray

NYSTROM, Paul (1929), *The Economics of Fashion*, New York: Ronalds Press

SAUNDERS, Edith (1954), *The Age of Worth*, London: Longmans

STEELE, Valerie (1985), *Fashion and Eroticism*, New York: Oxford University Press

STEELE, Valerie (1988), *Paris Fashion: A Cultural History*, Oxford: Oxford University Press

TAYLOR, Lou (1983), *Mourning Dress: A Costume and Social History*, London: Allen & Unwin

TOZER, Jane, and LEVITT, Sarah (1983), *Fabric of Society: A Century of People and their Clothes: 1770–1870*, Carno, Powys, Wales: Laura Ashley

WALKLEY, Christina (1981), *The Ghost in the Looking Glass*, London: Peter Owen

WAUGH, Nora (1973), *The Cut of Women's Clothes*, London: Faber & Faber

WILSON, Elizabeth (1985), *Adorned in Dreams: Fashion and Modernity*, London: Virago

We have also used a wide range of period magazines, such as *English Women's Domestic Magazine, Punch, Illustrated London News, Aglaia, The Ladies Treasury, Picture Post, Woman, Woman's Own, Vogue* and *Harper's Bazaar*. Another increasingly useful source of dress and social history study comes out of community bookshops and oral history publications, from groups such as Stepney Books, Centreprise, Hackney, and Queenspark Books, Brighton. Detailed listing of local history/memoirs, publications and organisations may be obtained from:

The Federation of Worker Writers and Community Publishers

c/o Centreprise Publishing Project

Tower Hamlets Art Project

178 White-Chapel

London E1 1BJ

PICTURE CREDITS

Colour

Page 129 Kunsthistorisches Museum, Vienna; 130 Metropolitan Museum of Art, New York/Sheldan Collins; 131 Private Collection; 132 Liberty's; 133 British Library; 134 Costume Study Centre, Bath; 135 Metropolitan Museum of Art, New York/Sheldan Collins; 136 Private Collection; 137 Department of Art and Design History Collection, Brighton Polytechnic; 138 Private Collection; 139 British Library; 140 Victoria & Albert Museum; 141 Metropolitan Museum of Art, New York/Sheldan Collins; 142 Condé Nast Publications Ltd; 143 Freeman's Catalogues; 144 Nial McInerney

Black & White

Frontispiece: *left* Hulton Picture Company, *right* National Magazine Company Ltd.
Page 10 Popperfoto; 15 Private Collection; 16 Cundall & Downes; 17 John Thomson; 18 Trinity College, Cambridge; 20 & 23 Hulton Picture Company; 24 Popperfoto; 29 Alan Felton; 31 William Morris Gallery, Walthamstow Borough Council; 32 *Punch*; 34 Hulton Picture Company; 36 Lou Taylor Collection; 39 York Castle Museum; 40 & 42 Hulton Picture Company; 44 Faculty of Art, Design & Humanities Library, Brighton Polytechnic; 47 *top & bottom* British Library; 50 Salford Cultural Services; 51 Lou Taylor Collection; 54 Buckman Papers; 55 St Hilda's College, Oxford; 58 Buckman Papers; 59 Hulton Picture Company; 61 Glasgow Art Gallery & Museum; 63 Private Collection; 65 & 67 Hulton Picture Company; 72 Leicester Museum; 74 Hulton Picture Company; 77 Maud Bunker; 80 Bianchini-Ferier; 82 Hulton Picture Company; 85 Jacques Damase; 87 Metropolitan Museum of Art, New York; 88 & 89 Hulton Picture Company; 91 & 92 Condé Nast Publications Ltd; 94 *top* British Library, *bottom* Madame Wright's, Cheltenham; 96 The Lock Museum, Willenhall; 98 Hulton Picture Company; 100 British Library; 103 Courtaulds Archive; 106 Hulton Picture Company; 109 Faculty of Art, Design & Humanities Library, Brighton Polytechnic; 111 Condé Nast Publications Ltd, 112 Hulton Picture Company; 115 Worthing Costume Museum/David Nicholls Photography; 116 Robert Opie Collection; 117 *Daily Express*/John Frost Newspapers; 118 Imperial War Museum; 120 Condé Nast Publications Ltd; 121 Kay's Catalogues/Faculty of Art, Design & Humanities Library, Brighton Polytechnic; 123 Condé Nast Publications Ltd; 126 Imperial War Museum; 146 Roger Viollet Collection; 147 Topham Picture Library; 151 *top* Popperfoto, *bottom* Topham Picture Library; 153 Hulton Picture Company; 154 Popperfoto; 159 *Woman's Day*; 160 & 162 Topham Picture Library; 164 *top* Town. *bottom* Roger Mayne; 166 Hulton Picture Company; 170 Topham Picture Library; 172 Popperfoto; 175 Condé Nast Publications Ltd; 176 & 179 Topham Picture Library; 182 *The Sunday Times*; 183 Faculty of Art, Design & Humanities Library, Kingston Polytechnic; 185 Roger Mayne; 187 Condé Nast Publications; 190 Popperfoto; 195 Hulton Picture Company; 197 Network; 198 London Institute/Central St Martin's; 201 Comme des Garçons; 202 Lee Apparel UK; 205 *The Sunday Times*; 206 Andrew Anderson; 209 Yves St Laurent; 211 *right* Tim Graham, *left* Freeman's Catalogues; 213 National Magazine Company Ltd/Robert Erdmann; 215 & 216 Next Catalogue; 218 Marks & Spencer plc; 223 Format Photographers plc/Brenda Price; 224 Jean Muir/Chris Moore; 226 C. O'Brien; 227 *ID Magazine*/Marc Lebon.

Every attempt has been made to trace the legal copyright holder of the material published in this book. The BBC apologise for any omissions.

$\mathcal{I}$ NDEX